PRENTICE HALL
Chemistry

Laboratory Manual

Antony C. Wilbraham
Dennis D. Staley
Michael S. Matta

PEARSON

Prentice
Hall

Boston, Massachusetts
Upper Saddle River, New Jersey

Cover photograph: Image from Getty Images, Inc.

ISBN 0-13-190359-4

24 18

CONTENTS

*Core experiment

TO THE STUDENT

Chemistry is exciting! Each day in the laboratory you are given the opportunity to confront the unknown, and to understand it. Each experiment holds many secrets. Look hard and you may uncover them. Work hard and you will understand them.

The word *science* comes from the Latin word *scire*, which means "to know." The goal of all science is knowledge. Scientists are men and women who devote their lives to the pursuit of knowledge.

In this class, you are given the opportunity to do what scientists do. You can wonder how things work, ask why and how, and then think of ways to answer your own questions. You are given the chance to understand what is unknown to you and to many other people.

It is a great opportunity. Do not waste it by being lazy or careless. Work hard. Master the scientist's skills of observation and experiment. These skills are tools for understanding the secrets of the unknown.

SAFETY

Chemistry is a laboratory science. As part of your laboratory experience you will handle many chemical substances and manipulate specialized laboratory equipment. Many of these substances pose a health risk if handled improperly, and some of the laboratory equipment can cause severe injury if used improperly. This section is a guide to the safe laboratory practices you will use throughout this course.

Preparation and Safety

To get the most out of your laboratory experience, you must be well prepared for each experiment. This means that you must read the experiment thoroughly before coming to the laboratory. Make sure you have a clear idea of what the experiment is about. Be sure that you understand each step of the procedure. If you are unsure of any part of the experiment, ask your teacher for help before the laboratory begins.

Preparation is important not only to understanding, but also to safety. If you are well prepared for the laboratory, it is much less likely that an accident will occur. In the laboratory, you are responsible not only for your safety, but also for the safety of your classmates. If an accident happens because you are not prepared, it can also affect your friends. This is all the more reason for you to take the time and make the effort to prepare for the laboratory.

Be sure to note the safety warnings listed in the Safety section of each experiment. Note that these warnings are emphasized by symbols appearing in the margins. The symbols mark those parts of the procedure that may be hazardous. In addition, be sure to observe the general safety precautions described in the safety section at the beginning of the manual. Finally, remember the most important safety advice of all: *Always wear safety goggles in the chemistry laboratory!*

Safety in the Chemistry Laboratory

Everyone who works in a chemistry laboratory should follow these safety precautions:

1. Wear safety goggles and a laboratory apron in the laboratory at all times.

2. Shoes must be worn in the laboratory. Avoid wearing overly bulky or loose-fitting clothing. Remove any dangling jewelry.

3. Conduct only assigned experiments, and do them only when your teacher is present.

4. Know the locations of safety equipment such as eyewash fountains, fire extinguishers, emergency shower, and fire blanket. Be sure you know how to use the equipment.

5. Do not chew gum, eat, or drink in the laboratory. Never taste any chemicals. Keep your hands away from your face when working with chemicals.

6. Wash your hands with soap and water at the end of each laboratory exercise.

7. Read all of the directions for a laboratory procedure before proceeding with the first part. Reread each instruction before you do it.

8. Notify your teacher immediately if any chemicals, especially concentrated acid or base, are spilled.

9. Report all accidents, no matter how slight, to the teacher immediately.

10. Pin or tie back long hair and roll up loose sleeves when working with flames.

11. Do not leave a lighted burner unattended.

12. Use a hot plate instead of an open flame whenever a flammable liquid is present.

13. Read the label on a reagent bottle carefully *before* using the chemical. After removing the chemical from the bottle, check to make sure that it is the correct chemical for that procedure.

14. To avoid contamination, do not return unused chemicals to a reagent bottle. Similarly, never put a pipet, spatula, or dropper into a reagent bottle. Instead, pour some of the reagent into a small clean beaker and use that as your supply.

15. Do not use chipped or cracked glassware. Discard it according to your teacher's instructions.

16. When diluting an acid, *always* pour the acid slowly into water, stirring to dissipate the heat generated. **CAUTION:** *Never pour water into a concentrated acid.*

17. When heating a liquid in a test tube, turn the mouth of the test tube away from yourself and others.

18. Clean up spills and broken glass immediately. Leave your work area clean at the end of the laboratory period.

Laboratory Hazards

You should be aware of possible hazards in the laboratory and take the appropriate safety precautions. By doing so, you can minimize the risks of doing chemistry. This safety section is intended to acquaint you with the hazards that exist in the laboratory and to indicate how you can avoid these hazards. In addition, information is provided on what to do if an accident should occur.

Thermal Burns

A thermal burn can occur if you touch hot equipment or come too close to an open flame. You can prevent thermal burns by being aware that hot and cold equipment look the same. If a gas burner or hot plate has been used, some of the equipment nearby may be hot. Hold your hand near an item to feel for heat before touching it. Treat a thermal burn by *immediately* running cold water over the burned area. Continue applying the cold water until the pain is reduced. This usually takes several minutes. In addition to reducing pain, cooling the burned area also serves to speed the healing process. Greases and oils should not be used to treat burns because they tend to trap heat. Medical assistance should be sought for any serious burn. *Notify your teacher immediately if you are burned.*

Chemical Burns

A chemical burn occurs when the skin or a mucous membrane is damaged by contact with a substance. The Materials section of each exercise indicates which substances can cause chemical burns. $\boxed{C}$ **stands for corrosive**. It indicates that the chemical can cause severe burns. $\boxed{I}$ **stands for irritant**. It indicates that the chemical can irritate the skin and the membranes of the eye, nose, throat, and lungs. Chemicals that are marked $\boxed{C}$ or $\boxed{I}$ should be treated with special care. Chemical burns can be severe. Permanent damage to mucous membranes can occur despite the best efforts to rinse a chemical from the affected area.

The best defense against chemical burns is prevention. *Without exception, wear safety goggles during all phases of the laboratory period— even during cleanup.* Should any chemical splash in your eye, immediately use a continuous flow of running water to flush your eye for a period of 20 minutes. Call for help. If you wear contact lenses, remove them immediately. This is especially crucial if the chemical involved is an acid or base. It can concentrate under the lens and cause extensive damage. Wear a laboratory apron and close-toed shoes (no sandals) to protect other areas of your body. If corrosive chemicals should contact your exposed skin, wash the affected area with water for several minutes.

An additional burn hazard exists when concentrated acids or bases are mixed with water. The heat released in mixing these chemicals with water can cause the mixture to boil, spattering corrosive chemical. The heat can also cause non-Pyrex containers to break, spilling corrosive chemical.

To avoid these hazards, follow these instructions: Always add acid or base to water, very slowly while stirring; never the reverse. One way to remember this critical advice is to think of the phrase "Pouring acid into water is doing what you ought-er."

Cuts from Glass

Cuts occur most often when thermometers or pieces of glass tubing are forced into rubber stoppers. Prevent cuts by using the correct technique for this procedure. The hole should be lubricated with glycerol or water to facilitate the movement of the glass tubing. The glass should not be gripped directly with the hands, but rather by means of cloth towels. The towels will protect your hands if the glass should break. Use a gentle twisting motion to move the tube smoothly into the stopper.

Avoid cuts from other sources by discarding chipped and cracked glassware according to your teacher's instructions. If you should receive a minor cut, allow it to bleed for a short time. Wash the injured area under cold running water, and notify your teacher. Serious cuts and deep puncture wounds require immediate medical help. Notify your teacher immediately. While waiting for assistance, control the bleeding by applying pressure with the fingertips or by firmly pressing with a clean towel or sterile gauze.

Fire

A fire may occur if chemicals are mixed improperly or if flammable materials come too close to a burner flame or hot plate. When using lab equipment, prevent fires by tying back long hair and loose-fitting clothing. Do not use a burner when flammable chemicals are present. **Flammable chemicals are designated with the symbol** F in the Materials section for each exercise. Use a hot plate as a heat source instead of a burner when flammable chemicals are present.

If hair or clothing should catch fire, *do not* run, because running fans a fire. Drop to the floor and roll slowly to smother the flames. Shout for help. If another person is the victim, get a fire blanket to smother the flames. If a shower is nearby, help the victim to use it.

In case of a fire on a laboratory bench, turn off all accessible gas outlets and unplug all accessible appliances. A fire in a container may be put out by covering the container with a nonflammable object. It could also be smothered by covering the burning object with a damp cloth. If not, call for a fire extinguisher. Spray the base of the fire with foam from the extinguisher. **CAUTION:** *Never direct the jet of a fire extinguisher into a person's face.* Use a fire blanket instead. If a fire is not extinguished quickly, leave the laboratory. Crawl to the door if necessary to avoid the smoke. Do not return to the laboratory.

Poisoning

Many of the chemicals used in this manual are toxic. **Toxic chemicals are identified in the Materials sections with the symbol** T .

You should do several things to prevent poisoning. Never eat, chew gum, or drink in the laboratory. Do not touch chemicals. Clean up spills. Keep your hands away from your face. In this way you will prevent chemicals from reaching your hands, mouth, nose, or eyes.

In some cases, the detection of an odor is used to indicate that a chemical reaction has taken place. It is important to note, however, that many gases are toxic when inhaled. If you must detect an odor, use your hand to waft some of the gas toward your nose. Sniff the gas instead of taking a deep breath. This will minimize the amount of gas sampled.

Safety Symbols

Take appropriate precautions whenever any of the following safety symbols appear in an experiment.

 Eye Safety
Wear safety goggles.

 Clothing Protection
Wear a lab coat or apron when using corrosive chemicals or chemicals that can stain clothing.

 Skin Protection
Wear plastic gloves when using chemicals that can irritate or stain your skin.

 Broken Glass
Do not use chipped or cracked glassware. Do not heat the bottom of a test tube.

 Open Flame
Tie back hair and loose clothing. Never reach across a lit burner.

 Flammable Substance
Do not have a flame near flammable materials.

 Corrosive Substance
Wear safety goggles, an apron, and gloves when working with corrosive chemicals.

 Poison
Don't chew gum, drink, or eat in the laboratory. Never taste a chemical in the laboratory.

 Fume
Avoid inhaling substances that can irritate your respiratory system.

 Thermal Burn
Do not touch hot glassware or equipment.

 Electrical Equipment
Keep electrical equipment away from water or other liquids.

 Sharp Object
To avoid a puncture wound, use scissors or other sharp objects only as intended.

 Disposal
Dispose chemicals only as directed.

 Hand Washing
Wash your hands thoroughly with soap and water.

 Corrosive

 Irritant

 Flammable

Toxic

Emergency Procedures

Report any injury, accident, or spill to your teacher immediately. Know the location of the closest eyewash fountain, fire blanket, fire extinguisher, and shower.

SITUATION	SAFE RESPONSE
burns	Immediately flush with cold water until the burning sensation subsides.
fainting	Provide fresh air (for instance, open a window). Move the person so that the head is lower than the rest of the body. If breathing stops, use CPR
fire	Turn off all gas outlets. Unplug all appliances. Use a fire blanket or fire extinguisher to smother the fire. **CAUTION:** *Do not cut off a person's air supply.*
eye injury	Immediately flush the eye with running water. Remove contact lenses. Do not allow eye to be rubbed if a foreign object is present in the eye.
minor cuts	Allow to bleed briefly. Wash with soap and water.
poisoning	Note what substance was responsible. Alert teacher immediately.
spills on skin	Flush with water.

Laboratory Equipment

Beaker

Mortar and pestle

Crucible and cover

Watch glass

Evaporating dish

Pneumatic trough

Florence flask

Wide-mouth collecting bottle

Plastic wash bottle

Dropper pipet

Funnel

Erlenmeyer flask

Safety goggles

Rubber stoppers

Glass rod with nichrome wire (for flame testing)

Test-tube holder

Scoopula

Crucible tongs

Clay triangle

Ring stand

Rubber tubing

Metal spatula

Test-tube brush

Ceramic square

Wire gauze

Triangular file

Burner

Tripod

Beaker: glass or plastic; common sizes are 50 mL, 100 mL, 250 mL, 400 mL; glass beakers may be heated.

Buret: glass; common sizes are 25 mL and 50 mL; used to measure volumes of solutions in titrations.

Ceramic square: used under hot apparatus or glassware.

Clamps: the following types of clamps may be fastened to support apparatus: buret/test-tube clamp, clamp holder, double buret clamp, ring clamp, 3-pronged jaw clamp.

Clay triangle: wire frame with porcelain supports; used to support a crucible.

Condenser: glass; used in distillation procedures.

Crucible and cover: porcelain; used to heat small amounts of solid substances at high temperatures.

Crucible tongs: iron or nickel; used to pick up and hold small items.

Dropper pipet: glass tip with rubber bulb; used to transfer small volumes of liquid.

Erlenmeyer flask: glass; common sizes are 100 mL, 250 mL; may be heated; used in titrations.

Evaporating dish: porcelain; used to contain small volumes of liquid being evaporated.

Florence flask: glass; common sizes are 125 mL, 250 mL, 500 mL; may be heated; used in making and for storing solutions.

Forceps: metal; used to hold or pick up small objects.

Funnel: glass or plastic; common size holds 12.5-cm diameter filter paper.

Gas burner: constructed of metal; connected to a gas supply with rubber tubing; used to heat chemicals (dry or in solution) in beakers, test tubes, and crucibles.

Gas collecting tube: glass; marked in mL intervals; used to measure gas volumes.

Glass rod with nichrome wire: used in flame tests.

Graduated cylinder: glass or plastic; common sizes are 10 mL, 50 mL, 100 mL; used to measure approximate volumes; must not be heated.

Graduated pipet: glass; common sizes are 10 mL, 25 mL; used to measure solution volumes; less accurate than a volumetric pipet.

Mortar and pestle: porcelain; may be used to grind crystals and lumpy chemicals to a powder.

Pipet bulb: rubber; used in filling a pipet with a solution; a pipet must never be filled by mouth.

Test-tube rack

Test tubes

Stirring rod

Graduated cylinder

Volumetric pipet

Thermometer

Buret/test tube clamp

Clamp holder

3-prong jaw clamp

Forceps

Condenser

Rubber policeman

Pinch clamp

Gas collecting tube

Screw clamp

Buret

Graduated pipet

Pipet bulb

Double buret clamp

Ring clamp

Platform balance (triple beam)

Plastic wash bottle: flexible plastic; squeeze sides to dispense water.

Platform balance: also known as a triple-beam balance.

Pneumatic trough: galvanized container with shelf; used in experiments where a gas is collected.

Ring stand: metal rod fixed upright in a heavy metal base; has many uses as a support.

Rubber stoppers: several sizes.

Rubber tubing: used to connect apparatus to transfer liquids or gases.

Safety goggles: plastic; must be worn at all times while working in the laboratory.

Screw clamp, pinch clamp: metal; used to block off rubber tubing.

Spatula, scoopula: metal or porcelain; used to transfer solid chemicals; the scoopula has a larger capacity.

Stirring rod and rubber policeman: glass with rubber sleeve; used to stir, assist in pouring liquids, and for removing precipitates from a container.

Test-tube brush: bristles with wire handle; used to scrub small-diameter glassware.

Test-tube holder: spring metal; used to hold test tubes or glass tubing.

Test-tube rack: wood or plastic; holds test tubes in a vertical position.

Test tubes: glass; common sizes small (13 mm × 100 mm), medium (20 mm × 150 mm), large (25 × 200 mm); may be heated.

Thermometer: non-mercury; common range −10°C to 110°C.

Triangular file: metal; used to scratch glass tubing prior to breaking to desired length.

Tripod: iron; used to support containers of chemicals above the flame of a burner.

Volumetric pipet: glass; common sizes are 10 mL, 25 mL; used to measure solution volumes accurately; must not be heated.

Watch glass: glass; used to cover an evaporating dish or beaker.

Wide-mouth bottle: glass; used with pneumatic trough.

Wire gauze: used to spread the heat of a burner flame.

EQUIPMENT

Working in the chemistry laboratory requires the use of a wide variety of specialized laboratory equipment. This section provides an illustrated listing of the equipment required in this course. Also provided is a brief description of each piece of equipment and an inventory list so you can keep track of the equipment assigned to you.

Student Equipment

At the beginning and end of the year, record how many of each item are in your equipment drawer.

Item	Quantity Checked In	Quantity Checked Out	Breakage
beaker, 100-mL			
beaker, 250-mL			
beaker, 400-mL			
ceramic plate			
crucible, with cover			
crucible tongs			
dropper pipet (eye dropper)			
evaporating dish			
flask, Erlenmeyer, 125-mL			
flask, Erlenmeyer, 250-mL			
forceps			
funnel			
graduated cylinder, 10-mL			
graduated cylinder, 25-mL			
graduated cylinder, 100-mL			
laboratory apron			
mortar and pestle			
safety goggles			
screw clamp or pinch clamp			
spatula, scoopula			
stirring rod and policeman			
test tube, 13 mm × 100 mm (small)			
test tube, 20 mm × 150 mm (medium)			
test tube holder			
thermometer ($-10°C$ to $110°C$), non-mercury			
triangle			
watch glass			
wire gauze			

LABORATORY TECHNIQUES

Working in the chemistry laboratory, you will be handling potentially dangerous substances and performing unfamiliar tasks. This section provides you with a guide to the safe laboratory techniques needed in this course. While performing experiments throughout the year, refer back to this section any time you are unsure of proper laboratory techniques.

Pouring Liquids

- Always read the label on a reagent bottle before using its contents.
- Always wear safety goggles when handling chemicals.
- Never touch chemicals with your hands.
- Never return unused chemicals to their original containers. To avoid waste, do not take excessive amounts of reagents.

Follow this procedure when pouring liquids:

1. Use the back of your fingers to remove the stopper from a reagent bottle. Hold the stopper between your fingers until the transfer of liquid is complete. Do not place the stopper on your workbench.

2. Grasp the container from which you are pouring with the palm of your hand covering the label.

3a. When you are transferring a liquid to a test tube or measuring cylinder, the container should be held at eye level. Pour the liquid slowly, until the correct volume has been transferred.

3b. When you are pouring a liquid from a reagent bottle into a beaker, the reagent should be poured slowly down a glass stirring rod (Figure 1). When you are transferring a liquid from one beaker to another, you can hold the stirring rod and beaker in one hand.

Figure 1 *Pouring from a reagent bottle into a beaker.*

Filtering a Mixture

Sometimes it is necessary to separate a solid from a liquid. The most common method of separating such a mixture is filtration.

1. Fold a filter paper circle in half and then quarters. Open the folded paper to form a cone, with one thickness of paper on one side and three thicknesses on the other (Figure 2).

2. Put the paper cone in a filter funnel. Place the funnel in an iron ring clamped to a ring stand. Moisten the filter paper with a small volume of distilled water, and gently press the paper against the sides of the funnel to achieve a good fit. (If the correct size of filter paper has been used, the top edge of the cone will be just below the rim of the filter funnel.)

3. Place a beaker beneath the funnel to collect the filtrate. The tip of the funnel should touch the inside surface of the beaker and extend about one inch below the rim (Figure 3).

Figure 2 *Folding the filter paper.*

Guide flow of liquid with a glass rod

Solid collects on filter paper

Mixture being filtered

Stem touches side of beaker

Filtrate

Figure 3 *Filtration assembly.*

Figure 4 *Laboratory gas burners.*

4. Decant the liquid from the solid by pouring it down a glass stirring rod into the funnel. Be careful to keep the liquid below the top edge of the cone of filter paper at all times; the liquid must not overflow. Finally, use a jet of distilled water from a wash bottle to wash the solid from the beaker into the filter.

5. When the filtration is complete, wash the solid residue on the filter paper with distilled water to remove traces of solvent. Dry the solid.

6. If the filtrate contains a dissolved salt, it may be recovered by evaporation if desired.

Using a Gas Burner

Laboratory gas burners produce various kinds of flames when different mixtures of gas and air are burned. The two most common models are the Bunsen burner and the Tirrell burner. Both have adjustable air vents; the Tirrell burner has a gas control valve in its base (Figure 4).

a. air vents closed

1. Examine your laboratory burner. Determine which model you have.

2. Connect the burner to the gas supply with rubber tubing.

3. Close the air vents. If your model is a Tirrell burner, also close the gas control valve at the base of the burner.

4. Hold a lighted match at the top of the burner tube and turn on the gas supply. Do this by opening the main gas supply valve located on top of the nozzle to which you attached the rubber tubing. (If your model is a Tirrell burner, first open the main gas supply valve, then open the gas control valve at the base approximately one-half-turn.) You should get a yellow, or luminous, flame (Figure 5). When a Tirrell burner is used, the main gas supply valve should be opened fully and the gas flow regulated by the gas control valve. Gas supply to a Bunsen burner is controlled by the main gas valve.

b. air vents open

Figure 5 *Burner flame characteristics.*

5. Open the air vents slowly, to admit more air into the flame, to produce a light blue (nonluminous) cone-shaped flame. If the flame "blows out" after lighting, the gas supply should be reduced.

6. Adjust the air vents and gas supply to produce the desired size of flame. For most laboratory work, the blue inner cone of the flame should be about 1 inch high and free of yellow color. If you want a smaller flame, close the air vent slightly and reduce the gas supply. You will learn how to control the burner flame by trial and error.

7. Turn the burner off at the main gas supply valve when done.

CAUTION: *Confine long hair and loose clothing when using a gas burner. Do not reach over a burner. Ensure that flammables are not being used when a burner is lit. Never leave a lit burner unattended. Know the location of fire extinguishers, the fire blanket, and safety shower.*

Figure 6 *Heating a liquid in a test tube.*

Heating Liquids

Heating a Liquid in a Test Tube

The correct procedure for heating liquids in the laboratory is important to laboratory safety.

1. Adjust your gas burner to produce a gentle blue flame.

2. Fill a test tube one-third full with the liquid to be heated.

3. Grasp the test tube with a test-tube holder, near the upper end of the tube.

4. Hold the test tube in a slanting position in the flame, and gently heat the tube a short distance below the surface of the liquid (Figure 6).

5. Shake the tube gently as it is being heated, until the liquid boils or reaches the desired temperature.

CAUTION: *Never point the open end of a test tube you are heating either toward yourself or anyone working nearby. Never heat the bottom of the test tube.*

Heating a Liquid in a Beaker

Many laboratory experiments require the use of a hot water or boiling water bath. This procedure describes how to assemble a water bath.

1. Fasten an iron ring securely to a ring stand so that it is 2–4 cm above the top of a gas burner placed on the ring stand base.

2. Place a 250-mL beaker one-half-filled with water on a wire gauze resting on the iron ring (Figure 7).

3. Light your gas burner and adjust it to produce a hot flame.

4. Place the burner beneath the wire gauze. For a slower rate of heating, reduce the intensity of the burner flame.

CAUTION: *Never heat plastic beakers or graduated glassware in a burner flame. Never let a boiling water bath boil dry; add water to it as necessary.*

Figure 7 *Heating a liquid in a beaker.*

Inserting Glass Tubing

In many experimental procedures, you are required to insert a thermo-meter or a length of glass tubing into a hole in a rubber stopper. It is essential that you know the correct way to do this. Otherwise, serious injury may result.

1. Lubricate the end of the glass tubing with a few drops of water, washing-up liquid, glycerol, or vegetable oil.

2. Hold the glass tubing close to where it enters the hole in the rubber stopper. Protect your hands with work gloves or pieces of cloth.

3. Ease the tubing into the hole with a gentle twisting motion. Push the tubing through the hole as far as is required. Do not use force!

4. Wipe excess lubricating material from the tubing before continuing with the experiment.

5. If the glass tubing is to be removed from the stopper, it should be done immediately after the experiment is completed.

CAUTION: *The end of the glass tubing should be fire-polished or smoothed with emery cloth before being inserted into a rubber stopper. Do not try to bend the glass tubing—it will break. Ensure that the palm of the hand holding the rubber stopper is not in line with the emerging glass tube.*

Measuring Mass

In many experiments you are required to determine the mass of a chemical used or produced in a reaction. An object's mass is determined by measuring it on a balance. When you determine the mass of an object, you are comparing its mass with a known mass. In SI, the base unit of mass is the kilogram.

There are many types of laboratory balances. The one used most fre-quently in schools is the centigram balance (Figure 8). The following general rules apply to the use of all balances:

Figure 8 *The centigram balance.*

- Check the balance before you start. The balance pan should be empty and clean, and all masses (or dials) should be set on zero. The balance must be level. Check the bubble level on the base. See your teacher if you need assistance with checking your balance.
- Objects to be placed directly on the balance pan must be clean, dry, and at room temperature. Solid chemicals and liquids must never be put directly on the balance pan. Liquid samples should be placed in beakers or sealed containers. Solid chemicals can be conveniently placed in beakers, disposable plastic weighing boats, or on 10-cm squares made of glossy paper.
- The balance is a precision instrument that must be handled with care. To avoid damaging it, always be sure that the balance is in an arrested position when objects are placed on or removed from the pan. Always turn all dials slowly.
- Never move or jar either a balance or the balance table.
- If you spill a chemical on or near the balance, clean it up immediately. If in doubt, inform your teacher. A camel-hair brush is usually provided to wipe minute traces of solid from the balance pan before you use it.
- Never attempt to measure an object with a mass greater than the maximum capacity of the balance.
- When you are done, return all the masses to zero, and make sure the balance pan is clean.

Do not attempt to use a balance until your teacher has demonstrated the proper technique.

Using a Centigram Balance

1. Examine a centigram balance. The maximum capacity for this balance is 300 g and the sensitivity (limit of detection) is 0.01 g. The balance has four beams and four riders.
2. Move all the riders to their zero points (to the left side of their respective beams). Ensure that the riders rest in the notches on the beams.
3. Check to see that the beam is balanced. The pointer should move the same distance above and below the zero line on the scale or come to rest at the zero line. Use the zero adjustment screw if necessary. Always zero the balance before you begin. When the balance has been checked and adjusted, you are ready to begin.
4. Place the object whose mass is to be determined on the pan. (It must be dry and at room temperature.)
5. Slide the riders gently along the beams, one at a time, beginning with the largest. If a beam is notched, be sure that the rider is in a notch. Note that all the beams have notches except the one carrying the smallest rider. When the added masses (the positions of the riders) are equal to the mass of the object on the pan, then the pointer will be on the zero line. It may also swing equal distances above and below the zero line.
6. To record the mass of the object, sum the masses indicated by the positions of the riders on their respective beams.
7. Return all riders to zero and remove your sample. Make sure that the balance pan is left clean.

Measuring Volume

Volume measurements are important in many experimental procedures. Sometimes volume measurements must be accurate; other times they can be approximate. Most volume measures in the laboratory are made using equipment calibrated in milliliters. Although some beakers have graduation marks, these marks are designed only for quick, rough estimates of volume. Accurate volumes must be measured with pipets, burets, or volumetric flasks.

Using a Graduated Cylinder

Half-fill a 100-mL graduated cylinder with water, and set the cylinder on your laboratory bench. Examine the surface of the water. Notice how the surface curves upward where the water contacts the cylinder walls. This curved surface is called a *meniscus.*

A volume measurement is always read at the bottom of the meniscus, with your eye at the same level as the liquid surface. To make the meniscus more visible, you can place your finger or a dark piece of paper behind and just below the meniscus while making the reading (Figure 9).

Graduated cylinders are available in many capacities. The 100-mL cylinder is marked in 1-mL divisions, and volumes can be estimated to the nearest 0.1 mL. The last digit in these measurements is therefore significant but uncertain.

Using a Pipet

A pipet is used to accurately measure and deliver volumes of liquids. Two types are in common use: volumetric pipets and graduated, or measuring, pipets (Figure 10). The use of a volumetric pipet will be described. A volumetric pipet has a single calibration mark and delivers the volume printed on the bulb of the pipet at the temperature specified. (A graduated pipet has calibrations along the length of the pipet.) Volumes can be measured more accurately with a volumetric pipet than with a graduated pipet.

1. Place the tip of the pipet below the surface of the liquid to be dispensed.

2. Compress a pipet bulb and press the hole in the bulb against the upper end of the pipet. **CAUTION:** *Never fill a pipet by applying suction with your mouth.* Never push the pipet bulb over the end of the pipet.

3. Slowly release pressure on the bulb so that liquid is drawn into the pipet to a level about 2 cm above the calibration mark.

4. Remove the bulb and simultaneously place your index finger over the end of the pipet. If you are right-handed, you should hold the pipet in your right hand and the pipet bulb in your left (Figure 11).

5. Keep your index finger pressed firmly against the end. Withdraw the pipet from the liquid, and carefully wipe the outside of the stem with a paper towel.

Figure 9 *Reading volume in a graduated cylinder.*

Figure 10 *(a) The volumetric pipet and (b) the graduated pipet.*

Figure 11 *Filling and emptying a pipet.*

6. Slowly reduce the pressure on your finger to allow the excess liquid to drain into a waste receiver, until the bottom of the meniscus is at the calibration mark.

7. Now, deliver the remaining liquid in the pipet into the designated receiver. When releasing liquid from a volumetric pipet, let it drain completely. Wait 20 seconds, then touch the pipet tip to the side of the flask or surface of the liquid. This action will remove some, but not all, of the liquid in the tip. The pipet delivers the stated volume when this procedure is followed. A small amount of liquid remains in the tip. Do not blow this out into your receiver.

Glassworking

Cutting and Fire Polishing

1. Place the glass tubing or glass rod on a flat surface (such as the laboratory bench).

2. Hold the glass tightly with one hand close to the area to be cut.

3. Using a firm stroke, make a *single* deep scratch with a triangular file (Figure 12).

   CAUTION: *Do not use a sawing motion or repeated scratching.*

4. Grasp the glass in both hands with the scratch facing away from you and both thumbs directly behind the scratch (Figure 13).

5. Push firmly with the thumbs and pull with your fingers. The glass should snap with a clean break.

   CAUTION: *Be careful with the cut ends of the glass. They may be sharp and jagged. Do not attempt to break glass tubing having an outside diameter greater than 6 mm.*

Figure 12

Figure 13

Correctly fire polished

Tube closed up (heated too much)

Figure 14

Properly adjusted flame

Wing top on burner

Figure 15

Heating glass tubing over a wing top prior to bending

Figure 16

6. The cut ends of the glass tubing should be fire-polished to make the tubing safe to handle. Rotate one end of the glass tube in the hottest part of a burner flame, until the sharp edges have softened and become rounded (Figure 14).

CAUTION: *Do not hold the tubing in the flame too long. If you do, the hole in the tube will close.*

7. Place the hot glass on a wire gauze square to cool.

CAUTION: *Hot glass and cold glass look alike. Make sure one end of a piece of glass has cooled before you attempt to fire-polish the other end.*

Bending Glass Tubing

1. Put a wing top or flame spreader on your gas burner.

2. Light the burner and adjust the flame to produce an even blue (hot) flame across the wing top (Figure 15).

3. Grasp a length of glass tubing that has been fire-polished at both ends. Hold the center of it lengthwise in the flame, just at the top of the blue region. This is the hottest part of the flame (Figure 16).

4. Rotate the tubing in the flame to heat approximately a 5-cm section uniformly, until it becomes soft and just begins to sag.

5. Remove the tubing from the flame and bend it to the desired shape in one movement (Figure 17). Examples of good and bad bends are shown in Figure 18.

6. When it has hardened, put the glass tubing on a wire gauze to cool.

CAUTION: *Hot and cold glass look alike.*

Bend and hold at desired angle

Figure 17

Good bend

Poor bend (glass heated too strongly at one point)

Poor bend (glass held too low in flame)

Figure 18

1 OBSERVING AND INFERRING

Text Reference
Section 1.3

PURPOSE

To practice making observations and to learn how to formulate hypotheses that account for these observations.

BACKGROUND

Throughout the day, you use your senses to observe the world. You hear your alarm clock go off in the morning, you smell familiar odors as you approach the school cafeteria, and you see your friend walking down the hall toward you.

Observation, followed by the development of a hypothesis, are often the first steps in a scientific method. Experiments are then designed and carried out to test the hypothesis under controlled conditions. If the results of the initial experiment support the hypothesis, additional testing is done to further test the hypothesis. If, however, the experimental results do not support the original hypothesis, then the hypothesis must be changed or modified. When the results of many, many experiments support a hypothesis, it may become a theory. A theory is a well-tested explanation for a broad set of observations.

Your teacher will do a series of demonstrations, and you will make and record observations. You will then formulate hypotheses to explain your observations.

MATERIALS

(Teacher demonstration)

2 insulated gloves	copper wire
crucible tongs	0.05*M* silver nitrate C T
safety goggles and apron	distilled water
3 watch glasses	manganese(IV) oxide T
3 100-mL beakers	3% hydrogen peroxide
4 glass stirring rods	wood splints
3 250-mL beakers	matches
plastic wash bottle	calcium ethanoate
2-L graduated cylinder	95% ethanol F T
ice	universal indicator solution
dry ice C	0.1*M* sodium hydroxide C T
cornstarch	

Figure 1.1
Copper wire tree

Name _____ Date _____ Class _____

SAFETY FIRST!

In this lab, your teacher will perform the demonstrations. Some of the solutions may contain harmful materials. Handle chemicals only when instructed to do so by the teacher. Observe all precautions, especially the ones listed below. If you see a safety icon beside a step in the Procedure, refer to the list below for its meaning.

 Caution: Do not touch the dry ice. It can cause frostbite. Use insulated gloves or tongs. (Step 1.)

 Caution: Wear your safety goggles. (All steps.)

 Caution: Avoid contact with silver nitrate solution. It can cause temporary skin discoloration and skin burns. (Step 3.)

 Caution: Ethanol is flammable. (Step 6.)

 Note: Your teacher will properly dispose of the materials.

PROCEDURE

Your teacher will perform the demonstrations. Record your observations in Data Table 1.

 1. Place a piece of ice and a piece of dry ice on separate watch glasses. Observe what happens with time.

2. Add 30 g of cornstarch to three 100-mL beakers containing 10 mL, 15 mL, and 20 mL of water, respectively. Observe what happens when each mixture is stirred with its own glass stirring rod and when some of each mixture is picked up with the rod.

 3. Place the copper wire tree (Figure 1.1) in a 250-mL beaker containing 200 mL of the silver nitrate solution. Observe this system at intervals during the class period.

4. Place several small pieces of dry ice in a plastic wash bottle half-filled with distilled water. Observe what happens when the jet assembly of the wash bottle is replaced and tightened.

5. Add a small amount of manganese(IV) oxide powder to 50 mL of hydrogen peroxide solution in a 250-mL beaker. Cover the beaker with a watch glass for 15 seconds. Observe what happens when a *glowing* wood splint is inserted into the upper part of the beaker.

 6. Observe what happens when 50 mL of calcium ethanoate solution is poured into a 250-mL beaker containing 50 mL of ethanol.

7. Add about 20 drops of universal indicator solution to 1500 mL of water in a 2-L graduated cylinder. Record what happens when 150 mL of sodium hydroxide solution is added and the mixture is stirred. Observe what occurs when several small pieces of dry ice are added.

OBSERVATIONS

DATA TABLE 1: OBSERVATIONS	
System	Observations
ice dry ice	
cornstarch 10 mL water cornstarch 15 mL water cornstarch 20 mL water	
copper silver nitrate	
dry ice wash bottle	
manganese(IV) oxide hydrogen peroxide	
calcium ethanoate ethanol	
water universal indicator sodium hydroxide dry ice	

ANALYSES AND CONCLUSIONS

For each demonstration, suggest at least one explanation for the behavior that you observed.

1. ice and dry ice

_____

_____

_____

2. cornstarch and water

_____

_____

3. copper and silver nitrate

_____

_____

_____

4. dry ice in water-filled wash bottle

_____

_____

_____

5. manganese(IV) oxide, hydrogen peroxide, and wood splint

_____

_____

_____

6. calcium ethanoate and ethanol

_____

_____

_____

7. sodium hydroxide, dry ice, and water with an indicator

_____

_____

_____

GOING FURTHER

Design an Experiment

Propose an experiment to test one of your explanations. If resources are available and you have your teacher's permission, perform the experiment.

2 PHYSICAL AND CHEMICAL CHANGE

Text Reference
Section 2.4

PURPOSE

To investigate the criteria used to distinguish between physical and chemical changes in matter.

BACKGROUND

Matter has both physical and chemical properties. A *physical property* is a quality or condition of a substance that can be observed or measured without changing the composition of the substance. Color is an example of a physical property. During a *physical change,* some properties of a sample of matter change, but the composition of the sample does not change. Melting and dissolving are examples of physical changes. A *chemical change* produces matter with a different composition than the original sample. A *chemical property* describes the ability of a substance to undergo a specific chemical change. The ability to rust is a chemical property of iron.

In this experiment, you will observe various materials and describe their physical properties. You will then cause some of the materials to undergo changes. Based upon your observations, you will determine whether the changes are physical changes or chemical changes.

MATERIALS (PER PAIR)

(Student Experiment)

safety goggles	crucible tongs
spatula	wire gauze
magnifying glass	test-tube holder
magnet	9 pieces paper, 10 cm × 10 cm
12 small test tubes	magnesium ribbon, Mg F T
test-tube rack	sulfur, powdered, S F T
2 100-mL beakers	iron filings, Fe
glass stirring rod	sodium hydrogen carbonate,
funnel	NaHCO$_3$
ring stand	sodium chloride, NaCl
ring support	sucrose, C$_{12}$H$_{22}$O$_{11}$
evaporating dish	sand
gas burner	distilled water
watch glass	coarse filter paper
plastic wash bottle	2 pieces of exposed film
	6*M* hydrochloric acid, HCl C T

(Teacher Demonstration)

small test tube	gas burner
centigram balance	test-tube holder
fume hood	magnet

Name _____ Date _____ Class _____

SAFETY FIRST!

In this lab, observe all precautions, especially the ones listed below. If you see a safety icon beside a step in the Procedure, refer to the list below for its meaning.

 Caution: Wear your safety goggles. (All steps.)

 Caution: Hydrochloric acid is very corrosive and can cause burns. (Steps 10, 12.)

 Caution: Do not look directly at burning magnesium. The intense light may damage your eyes. View the magnesium reaction through exposed pieces of film. Do not inhale the smoke that is produced when magnesium burns. (Step 9.) Powdered sulfur is irritating to the moist membranes of the eyes, nose, and throat. Avoid getting the dust into the air. (Step 6.)

 Caution: Do not taste any of the substances or touch them with your hands. (All steps.)

 Caution: Hot glass looks just like cool glass. Once a test tube has been heated over an open flame, it may take several minutes for it to cool. Be sure that test tubes are cool before handling them. (Step 11.)

 Caution: Magnesium is extremely flammable. Keep unused strips away from open flames. (Step 9.)

 Note: Return or dispose of all materials according to the instructions of your teacher. (Steps 5, 13, 15.)

PROCEDURE

Part A. The Physical Properties of Matter

Record your observations for Part A in Data Table 1.

 1. Label a separate piece of paper for each of the seven substances to be examined. Place two pieces of magnesium ribbon, one 5 cm long and one 1 cm long, on the paper labeled "magnesium." Using the spatula supplied for each substance, transfer a pea-sized sample of the other substances to their correctly labeled papers.

2. Examine each substance with a magnifying glass. Record your observations in Data Table 1.

3. Test the effect of a magnet on each substance by passing the magnet under the sheet of paper.

4. In separate small test tubes, test the solubility of each substance by mixing a small amount of each sample with 3 mL of distilled water. "Flick" each test tube to mix the contents.

 5. Return the strip of magnesium ribbon in the test tube to its paper. Follow your teacher's instructions for proper disposal of the other materials.

26 *Chemistry Laboratory Manual*

Part B. Causing a Physical or Chemical Change

Record your observations for Part B in Data Table 2.

6. Mix the iron filings and sulfur on a clean piece of paper. Examine the mixture with a magnifying glass. Test the effect of a magnet by passing the magnet under the paper. Give this mixture to your teacher for use in Part C.

7. Mix the sodium chloride and sand on a clean piece of paper. Examine the mixture with a magnifying glass, and test the effect of a magnet.

8. Transfer the salt-sand mixture to a clean 100-mL beaker. Add about 30 mL of tap water and stir. Record your observations. Prepare a filtration setup as shown in Figures 2.1 and 2.2. Filter the mixture and record your observations. Pour about 10 mL of the filtrate into an evaporating dish. Convert your filtration setup into a setup you can use to heat the liquid in the evaporating dish. Heat the dish gently until the filtrate has completely evaporated. Examine both the dry residue in the evaporating dish and the wet residue on the filter paper.

Figure 2.1

Put cone in funnel and moisten with water

Press moistened filter paper against filter funnel to seal

Guide flow of liquid with a glass rod

Solid collects on filter paper

Mixture being filtered

Stem touches side of beaker

Filtrate

Figure 2.2

9. **CAUTION:** *Do not look directly at burning magnesium; look through the exposed film.* Position a watch glass near the gas burner. Using crucible tongs, grasp one end of the 5-cm strip of magnesium ribbon and hold it in the burner flame until the magnesium ignites. Quickly position the burning magnesium so that the combustion products fall on the watch glass. Compare the appearance of this product with that of the original magnesium ribbon.

10. Place the unburned 1-cm strip of magnesium and the combustion product from the watch glass into separate test tubes. Add 10 drops of 6*M* hydrochloric acid to each tube. Feel the bottom of each test tube. Record your observations.

11. Put half of your sucrose sample into a test tube. **CAUTION:** *When heating a test tube, never point the mouth of it at yourself or anyone else.* Heat the tube gently in a burner flame and watch carefully for changes. Periodically remove the tube from the flame and check for odors by fanning the fumes toward your nose. Grasp the test tube with a test-tube holder and hold the test tube about 3–5 inches from your nose while fanning the vapors toward your nose.

Now heat the residue in the test tube more vigorously for 1–2 minutes. **CAUTION:** *Be sure the tube is cool before handling it.* After cooling the tube, use a spatula to scrape some of the residue into a clean test tube. Examine the residue and test its solubility in water.

12. Transfer the sodium hydrogen carbonate sample to a test tube. Carefully add 5 drops of 6*M* hydrochloric acid. Touch the bottom of the test tube with your hand. Record your observations.

13. Follow your teacher's instructions for proper disposal of the materials.

Part C. Conservation of Mass (Teacher Demonstration)

Record your observations for Part C in Data Table 2.

14. Several samples of the iron-sulfur mixture from Part B will be combined in a clean, dry test tube. The mass of the test tube and its contents will be determined and recorded. The test tube is heated gently, then vigorously, for several minutes. **CAUTION:** *This heating must be done in a fume hood.* After heating is complete, the mass is remeasured and recorded. Examine the reaction product. The effect of a magnet on the reaction product will be tested.

15. Your teacher will properly dispose of the materials.

Name _____ Date _____ Class _____

OBSERVATIONS

DATA TABLE 1: PHYSICAL PROPERTIES OF MATTER

Substance and Formula	Physical State	Color	Odor	Dissolves in water	Effect of Magnet
sulfur, S					
iron filings, Fe					
sodium hydrogen carbonate, $NaHCO_3$					
sodium chloride, NaCl					
sucrose, $C_{12}H_{22}O_{11}$					
sand, SiO_2					
magnesium, Mg					

DATA TABLE 2: OBSERVATIONS OF PHYSICAL AND CHEMICAL CHANGES

System	Observations
Fe and S mixture —tested with magnet	
NaCl and sand mixture —mixed with water —filtered —filtrate allowed to evaporate	
Mg —burned in air	
Mg —reacted with 6M HCl	
product of burning —reacted with 6M HCl	
$C_{12}H_{22}O_{11}$ —heated	
$NaHCO_3$ —reacted with 6M HCl	
Fe and S mixture —heated initial mass final mass	

Name _____ Date _____ Class _____

ANALYSES AND CONCLUSIONS

1. The following is a list of changes you observed in Parts B and C. Indicate whether each change was a physical change or a chemical change and give reasons for your answer.

   a. Mixing iron and sulfur. (Part B, Step 6)

   _____

   _____

   _____

   b. Mixing salt, sand, and water. (Part B, Step 8)

   _____

   _____

   _____

   c. Burning magnesium. (Part B, Step 9)

   _____

   _____

   _____

   d. Mixing magnesium and the product of burning magnesium with hydrochloric acid. (Part B, Step 10)

   _____

   _____

   _____

   _____

   e. Heating sucrose. (Part B, Step 11)

   _____

   _____

   _____

   _____

   f. Mixing sodium hydrogen carbonate and hydrochloric acid. (Part B, Step 12)

   _____

   _____

   _____

   _____

   g. Heating iron and sulfur. (Part C, Step 14)

   _____

   _____

   _____

2. Was mass conserved in the reaction of iron and sulfur? Explain.

_____

_____

_____

3. Except for the reaction between iron and sulfur, none of the reactions in this experiment can be used to demonstrate the law of conservation of mass. Explain why.

_____

_____

_____

_____

_____

_____

4. How do you decide whether an observed property of matter is a physical or chemical property?

_____

_____

_____

_____

_____

_____

5. What criteria are used to distinguish between a chemical change and a physical change?

_____

_____

_____

6. State in your own words the law of conservation of mass.

_____

_____

_____

_____

GOING FURTHER

Develop a Hypothesis

The black residue left in Step 11 has a smaller mass than the original sucrose sample. Propose a hypothesis to explain this loss of mass.

_____

_____

_____

_____

Design an Experiment

Propose an experiment to test your hypothesis. If resources are available and you have your teacher's permission, perform the experiment.

_____

_____

_____

_____

_____

　　　　　　　　　　　　　　　　　　　　　　　EXPERIMENT

3 OBSERVING A CHEMICAL REACTION

Text Reference
Section 2.4

PURPOSE

To learn how qualitative and quantitative observations of a chemical reaction are used to formulate a hypothesis.

BACKGROUND

You and a friend may have very different feelings about a movie you've just seen. You may disagree about whether you liked the movie or about the movie's intended meaning. Although you both have observed the same movie, your interpretations of the movie may differ. Distinguishing between observation and interpretation is very important in chemistry. An *observation* is a statement of fact, based on what you detect by your senses. An *interpretation* is your judgment or opinion about what you have observed. A statement such as "the liquid is clear and colorless" is an observation. It would be an interpretation to say, without further testing, that the clear and colorless liquid is water.

The purpose of this experiment is to help you distinguish observation from interpretation while examining a chemical reaction. Try to make as many observations of the reaction as possible. There are two types of observations. A *quantitative* observation is an observation that involves a measurement; a *qualitative* observation is a general description and does not involve a measurement. "The liquid is hot" is a qualitative observation. "The temperature of the liquid is 95.0°C" is a quantitative observation.

MATERIALS (PER PAIR)

safety goggles
100-mL beaker
plastic spoon
glass stirring rod
thermometer

copper(II) chloride dihydrate,
　　$CuCl_2 \cdot 2H_2O$　T　I
distilled water
aluminum foil, 8 cm × 8 cm

SAFETY FIRST!

In this lab, the solution you are working with may become quite hot following the addition of aluminum foil. Observe all precautions, especially the ones listed below. If you see a safety icon beside a step in the Procedure, refer to the list below for its meaning.

 Caution: Wear safety goggles. (All steps.)

 Caution: Copper(II) chloride is an irritant. Avoid skin contact with this chemical. (All steps.)

Name _____ Date _____ Class _____

 Caution: Copper chloride is toxic by ingestion and inhalation. (Step 1.)

 Note: Return or dispose of all materials according to the instructions of your teacher. (Step 5.)

PROCEDURE

© Pearson Education, Inc., publishing as Pearson Prentice Hall. All rights reserved.

As you perform the experiment, record your observations in Data Table 1.

 1. Obtain and describe a sample of copper(II) chloride dihydrate, $CuCl_2 \cdot 2H_2O$.

 2. Fill the 100-mL beaker about one-fourth full with distilled water. Without stirring, add 1 level teaspoonful of the solid to the water. Record your observations of both the solid and the water.

3. Use the glass stirring rod to stir the mixture until the solid is completely dissolved. Record your observations of the solution.

 4. Place the thermometer in the copper(II) chloride solution and record the temperature. **CAUTION:** *Observe the mixture from the side; do not look directly down into the beaker.* Place a loosely crumpled ball of aluminum in the solution and record your observations. Stir the mixture occasionally and observe for at least 10 minutes. Record any change in temperature.

 5. Follow your teacher's instructions for proper disposal of the materials.

Name _____ Date _____ Class _____

OBSERVATIONS

DATA TABLE 1: OBSERVATIONS	
System	Observations
dry copper(II) chloride dihydrate	
copper(II) chloride in water	
stirred copper(II) chloride in water	
copper(II) chloride solution plus aluminum foil	
initial temperature:	
final temperature:	

ANALYSES AND CONCLUSIONS

1. Check your observations. Cross out any that are interpretations rather than observations.

2. List each of your observations in one of four following sections. Number your observations consecutively. Circle the number of any observation that is quantitative.

   a. observations of the dry solid

   _____

   _____

   b. observations of the wet solid before stirring

   _____

   _____

   _____

   c. observations of the solution before addition of aluminum

   _____

   _____

   _____

    d. observations of the reaction that occurs when the aluminum is added to the solution

_____

_____

_____

3. Would you expect your observations or your interpretations to most closely match those of your classmates? Explain.

_____

_____

_____

_____

GOING FURTHER

Develop a Hypothesis

Based on the observations you made during this lab, develop a hypothesis about what happened when aluminum metal was added to the solution of copper(II) chloride.

_____

_____

_____

_____

Design an Experiment

Propose an experiment to test your hypothesis. If resources are available and you have the permission of your teacher, perform the experiment.

_____

_____

_____

_____

_____

_____

Chapter 3 • *Scientific Measurement* **EXPERIMENT**

4 MASS, VOLUME, AND DENSITY

Text Reference
Section 3.2, 3.3, and 3.4

PURPOSE

To determine the densities of unknown metals.

BACKGROUND

An old riddle asks "Which is heavier, a pound of feathers or a pound of lead?" The question is nonsensical, of course, since a pound of feathers and a pound of lead both weigh the same, one pound. Nevertheless, there is a clearly something different about a small lead brick and a large bag of feathers, even though they weigh the same. The key to answering the riddle is understanding the relationship that exists between a substance's mass and the volume it occupies. This relationship is expressed by the physical property called density. *Density* is defined as the ratio of a substance's mass to the volume it occupies.

$$\text{Density} = \frac{\text{mass of substance (g)}}{\text{volume of substance (mL)}}$$

In this experiment, you will measure the mass and volume of several unknown materials. You will then use your data to explore the relationship between the mass and volume of the materials and to calculate their density.

After performing this lab, if someone asks you the riddle about feathers and lead, you can explain to them the difference between weight and density.

MATERIALS (PER PAIR)

safety goggles   ruler
centigram balance   metal samples
25-mL graduated cylinder   paper towels

SAFETY FIRST!

In this lab, observe all precautions, especially the ones listed below. If you see a safety icon beside a step in the Procedure, refer to the list below for its meaning.

 Caution: Wear your safety goggles. (All steps.)

 Note: Your teacher will properly dispose of the materials.

PROCEDURE

As you perform the experiment, record your data in Data Tables 1 and 2.

1. Determine the mass of two different unknown metal samples to the nearest 0.01 gram, using a centigram balance. Record the masses in Data Tables 1 and 2.

2. Find the volume of each metal sample by water displacement. Fill a 25-mL graduated cylinder about half-full with water, measure the volume, and record as "volume of water alone" in Data Table 1. Tilt the graduated cylinder and carefully slide one of the metal samples down the side. Make sure the metal sample is completely submerged in the water. Measure the volume and record the measurement as "volume of water + metal" in Data Table 1.

3. Repeat Step 2, using the other metal sample. Dry both samples and return them to your teacher.

Name _____ Date _____ Class _____

OBSERVATIONS

DATA TABLE 1: INDIVIDUAL DATA AND CALCULATIONS			
	Metal A	Metal B	Additional Metal Sample
mass (g)			
volume of water alone (mL)			
volume of water + metal (mL)			
volume of metal (mL)			
density of metal (g/mL)			

DATA TABLE 2: CLASS DATA: MASS AND VOLUME OF METAL SAMPLES						
	Metal A		Metal B		Additional Metal Sample	
Lab Pair	mass (g)	volume (mL)	mass (g)	volume (mL)	mass (g)	volume (mL)
1						
2						
3						
4						
5						
6						
7						
8						
9						

ANALYSES AND CONCLUSIONS

1. Compute the volume of each metal sample, using data from Data Table 1. Compute the density of each metal sample, showing your work (including units), in Data Table 1. Remember,

$$\text{density} = \frac{\text{mass (g)}}{\text{volume (mL)}}.$$

2. Complete Data Table 2 by recording the mass and volume data collected by you and your classmates.

3. Using the class data, plot a graph of mass versus volume. Represent the plotted points for each metal with a different symbol. Draw a "best fit" straight line through each group of plotted points.

4. Determine the slope of each of the lines on your graph. Record the slope of each line and your method of calculation in Data Table 3. (**Hint:** The general equation for a line is $y = mx + b$ where m is the value for the slope and b is the value for the y-intercept.) Pay special attention to the units of the slope.

DATA TABLE 3: DENSITY CALCULATIONS FROM CLASS DATA (SLOPES)	
Metal A	Metal B
$\dfrac{y}{x} = \dfrac{\text{g}}{\text{. mL}} = \underline{\quad}$ g/mL	$\dfrac{y}{x} = \dfrac{\text{g}}{\text{mL}} = \underline{\quad}$ g/mL

5. What does the slope of the line for each metal represent? (**Hint:** Look back at Data Table 1.)

_____

_____

_____

_____

_____

6. Looking at your graph, what does this experiment demonstrate about the density of a metal? What does it demonstrate about the densities of different metals?

_____

_____

_____

_____

_____

_____

Name _____ Date _____ Class _____

7. Calculate the percent error in the density calculations for the two samples. (See Analyses and Conclusions, Step 1.) Your teacher will provide the accepted value for the density of each metal.

$$\text{percent error} = \frac{|\text{experimental value} - \text{accepted value}|}{\text{accepted value}} \times 100\%$$

8. Calculate the percent error in the values of density obtained from the slopes of the lines in your graph. (See Analyses and Conclusions, Step 4.)

9. Look back at the percent errors calculated in problems 7 and 8. Generally, the slope of the line will give a more accurate value for density than a single sample. Explain why this is usually true.

_____

_____

_____

_____

_____

_____

10. Can you identify a metal if you know its density? Explain your answer. Try to identify the metals used in this experiment by referring to tables of density.

_____

_____

_____

_____

_____

_____

11. Do you think that determining the volumes of your metal samples by measuring their dimensions and calculating would be more accurate or less accurate than determining these volumes by water displacement? Explain. Would measuring the dimensions of a solid always be possible? Explain.

_____

_____

_____

_____

_____

_____

_____

12. How would you modify this experiment to determine the density of table sugar, wood chips, and milk?

_____

_____

_____

_____

_____

_____

GOING FURTHER

Develop a Hypothesis

Based on the results of this lab, develop a hypothesis about how and why unknown substances can be distinguished from one another by measuring their densities.

_____

_____

_____

_____

Design an Experiment

Propose an experiment to test your hypothesis. If resources are available and you have your teacher's permission, perform the experiment.

_____

_____

_____

_____

ATOMIC STRUCTURE: RUTHERFORD'S EXPERIMENT

Text Reference
Section 4.2

PURPOSE

To discover how the physical properties, such as size and shape, of an object can be measured by indirect means.

BACKGROUND

As you have done experiments, you have learned to make useful observations and to draw reasonable conclusions from data. But imagine how little you would be able to accomplish if the room in which you worked were so dark that you could not see the materials you were working with. Imagine how limited your observations would be if the object of your scrutiny were so small that it could not be seen, even with a microscope. When you think of how difficult experimentation would be under such adverse conditions, you will gain some appreciation for the enormous technical problems confronting early atomic scientists.

These scientists had as their target the atom—a bit of matter so small that there was no hope of seeing it directly. Nevertheless, these ingenious experimenters were able to infer that the atom had a nucleus.

It is impractical to reproduce the classic experiments that led to the discovery of the nucleus in a high school laboratory. You can get some idea of the challenge that these researchers faced, however, by playing the game described in this experiment. You will infer the size and shape of an object you cannot see or touch.

MATERIALS (PER PAIR)

safety goggles
sheet of heavy cardboard or thin
    plywood sheet, 60 cm × 60 cm
plastic-foam shape

marble
sheet construction paper
sheet notebook paper

SAFETY FIRST!

 Caution: Wear your safety goggles. (All steps.)

Name _____ Date _____ Class _____

PROCEDURE

1. At your lab station, you will find a sheet of cardboard resting on top of a hidden object. *Do not look under the cardboard!* Roll a marble under the cardboard from various directions and observe where it comes out. (Have your teacher retrieve the marble if it stays under the board; no peeking!)

2. Place a sheet of construction paper on top of the board and trace the entry and exit path for each roll of the marble.

3. Continue rolling the marble and recording its path until you think you know the size and shape of the object. Draw a full-sized sketch of the object on a sheet of paper. Check your results with your teacher. Do not look under the board until your teacher confirms your results.

4. Ask your teacher for a second mystery object if you have time to repeat the game.

ANALYSES AND CONCLUSIONS

1. How does this game simulate early efforts to determine the structure of the atom? In what ways is it different?

_____

_____

_____

_____

_____

_____

_____

_____

_____

2. You eventually had the satisfaction of seeing the shape under the board. Did the early atomic scientists have this same opportunity? Do scientists today have this opportunity?

_____

_____

_____

GOING FURTHER

Develop a Hypothesis

On the basis of the results in this lab, develop a hypothesis about how the size, shape, or identity of other kinds of objects could be determined by indirect means.

_____

_____

_____

_____

Design an Experiment

Propose an experiment to test your hypothesis. If resources are available and you have your teacher's permission, perform the experiment.

_____

_____

_____

_____

_____

_____

_____

_____

_____

_____

_____

Chapter 5 • *Electrons in Atoms*   **EXPERIMENT**

6 FLAME TESTS FOR METALS

Text Reference
Section 5.3

PURPOSE

To observe and identify metallic ions, using flame tests.

BACKGROUND

Have you ever wondered why a candle flame is yellow? The characteristic yellow of a candle flame comes from the glow of burning carbon fragments. The carbon fragments are produced by the incomplete combustion reaction of the wick and candle wax. When elements, such as carbon, are heated to high temperatures, some of their electrons are excited to higher energy levels. When these excited electrons fall back to lower energy levels, they release excess energy in packages of light called photons, or light quanta. The color of the emitted light depends on its energy. Blue light is more energetic than red light, for example. When heated, each element emits a characteristic pattern of light energies, which is useful for identifying the element. The characteristic colors of light produced when substances are heated in the flame of a gas burner are the basis of flame tests for several elements.

In this experiment, you will perform the flame tests used to identify several metallic elements.

MATERIALS (PER PAIR)

safety goggles	potassium nitrate, KNO_3 T
8 small test tubes	calcium nitrate, $Ca(NO_3)_2$ T
test-tube rack	strontium nitrate, $Sr(NO_3)_2$ T
paper towel	lithium nitrate, $LiNO_3$
scoopulas	copper(II) nitrate, $Cu(NO_3)_2$ T
50-mL beaker	sodium nitrate, $NaNO_3$ T
platinum wire or nichrome	barium nitrate, $Ba(NO_3)_2$ T C
wire loop	6M hydrochloric acid, HCl C T
gas burner	unknown salt
cobalt-blue glass	

SAFETY FIRST!

In this lab, the solutions you will be using contain harmful materials. Avoid skin contact with these chemicals. Observe all precautions, especially the ones listed below. If you see a safety icon beside a step in the Procedure, refer to the list below for its meaning.

 Caution: Wear your safety goggles. (All steps.)

Caution: Hydrochloric acid is corrosive and can cause severe burns. (Step 2.)

 Caution: Do not taste any of the substances or touch them with your hands. (Step 1.)

 Caution: Do not at any time touch the end of the wire loop used in the flame tests. This wire gets extremely hot and can cause severe burns. (Steps 2–5.)

 Note: Return or dispose of all materials according to the instructions of your teacher. (Step 6.)

PROCEDURE

As you perform the experiment, record your observations in Data Table 1.

1. Place a test-tube rack on a paper towel. Write the chemical name for each of the seven metal salts next to a position in the rack where a test tube will be placed. Use scoopulas supplied with each salt to place pea-sized samples of each metal salt into a test tube. Place the tubes in the test-tube rack.

2. Pour about 15 mL of $6M$ HCl into a clean, labeled 50-mL beaker. Dip the wire loop into the $6M$ HCl and then heat it in the hot flame of a gas burner, as shown in Figure 6.1a. Continue this procedure until no color comes from the wire when it is put into the flame.

3. Dip the clean wire loop into a sample of metal salt and heat the sample in the burner flame, as shown in Figure 6.1b. Record the color of the flame in Data Table 1. Test the remaining samples, cleaning the wire loop as described in Step 2, before each new sample is tested. Record your observations.

4. View the flame colors produced by $NaNO_3$ and KNO_3 through cobalt-blue glass. Record your observations.

5. Perform a flame test on your unknown salt. Record your observations.

 6. Dispose of the unused portions of your samples as directed by your teacher.

Figure 6.1a

Figure 6.1b

Name _____ Date _____ Class _____

OBSERVATIONS

DATA TABLE 1: FLAME TESTS	
Ion	Flame Color
sodium, Na^+	
potassium, K^+	
calcium, Ca^{2+}	
barium, Ba^{2+}	
strontium, Sr^{2+}	
lithium, Li^+	
copper, Cu^{2+}	
sodium, Na^+ (cobalt glass)	
potassium, K^+ (cobalt glass)	
unknown	

ANALYSES AND CONCLUSIONS

1. List the elements that produced the most easily identified colors.

_____

_____

2. Which elements are least easily identified? Explain.

_____

3. Which element produces the most intense color?

_____

_____

4. Would flame tests be useful for detecting metal ions present in a mixture of metal ions? Explain.

_____

_____

_____

5. The energy of colored light increases in the order red, yellow, green, blue, violet. List the metallic elements used in the flame tests in increasing order of the energy of the light emitted.

6. What is the purpose of using the cobalt glass in the identification of sodium and potassium?

_____

_____

_____

_____

_____

GOING FURTHER

Do Research

In this lab, you observed that each element emits a unique color of light when heated in a flame. If these light emissions were examined through a prism, you would observe that the emitted light is actually composed of different wavelengths of light that may lie in the violet region, the green region, or the red region of the visible spectrum. Each element has a unique *emission spectrum*. Look up the emission spectra for the elements tested in this lab. Do research on how scientists apply these emission spectra to investigate the chemical composition of stars. For example, what is the emission spectrum of the sun, and what does this spectrum reveal about the types of elements in the sun?

_____

_____

_____

_____

Chapter 5 • *Electrons in Atoms*

7 ENERGIES OF ELECTRONS

Text Reference
Section 5.3

PURPOSE

To construct a simple flame spectrograph and measure a wavelength of light produced by the electronic excitations of sodium ions.

BACKGROUND

You should recall from Experiment 6 that flame tests are useful for identifying metal ions that produce characteristic colors. Separating these characteristic colors into discrete wavelengths of light produces a pattern of individual lines that uniquely identifies the metal ion. This pattern of lines is called an *emission spectrum*. With a reference source of emission spectra, you would find it relatively easy to identify a particular metal ion.

You can separate the lines in the visible region of a flame emission spectrum by using an optical prism or a diffraction grating. A *spectrograph* is an instrument designed to produce electronic excitations, separate the emitted light into its component wavelengths, and then record the wavelengths of emitted light. In this experiment, you will construct a simple spectrograph and measure the wavelength of a strong excitation of sodium ions.

MATERIALS (PER PAIR)

safety goggles
2 meter sticks
diffraction grating
cardboard piece with narrow
   slit
50-mL beaker

watch glass
platinum or nichrome wire
   loop
gas burner
6M hydrochloric acid, HCl [C] [T]
1M sodium chloride, NaCl

SAFETY FIRST!

In this lab, observe all precautions, especially the ones listed below. If you see a safety icon beside a step in the Procedure, refer to the list below for its meaning.

 Caution: Wear your safety goggles. (All steps.)

 Caution: Hydrochloric acid is corrosive and can cause severe burns. (Step 2.)

 Caution: Do not let your skin or clothing contact the burner flame or the hot wire used in the flame tests. (Steps 2–4.)

Caution: Exercise care when working with an open flame. Tie back hair and loose clothing. Do not use the burner near flammable materials. (Steps 2–4.)

Note: Return or dispose of all materials according to the instructions of your teacher. (Step 7.)

PROCEDURE

As you perform the experiment, record your data and calculation results in Data Table 1.

1. Set up the apparatus shown in Figure 7.1.

2. Pour approximately 15 mL of 6*M* hydrochloric acid, HCl, into a 50-mL beaker. Always cover the beaker with a watch glass when the beaker is not being used. Clean the wire loop by first dipping it into the HCl and then heating it in the hot flame of a gas burner. Continue to dip and heat the wire until no color comes from the wire as it is heated.

3. Dip the clean wire loop into the NaCl solution.

4. Place the wire loop in the burner flame. Observe the flame through the slit in the cardboard and the diffraction grating, as shown in Figure 7.1. You should see a series of lines to the left and right of the slit. Pick out the brightest line to the left side of the slit and have your partner record this position on the meter stick as position A. Repeat this procedure on the right side of the slit and record this as position B.

5. Measure the distance from the diffraction grating to the slit and record this as distance Y.

6. Dispose of the solutions as directed by your teacher.

Figure 7.1

OBSERVATIONS

DATA TABLE 1: WAVELENGTH FOR THE SODIUM EMISSION LINE	
left image (A)	cm
right image (B)	cm
distance X (average of left and right images)	cm
distance Y	cm
distance Z	cm
diffracting grating constant (d)	cm/line
sin θ	
wavelength (λ)	nm

ANALYSES AND CONCLUSIONS

1. Find the average of distances A and B (in centimeters). Record this answer as distance X in your data table.

2. Calculate the distance Z, using the Pythagorean theorem. Refer to Figure 7.1 for relationship of distances.

$$Z = \sqrt{X^2 + Y^2}$$

Record the value of Z in the data table.

3. Calculate sin θ, using the following relationship:

$$\sin \theta = \frac{X}{Z}$$

Record sin θ in the data table.

4. The wavelength (λ) of the sodium flame emission line being investigated in this experiment is given, in nanometers, by the Bragg equation:

$$\lambda = d \times \sin \theta \times \left(\frac{1 \times 10^7 \text{ nm}}{1 \text{ cm}} \right)$$

d represents a diffraction grating constant: $d = \dfrac{1}{n}$ where n is the number of lines, per centimeter, scribed on the diffraction grating. Calculate the value of d for your grating and enter it in Data Table 1.

5. Compute the wavelength of the bright line you viewed on the meter stick, using the Bragg equation. Record this value in the data table.

6. The accepted value of λ for the observed transition is 589.0 nm. Calculate the percent error in your value.

7. Identify the possible sources of error in your determination of λ.

_____

_____

8. How can a spectrographic experiment help identify a particular metal ion?

_____

_____

_____

_____

GOING FURTHER

Do Research

Atomic absorption spectroscopy is one of the most sensitive methods available for the detection of various metals. Do research to find out how this method is used to quantify the amount of an element in a particular sample and compare the detection limits of this method with other spectroscopic methods of analysis.

_____

_____

_____

Chapter 5 • *Electrons in Atoms*   **EXPERIMENT**

8 INTRODUCTION TO THE SPECTROPHOTOMETER

PURPOSE

To determine the absorption spectrum of an aqueous solution of chromium(III) ions.

Text Reference
Section 5.3

BACKGROUND

Many compounds absorb light from regions of the electromagnetic spectrum. A *spectrophotometer* is a device designed to determine the wavelengths of light that a compound absorbs. When an aqueous sample of a compound is placed in the light path of a spectrophotometer, the sample may absorb all the light, some of the light, or no light at all. The absorption of light depends upon the materials in the sample and the wavelength of the light. Light absorption occurs at wavelengths whose energy corresponds to the energy necessary to cause electronic excitations of atoms, ions, or molecules in the sample. From the spectrophotometer data, a graph can be made that plots the light intensity transmitted through the sample versus the wavelength of the light; such a graph is called an *absorption spectrum*. The range of wavelengths absorbed by the sample appear as bands of minimum intensity.

Absorption spectra are useful for two reasons. First, the absorption spectrum of a substance is a unique characteristic of that substance. This makes the spectrum useful for the identification of unknown substances. Second, the intensity of the absorption bands can be related to the concentration of the substance in the sample. Thus, the intensity of the absorption band can be used to determine the amount of a particular substance in a mixture.

In this experiment, you will determine the absorption spectrum of an aqueous solution of chromium(III) ions.

MATERIALS (PER PAIR)

safety goggles
Spectronic 20
   spectrophotometer
2 small test tubes or 2 glass
   cuvettes
10-mL graduated cylinder

plastic wash bottle
distilled water
0.02M chromium(III) nitrate,
   $Cr(NO_3)_3$ T I
tissue paper

SAFETY FIRST!

In this lab, observe all precautions, especially the following ones. If you see a safety icon beside a step in the Procedure, refer to the following list for its meaning.

Caution: Wear your safety goggles. (All steps.)

 Caution: Chromium(III) nitrate is toxic and can irritate your skin. (Steps 5–8.)

 Note: Return or dispose of all materials according to the instructions of your teacher. (Step 8.)

PROCEDURE

As you perform the experiment, record your percent transmittance data in Data Table 1.

 1. Turn on the spectrophotometer and allow it to warm up for about 20 minutes.

2. Set the wavelength control knob to 375 nanometers (375 nm). Adjust the amplifier control knob to produce 0 percent transmittance (0%T) at this wavelength.

3. Add 3 mL of distilled water to a clean, small test tube. Wipe the outside of the tube with a tissue to make certain that it is clean and dry. Avoid getting fingerprints on the tube. Dislodge any air bubbles present in the water by gently tapping the tube with a finger.

4. Place the tube in the sample holder and close the cover. Adjust the light control knob until the spectrophotometer reads 100%T.

 5. Remove the first sample from the spectrophotometer. Add 3 mL of 0.02M chromium(III) nitrate, $Cr(NO_3)_3$, to another clean test tube. Use a tissue to clean and dry the tube. Insert the tube of chromium(III) nitrate into the sample holder. Close the cover of the holder. Read the percent transmittance and record the reading in Data Table 1. Remove the sample from the holder.

6. Turn the wavelength dial to 400 nm. Use the amplifier control knob to adjust the percent transmittance to 0%T. Place the water sample in the holder. With the light control knob, adjust the meter to 100%T. Replace the water sample with the chromium(III) nitrate sample. Measure and record the percent transmittance at 400 nm.

7. For the remainder of the wavelengths listed in Data Table 1, continue the procedure of setting 0%T, setting 100%T, and measuring the percent transmittance of the chromium(III) nitrate solution.

8. Unless directed otherwise by your teacher, return the aqueous chromium(III) nitrate to the dropper bottle.

Name _____ Date _____ Class _____

OBSERVATIONS

DATA TABLE 1: PERCENT TRANSMITTANCE AND ABSORBANCE OF 0.02M Cr(NO_3)$_3$ SOLUTION AT VARIOUS WAVELENGTHS		
Wavelength (nm)	% Transmittance (%T)	Absorbance
375		
400		
405		
415		
425		
440		
455		
470		
490		
500		
520		
530		
540		
550		
570		
575		
580		
600		
625		

ANALYSES AND CONCLUSIONS

1. Graph percent transmittance versus wavelength. The curve you plot is the absorption spectrum of chromium(III) ions in the visible region of the electromagnetic spectrum.

2. At what wavelengths do chromium(III) ions absorb the maximum amounts of light? What colors of light correspond to these wavelengths?

_____

_____

_____

_____

_____

_____

Name _____ Date _____ Class _____

3. Based on the answer to problem 2, would you expect a red solution to absorb or transmit red light? Explain.

_____

_____

_____

_____

_____

4. The amount of light that is absorbed by a solution is commonly expressed either in terms of percent transmittance, as in this experiment, or in terms of absorbance (A). Absorbance is defined as: 2 − log of percent transmittance

   or

$$A = 2 - \log \%T$$

Given the relationship shown in the preceding formula, convert the percent transmittance values in Data Table 1 to absorbance values. Plot a graph of absorbance versus wavelength. Compare and analyze the shapes of the two curves. Might it be more useful to use transmittance values sometimes and absorbance values at other times? Explain the advantages and disadvantages of using these different units.

_____

_____

_____

_____

_____

_____

_____

_____

GOING FURTHER

Develop a Hypothesis

Based on the results of this lab, propose a hypothesis about how the absorption of light by a solution of $Cr(NO_3)_3$ varies with the concentration of Cr^{3+} ions in solution.

_____

_____

_____

_____

Design an Experiment

Propose an experiment to test your hypothesis. In your protocol, include a method for determining the concentration of Cr^{3+} ions in an unknown solution of $Cr(NO_3)_3$. If resources are available and you have your teacher's permission, perform the experiment.

_____

_____

_____

_____

_____

_____

Chapter 6 • *The Periodic Table*

9 PERIODIC PROPERTIES

Text Reference
Section 6.2

PURPOSE

To investigate the periodic variation of density in Group 4A elements.

BACKGROUND

When the elements are arranged in order of increasing atomic number, they exhibit a periodic recurrence of properties. Elements in the same group in the periodic table tend to have similar physical and chemical properties. These similarities are due, in large part, to similarities among the electron configurations of the elements in a group. You can find periodic trends in certain properties, such as density, among the elements within a given group.

In this experiment, you will investigate the variation in density among three Group 4A elements. You will use your results to predict the density of another Group 4A element.

MATERIALS (PER PAIR)

safety goggles and apron
centigram balance
100-mL graduated cylinder
tin, Sn

lead shot, Pb T
silicon, Si
distilled water

SAFETY FIRST!

In this lab, observe all precautions, especially the ones listed below. If you see a safety icon beside a step in the Procedure, refer to the list below for its meaning.

 Caution: Wear your safety goggles. (All steps.)

 Note: Return or dispose of all materials according to the instructions of your teacher. (Step 4.)

 Note: Wash your hands thoroughly after completing this experiment.

Name _____ Date _____ Class _____

PROCEDURE

You will determine the densities of the tin (Sn), lead (Pb), and silicon (Si) samples by water displacement. As you perform the experiment, record your data in Data Table 1. Note the appearance of these elements.

1. Determine the mass of the samples to the nearest 0.01 gram, using a centigram balance. Record the masses in Data Table 1.

2. Fill a 100-mL graduated cylinder about three quarters full with water, measure the volume, and record the measurement as "volume of water alone" in Data Table 1. Tilt the graduated cylinder and carefully slide one of the samples down the side. Make sure the sample is completely submerged in the water. Measure the volume and record the measurement as "volume of water + sample" in Data Table 1.

3. Repeat Step 2, using the other samples.

4. Dry the samples and return them to your teacher. Then wash your hands thoroughly with soap or detergent.

OBSERVATIONS

DATA TABLE 1: DENSITIES OF GROUP 4A ELEMENTS			
	tin (Sn)	lead (Pb)	silicon (Si)
mass of sample (g)			
volume of water alone (mL)			
volume of water + sample (mL)			
volume of sample (mL)			
density of sample (mass/volume)			
appearance			

Name _____ Date _____ Class _____

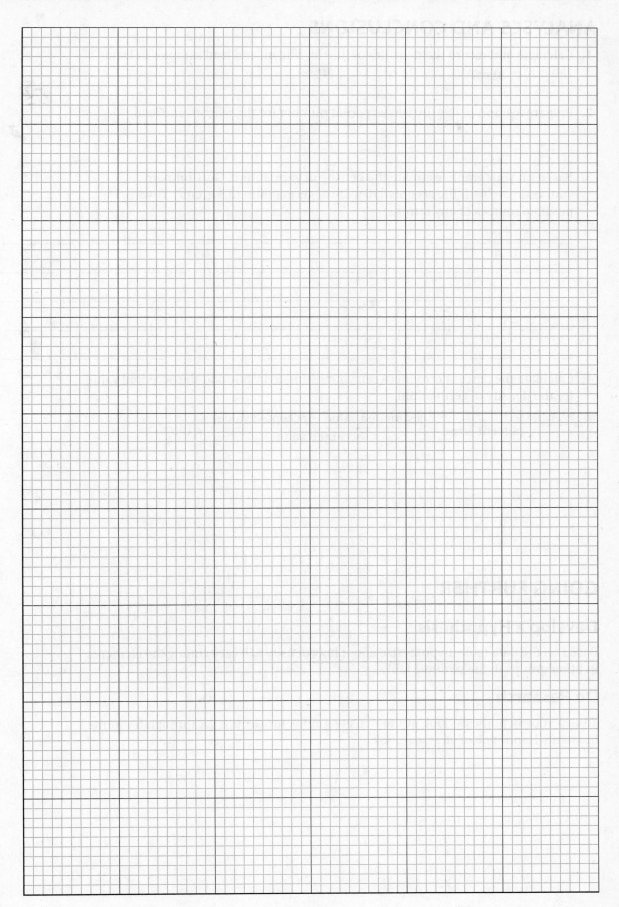

Name _____ Date _____ Class _____

ANALYSES AND CONCLUSIONS

1. Calculate and record the densities of the tin, silicon, and lead samples in Data Table 1.

2. Prepare a graph of density versus period number for tin, silicon, and lead.

3. Based on your graph, estimate the density of germanium, Ge. Compare your estimate with the accepted density of germanium (5.3 g/cm^3). Give possible sources of any errors.

   _____

   _____

   _____

   _____

   _____

4. Calculate the percent error between your estimated value and the accepted value for the density of germanium.

$$\text{percent error} = \frac{|\text{estimated value} - \text{accepted value}|}{\text{accepted value}} \times 100\%$$

GOING FURTHER

Develop a Hypothesis

Based on the data table, hypothesize about how density will vary among the elements in other groups in the periodic table.

Do Research

To test your hypothesis, look at the density graphs for Groups 1A through 8A in the Elements Handbook of your textbook.

Name _____ Date _____ Class _____

10   CRYSTAL STRUCTURES

Text Reference
Sections 7.2 and 7.3

PURPOSE

To investigate the geometric arrangement of atoms in crystalline solids.

BACKGROUND

The regular geometric shapes of crystals reflect the orderly arrangement of the atoms, ions, or molecules making up the crystal lattice. In this experiment, you will gain insight into the ways crystals are formed. To do this, you will model crystal structures using plastic-foam spheres. Using the models, you will determine the number of nearest neighbors (the coordination number) of the particles in each of these structures. The effect of the size of the anions and cations in the crystal structure on determining the coordination number will also be investigated. Your investigation will include three types of packing: hexagonal closest packing, face-centered cubic packing, and body-centered cubic packing.

MATERIALS (PER 8-STUDENT GROUP)

safety goggles
box of toothpicks, or 3 packs
   of plastic coffee stirrers, or
   box of pipe cleaners
62 plastic-foam balls, 2-inch
   diameter

13 plastic-foam balls, 1-inch
   diameter
13 plastic-foam balls, 3/4-inch
   diameter
scissors
centimeter ruler

SAFETY FIRST!

 Caution: Wear safety goggles when you are working in the lab. (All steps.)

PROCEDURE

As you perform the experiment, answer the questions in the Analyses and Conclusions section.

Part A. Hexagonal Closest Packing

 1. Use toothpicks (or plastic coffee stirrers) to connect three sets of 2-inch spheres, as shown in Figure 10.1.

   2. Place one of the sets of three spheres on a table. This is the first layer.

Figure 10.1

3. Place the set of seven spheres on the three spheres so that its center sphere fits snugly into the depression in the first layer.

4. Place the second set of three spheres over the center sphere of the second layer. The spheres in this third layer should be directly above the spheres in the first layer. The arrangement you have constructed, hexagonal closest packing, is found in crystals of zinc, magnesium, and many other metals. Record the number of nearest neighbors (the coordination number) of the central sphere in the structure you formed. Retain your model for Part C.

Part B. Face-Centered Cubic Packing

5. Construct the layers shown in Figure 10.2. Use 2-inch foam spheres and toothpicks, as before.

Figure 10.2

6. Place the first layer (five spheres) on the table. Place the second layer (four spheres) over the first in such a way that the spheres of the second layer rest in the spaces between the corner spheres of the first layer.

7. Place the third layer on the second layer so that the spheres of the third layer are directly over the spheres in the first layer. Study this model carefully to determine why crystals with this structure are described as face-centered cubic packing. This is the type of packing that is found in copper, silver, aluminum, and many other metals.

Part C. Comparison of Hexagonal Closest Packing and Face-Centered Cubic Packing

8. Rearrange the model from Part A so the top layer (three spheres) is no longer directly over the first layer, but is rotated 60° with respect to it.

9. Rotate this rearranged model and look for four spheres forming a square facing you. Once you have found the four-sphere square, obtain the model made in Part B. Remove the top layer of the Part B model and place it over the four-sphere square of rearranged model A. Note that this new model contains a face-centered cube, just as model B did.

Part D. Body-Centered Cubic Packing

10. Use 2-inch foam spheres to construct the layers depicted in Figure 10.3. Leave a space of approximately 0.5 cm between the spheres.

11. Place the single sphere in the center of the first layer, and then position the third layer in such a way that its spheres are directly over the spheres of the first layer. Examine the symmetry of this model and comment on the term *body-centered cubic*. This type of packing is typical of the alkali metals, which include sodium and potassium.

Figure 10.3

Part E. The Sodium Chloride Lattice

12. Ionic crystals are formed by packing positive and negative ions alternately into a lattice. A single sodium ion has a diameter of 0.19 nm; a chloride ion has a diameter of 0.36 nm. Because the diameters are in a ratio of roughly 1:2, the relative sizes of Na^+ and Cl^- can be approximated by using 1-inch and 2-inch spheres.

13. Use model B, with its 2-inch spheres, to represent the face-centered cubic arrangement of the chloride ions in a sodium chloride crystal. Insert thirteen 1-inch spheres, representing sodium ions, into the holes between the chloride ions in each layer. Note that the sodium chloride lattice is an interpenetrating set of face-centered cubes, one set of cubes made up of Na^+ ions and the other made up of Cl^- ions.

Part F. The Zinc Sulfide (Wurtzite) Lattice

14. Because each individual zinc ion has a diameter of 0.15 nm and the diameter of the sulfide ion is 0.37 nm, use 3/4-inch spheres for the Zn^{2+} ion and 2-inch spheres for the S^{2-} ion to approximate the relative sizes of these ions.

15. Use model A, with its hexagonal closest-packing orientation, to represent the lattice of the larger sulfide ions. Secure one 3/4-inch sphere directly above each of the larger spheres in each of the three layers of model A. The 3/4-inch spheres represent Zn^{2+} ions.

16. Place the largest layer of spheres on the table with the small spheres down. Place one of the smaller layers on the top of this layer so the smaller spheres fit into alternate depressions. Invert the two layers and place the other small layer, with small spheres upward, above the larger layer so that the spheres in the top layer are directly above the spheres in the bottom layer.

ANALYSES AND CONCLUSIONS

Part A. Hexagonal Closest Packing

1. What is the coordination number of the central atom in the model of hexagonal closest packing?

_____

_____

Part B. Face-Centered Cubic Packing

2. Explain the appropriateness of this name for describing the model you constructed.

_____

_____

_____

_____

Part C. Comparison of Hexagonal Closest Packing and Face-Centered Cubic Packing

3. Compare the coordination numbers for the two types of closest packing.

_____

_____

4. If both a hexagonal closest-packed model and a cubic closest-packed model were constructed from spheres of the same size and mass, would the densities of the models differ? Explain.

_____

_____

_____

Part D. Body-Centered Cubic Packing

5. Below 906°C, metallic iron crystallizes in a body-centered cubic form called alpha-ferrite. Above this temperature, the stable form is gamma-ferrite, which is a face-centered cube. At 140°C, the crystal form changes back to a body-centered cube form called delta-ferrite. What is the coordination number of iron in each of these forms?

_____

_____

_____

Part E. The Sodium Chloride Lattice

6. What ions most closely surround each Na^+ ion? What ions most closely surround each Cl^- ion?

_____

_____

_____

7. What is the coordination number of the Na^+ ions? What is the coordination number of the Cl^- ions?

_____

_____

Part F. The Zinc Sulfide (Wurtzite) Lattice

8. What is the coordination number of the Zn^{2+} ions?

_____

_____

9. Use plastic-foam balls and toothpicks to explore some other types of crystal structures. Possibilities include cesium chloride (both ions have a coordination number of 8) and titanium dioxide (coordination numbers of 6 and 3, respectively).

GOING FURTHER

Do Research

Many physical properties of a solid, such as melting point, hardness, and electrical conductivity, can be directly related to its structure. Do research on the properties and structures of other crystalline solids including alloys and minerals and compare their properties to the crystalline solids studied in this lab. What trends if any are observed?

Chapter 8 • *Covalent Bonding*   **EXPERIMENT**

11 MOLECULAR MODELS

Text Reference
Section 8.3

PURPOSE

To investigate the three-dimensional shapes of molecules by building molecular models.

BACKGROUND

You can represent a molecule on paper with either a molecular formula or a structural formula. However, molecular formulas, such as NH_3, provide no information concerning the actual arrangement of atoms in the molecule. Structural formulas, such as the following, give some information about the arrangement of atoms in the molecule.

$$H-O-H \qquad H-N-H \qquad H-C-H$$

However, these structural formulas provide only limited information because they are two-dimensional. Actual molecular shapes are three-dimensional. A molecular model is far superior to a structural formula when it comes to visualizing atomic arrangement. Compared to molecular formulas and structural formulas, molecular models provide much more information about the true shapes of the molecules.

In this experiment, you will use ball-and-stick models to help you visualize the shapes of molecules. The balls are color-coded and sized to represent different atoms. The balls are also drilled with holes to accept sticks and springs; the number of holes in a ball reflects the maximum number of bonds a given atom can form. Single bonds are represented by short wooden sticks; double and triple bonds are represented by springs.

MATERIALS (PER 6-STUDENT GROUP)

safety goggles
ball-and-stick model set

SAFETY FIRST!

 Caution: Wear your safety goggles. (All steps.)

PROCEDURE

Data Table 1 shows color codes for balls representing different atoms. As you build the models, draw the structural formulas of the molecules in Data Table 2.

DATA TABLE 1: Description of Model Set				
Atom	Symbol	Color of Ball	Number of Holes	Maximum Number of Bonds
hydrogen	H	yellow	1	1
carbon	C	black	4	4
oxygen	O	red	2	2
nitrogen	N	blue	3 or 5*	3
chlorine	Cl	green	1	1
bromine	Br	orange	1	1
iodine	I	purple	1	1

* If the nitrogen has five holes, connect two adjacent holes with a spring bond.

1. Using the ball-and-stick model set, construct models of water, H_2O; ammonia, NH_3; and methane, CH_4. Draw a sketch of each molecule in Data Table 2. The shape shown by the water molecule is described as *bent*, the shape of the ammonia molecule is called *trigonal pyramidal*, and the shape of the methane molecule is called *tetrahedral*. Write these names below the matching structures you have drawn in the table.

2. Construct models of hydrogen sulfide, H_2S; carbon tetrachloride, CCl_4; dichlorodifluoromethane, CCl_2F_2; and ethane, C_2H_6. Give the molecular formula for each of these compounds, and draw a sketch of each molecule in Data Table 2. Name the shape of each molecule.

3. The air above a burning candle contains nitrogen gas, carbon dioxide gas, and oxygen gas. Construct models of these substances. In Data Table 2, draw a sketch of each molecule.

4. The compound urea has the molecular formula $CO(NH_2)_2$. The structural formula of urea is:

$$
\begin{array}{c}
\quad\;\; O \\
\quad\;\; \| \\
H-N-C-N-H \\
\;\;\; | \qquad | \\
\;\;\; H \qquad H
\end{array}
$$

Construct a model of urea and sketch its shape in Data Table 2.

5. Construct a model of butane, C_4H_{10}. (**Hint:** The carbons are bonded to one another in a continuous, unbranched chain.) Draw a sketch of this molecule in Data Table 2. Can you construct a model of a different molecule that has the same molecular formula as butane? Make a model of such a molecule and sketch its structure in the data table.

The two different compounds having the molecular formula C_4H_{10} are called *structural isomers*. They have identical molecular formulas but different structural formulas. They also have different physical and chemical properties. Structural isomers play a very important role in organic chemistry.

6. Construct a model of bromochlorofluoromethane, CHBrClF. Sketch the compound in the table. Can you construct an isomer of this compound? (**Hint:** Is your left hand identical to your right?) Draw the new compound if you can.

The compound and the isomer have the same molecular formula, CHBrClF, but they are different from each other in the way that a left hand is different from a right hand. The compounds are mirror images of each other and are called *stereoisomers*. The phenomenon of "handedness" exhibited by pairs of stereoisomers is very important in organic chemistry and biochemistry.

Name _____ Date _____ Class _____

OBSERVATIONS

DATA TABLE 2: SKETCHES OF MOLECULES
H_2O NH_3 CH_4
H_2S CCl_4 CCl_2F_2 C_2H_6
N_2 CO_2 O_2
$CO(NH_2)_2$ CHBrClF, stereoisomers
C_4H_{10}, structural isomers

GOING FURTHER

Develop a Hypothesis

Although the VSEPR model allows one to predict the geometry of a molecule, the prediction must still be verified through experiment. One experimental method involves measuring the dipole moment of a molecule, a quantity that reflects the degree of charge separation in a molecule—the polarity. Based on your models of CCl_4 and NH_3, propose a hypothesis about the polarities of these molecules.

_____

_____

_____

Design an Experiment

To test your hypothesis, look up dipole moments of each molecule in a chemistry handbook.

_____

_____

_____

Chapter 10 • *Chemical Quantities*   **EXPERIMENT**

12 THE MASSES OF EQUAL VOLUMES OF GASES

Text Reference
Section 10.2

PURPOSE

To determine the ratio of masses of equal volumes of argon and carbon dioxide gases.

BACKGROUND

Because many gases are colorless, odorless, and have low densities, you might think they would be difficult to work with in the laboratory. For example, you cannot place an unconfined gas on a balance and find its mass. However, surprisingly, many experiments involving gases are quite easy to perform. In fact, you can easily find the mass of a volume of a contained gas by using a simple laboratory balance.

Molecules of different gases have different masses. A molecule of oxygen (O_2) has a mass of 32 atomic mass units (amu); a molecule of nitrogen (N_2) has a mass of 28 amu. Thus, the mass ratio of oxygen molecules to nitrogen molecules is 32/28. As a result of Avogadro's hypothesis, if equal volumes of oxygen and nitrogen are compared at the same temperature and pressure, the mass ratio between the molecules will always be 32/28. This fact forms the basis of the investigation in this experiment.

In this experiment, you will determine the masses of equal volumes of two different gases—argon and carbon dioxide. The volumes you will work with will contain only about 0.01 mol of gas molecules. You will calculate the ratio between these masses and compare this ratio with the established value for the ratio between the molar masses of these gases.

MATERIALS (PER PAIR)

safety goggles
250-mL Erlenmeyer flask
rubber stopper
glass delivery tube
rubber connecting tube
pinch clamp
centigram balance

glass-marking pencil
500-mL graduated cylinder
thermometer
barometer
argon, Ar
carbon dioxide, CO_2
distilled water

SAFETY FIRST!

 Wear your safety goggles. (All steps.)

PROCEDURE

As you perform this experiment, record your data in Data Table 1.

1. Obtain a 250-mL Erlenmeyer flask and set it up as shown in Figure 12.1. Keep the assembly dry throughout the experiment. Adjust the glass delivery tube so that it does not touch the bottom of the flask when the stopper is pushed firmly into the neck.

2. Determine and record the mass of the flask assembly to the nearest 0.01 g.

3. Attach the rubber tube to the delivery jet on the argon tank. Loosen the rubber stopper in the flask and loosen the pinch clamp on the rubber tube so the tube is open. Allow argon gas to flow into the flask for 20–30 seconds—this flushes out all the air in the flask. Quickly push the stopper firmly into the neck of the flask and close the pinch clamp on the rubber tube. Shut off the argon gas and disconnect the rubber tube from the delivery jet. Remeasure the mass of the flask, now full of argon, to the nearest 0.01 g.

4. Repeat Step 3 until you obtain a constant measurement for the mass of the argon-filled flask. Measurements that agree within 0.01 g can be considered constant.

5. Repeat Steps 3 and 4, using carbon dioxide gas.

6. Use a glass-marking pencil to draw a line on the neck of the flask, at the bottom of the rubber stopper. Set the stopper assembly aside to keep it dry.

7. Fill the Erlenmeyer flask with water to the height of the pencil mark. Carefully pour the water into a 500-mL graduated cylinder. Measure and record the volume.

8. Measure and record the room temperature and pressure.

Rubber connecting tube

Pinch clamp

Glass delivery tube

Rubber stopper

Figure 12.1

Name _____ Date _____ Class _____

OBSERVATIONS

DATA TABLE 1: QUANTITATIVE DATA		sample data
mass of flask assembly with air		
mass of flask assembly with Ar	(1) (2)	
mass of flask assembly with CO_2	(1) (2)	
volume of flask		
room temperature		
room pressure		

ANALYSES AND CONCLUSIONS

1. Calculate the mass of air in the flask. To do this, use the density relationship between mass and volume.

$$density = mass/volume$$

Solve this equation for mass. In your calculation, use Data Table 2 to find the density of air at the conditions recorded in Data Table 1, and use the volume determined in Step 7.

DATA TABLE 2: DENSITY OF DRY AIR (g/cm³)						
	Pressure (mm Hg)					
Temperature (°C)	**720**	**730**	**740**	**750**	**760**	**770**
20	0.001141	0.001157	0.001173	0.001189	0.001205	0.001221
21	0.001137	0.001153	0.001169	0.001185	0.001201	0.001216
22	0.001134	0.001149	0.001165	0.001181	0.001197	0.001212
23	0.001130	0.001145	0.001161	0.001177	0.001193	0.001208
24	0.001126	0.001142	0.001157	0.001173	0.001189	0.001204
25	0.001122	0.001138	0.001153	0.001169	0.001185	0.001200
26	0.001118	0.001134	0.001149	0.001165	0.001181	0.001196
27	0.001115	0.001130	0.001146	0.001161	0.001177	0.001192

2. Calculate the mass of the flask by subtracting the mass of the air in the flask from the mass of the flask when it was full of air.

3. Use the mass of the flask to calculate the masses of argon and carbon dioxide contained in the flask.

4. Determine the ratio of the mass of carbon dioxide contained in the flask to the mass of argon gas contained in the flask.

5. Using data from the periodic table, calculate the actual ratio of the molar masses of carbon dioxide and argon.

6. Avogadro's hypothesis states that equal volumes of different gases, at the same temperature and pressure, contain equal numbers of particles (or moles) of gases. Explain why similarity between the ratios calculated in problems 4 and 5 would support Avogadro's hypothesis.

_____

_____

_____

_____

_____

_____

7. Calculate the percent error in the experimentally determined mass ratio of equal volumes of argon and carbon dioxide. Use the ratio of the actual molar masses as the accepted value.

$$\text{Percent error} = \frac{|\text{accepted value} - \text{experimental value}|}{\text{accepted value}} \times 100\%$$

8. Why must the flask assembly be kept absolutely dry during this experiment? How would your results be affected if the flask became wet any time after Step 2 in the procedure?

_____

_____

_____

_____

9. Is it still accurate to call Avogadro's hypothesis a *hypothesis*? Explain.

_____

_____

_____

_____

_____

10. Could you find the relative mass of helium by using the procedure in this experiment? Propose a modified experimental procedure for helium and other "light" gases.

_____

_____

_____

_____

11. Demonstrate with calculations how this procedure could be used to identify an unknown gaseous element.

GOING FURTHER

Develop a Hypothesis

In this experiment, it was important to compare the masses of the gases at the same temperature and pressure. Hypothesize about how the ratio of the masses of the two gases would be affected if they were each measured under different conditions of temperature and pressure.

_____

_____

_____

Design an Experiment

Propose an experiment to test your hypothesis. If resources are available and you have your teacher's permission, perform the experiment.

_____

_____

_____

13 · EMPIRICAL FORMULA DETERMINATION

Text Reference
Section 10.3

PURPOSE

To determine the empirical formula of magnesium oxide.

BACKGROUND

Carbon dioxide (CO_2), water (H_2O), and ammonia (NH_3) are three out of many chemical compounds that you are familiar with. Have you ever seen a compound with a formula such as $Na_{2.3}Cl_{3.9}$? In fact, such a formula is impossible. Only whole atoms, not fractions of atoms, react with each other to form products. Also, although elements may react in different proportions to form more than one compound, the proportions of atoms in those compounds will always be a ratio of small whole numbers.

An empirical formula gives the simplest whole-number ratio of the different atoms in a compound. For example, while the molecular formula for hydrogen peroxide is H_2O_2, the simplest whole-number ratio of hydrogen and oxygen atoms can be expressed as HO. Thus, the empirical formula of hydrogen peroxide is HO.

In this lab, you will experimentally determine the empirical formula of magnesium oxide, the compound formed when magnesium metal reacts with oxygen.

MATERIALS (PER PAIR)

safety goggles
crucible
crucible lid
clay triangle
ring stand
ring support

crucible tongs
gas burner
centigram balance
magnesium ribbon, Mg ⬚F
2 pieces of exposed film

SAFETY FIRST!

In this lab, the crucible you are using will become quite hot and could cause a severe burn if handled improperly. Observe all precautions, especially those listed below. If you see a safety icon beside a step in the Procedure, refer to the list below for its meaning.

 Caution: Wear your safety goggles. (All steps.)

 Caution: Do not look directly at burning magnesium. Do not inhale the smoke produced when the magnesium is burned. (Steps 3, 4.)

Figure 13.1

 Caution: Always handle the crucible and crucible lid with crucible tongs, as shown in Figure 13.1. (Steps 3, 4.)

 Note: Return or dispose of all materials according to the instructions of your teacher. (Step 7.)

PROCEDURE

As you perform the experiment, record your data in Data Table 1.

 1. Set up the equipment, as shown in Figure 13.2. Clean a crucible and its cover with water. Dry them by heating in the hottest part of the flame for 5 minutes. Allow them to cool for at least 10 minutes. Measure and record the combined mass of the crucible and lid to the nearest 0.01 g.

2. Place a coiled 25-cm length of magnesium ribbon in the crucible. Measure and record the combined mass of the crucible, lid, and magnesium.

 3. **CAUTION:** *Do not look directly at the burning magnesium. View the reaction through the pieces of film provided by your teacher.* Over a high flame, heat the uncovered crucible on the triangle until the magnesium ignites. **CAUTION:** *Do not inhale the smoke produced.* When the magnesium begins to burn, immediately cover the crucible (using tongs) and remove the burner.

4. After smoke production has ceased, replace the burner and continue heating the crucible. **CAUTION:** *Do not lean over the crucible.* Remove the burner and carefully lift the lid and check the reaction every 2 or 3 minutes. After heating for a total of 10 minutes, check to see if the reaction is complete. The magnesium should be wholly converted to a light gray powder, magnesium oxide. If ribbonlike material remains in the crucible, replace the burner and continue heating.

5. Turn off and remove the burner. Allow the crucible to cool completely (at least 10 minutes).

6. Measure and record the combined mass of the crucible, crucible lid, and magnesium oxide.

7. Follow your teacher's instructions for proper disposal of the materials.

Figure 13.2

OBSERVATIONS

DATA TABLE 1: MASS MEASUREMENTS	
Item	Mass
empty crucible and lid	
crucible, lid, and Mg (before heating)	
crucible, lid, and combustion product (Mg_xO_y)	

ANALYSES AND CONCLUSIONS

1. Determine the mass of magnesium used.

2. Determine the number of moles of magnesium used.

   Hint: mol Mg = (mass Mg/molar mass Mg)

3. Determine the mass of magnesium oxide formed.

4. Determine the mass of oxygen that combined with the magnesium.

5. Calculate the number of moles of oxygen atoms that were used.

6. Calculate the ratio between moles of magnesium used and moles of oxygen used. Express this ratio in simplest whole-number form.

7. Based on your experimental data, write the empirical formula for magnesium oxide.

_____

_____

8. Calculate the percent error in your determination of the magnesium:oxygen mole ratio, using the accepted value provided by your teacher.

$$\text{Percent error} = \frac{|\text{accepted value} - \text{experimental value}|}{\text{accepted value}} \times 100 \text{ percent}$$

9. Identify major sources of error in this experiment. Explain how the magnesium: oxygen ratio would be affected by each error you identify.

_____

_____

_____

_____

_____

_____

_____

_____

10. Is there agreement among the results obtained by others in the class? What does the class data tell you about the empirical formula of a compound?

_____

_____

_____

_____

_____

_____

_____

_____

_____

_____

11. Interpret, in terms of atoms and in terms of moles, the subscripts in the chemical formula for ethane (C_2H_6).

_____

_____

_____

_____

_____

_____

_____

_____

GOING FURTHER

Develop a Hypothesis

At the high temperature at which this reaction takes place, a green-yellow solid may also be formed. Propose a hypothesis about the chemical nature of this product.

_____

_____

_____

Design an Experiment

Propose an experiment to test your hypothesis. If resources are available and you have your teacher's permission, perform the experiment.

_____

_____

Name _____ Date _____ Class _____

14 TYPES OF CHEMICAL REACTIONS

Text Reference
Section 11.2

PURPOSE

To identify and classify chemical reactions based on five general categories.

BACKGROUND

Although countless chemical reactions exist, nearly all of them can be classified into a few specific categories. In this experiment, you will learn to differentiate five general types of chemical reactions. Some of the reactions you will perform; others will be demonstrated by your teacher. From observations, you will identify the products of each reaction and determine the type of reaction that has taken place. You will consider the following reaction types: *combination reactions, decomposition reactions, single-replacement reactions, double-replacement reactions,* and *combustion reactions.* The majority of common chemical reactions can be classified as belonging to one of these categories.

MATERIALS (PER PAIR)

(Student Experiment)
safety goggles and apron
2 small test tubes
centigram balance
dropper pipet
2 medium test tubes
test-tube rack
crucible tongs
gas burner
ring stand
utility clamp

0.1M copper(II) sulfate, $CuSO_4$ [T]
iron filings, Fe
0.1M lead(II) nitrate, $Pb(NO_3)_2$ [T]
0.1M potassium iodide, KI [T]
6M hydrochloric acid, HCl [C][T]
magnesium turnings, Mg [F]
2 wood splints
book of matches
3% hydrogen peroxide, H_2O_2

(Teacher Demonstration)
electrolysis apparatus
rubber stopper, one-holed
large test tube
glass tube, 25-cm length, bent
    at 90° angle in center
gas burner
ring stand

utility clamp
sodium hydrogen carbonate,
    $NaHCO_3$
wood splints
matches
limewater, saturated solution of
    calcium oxide, CaO [I][C]

SAFETY FIRST!

In this lab, observe all precautions, especially the ones listed below. If you see a safety icon beside a step in the Procedure, refer to the list below for its meaning.

 Caution: Wear your safety goggles. (All steps.)

 Caution: Hydrochloric acid is corrosive and can cause severe burns. (Step 3.)

 Caution: Lead and copper compounds are toxic. Use as little of these compounds as practical. (Steps 1, 2.)

 Caution: Exercise care when working with an open flame. Tie back hair and loose clothing. Do not use the burner near flammable materials. (Step 4.)

 Note: Return or dispose of all materials according to the instructions of your teacher. (Step 7.)

 Note: Wash your hands thoroughly after completing this experiment.

PROCEDURE

As you perform the experiment, record your observations in Data Table 1.

Part A. Student Experiments

 1. **Iron metal and copper(II) sulfate solution.** Half-fill a small test tube with copper(II) sulfate solution. Add about 2 g of iron filings to the solution. After 5 minutes, record your observations.

2. **Lead(II) nitrate and potassium iodide solutions.** Put 2 mL of lead(II) nitrate solution into a small test tube. Add 5–10 drops of potassium iodide solution. Record your observations.

 3. **Magnesium metal and hydrochloric acid. CAUTION:** *Hydrochloric acid is corrosive.* Half-fill a medium-sized test tube with 6*M* hydrochloric acid. Place the test tube in a test-tube rack and add several magnesium turnings. Identify any gas that forms by using crucible tongs to hold a *burning* wood splint at the mouth of the test tube. Record your observations.

 4. **Action of heat on hydrogen peroxide.** Add 2 mL of 3% hydrogen peroxide solution to a medium-sized test tube. Clamp the test tube to a ring stand, as shown in Figure 14.1. **CAUTION:** *Make sure that the mouth of the tube is pointed away from you and away from everyone else.* Heat the solution *very gently.* Identify any gas that forms by using crucible tongs to insert a *glowing* wood splint into the mouth of the test tube. Record your observations.

Figure 14.1

Part B. Teacher Demonstrations

5. **Action of electricity on water (electrolysis).** Water can be broken down into its component elements by passing electricity through it. This process is called *electrolysis*. Your teacher will explain the apparatus shown in Figure 14.2. Make observations of the reaction during a 10-minute period.

Figure 14.2

6. **Action of heat on sodium hydrogen carbonate.** Solid sodium hydrogen carbonate will be heated strongly in a large test tube for 2 minutes. The gas that is given off will be tested by exposing it to a burning splint and by bubbling it through limewater. Record your observations of these tests.

 7. Follow your teacher's instructions for proper disposal of the materials.

Name _____ Date _____ Class _____

OBSERVATIONS

DATA TABLE 1: CHEMICAL REACTION TYPES

Reaction	Observations	Reaction Type
Fe and $CuSO_4$		
$Pb(NO_3)_2$ and KI		
Mg and HCl		
H_2O_2 and heat		
electrolysis of H_2O		
$NaHCO_3$ and heat		

ANALYSES AND CONCLUSIONS

1. Classify each of the observed reactions as one of the five reaction types listed in the Background section. Record your answers in Data Table 1.

2. Write an equation for each reaction observed. Indicate the state (*s, l, g, aq*) for each reactant and product, then balance each equation.

_____

_____

_____

_____

_____

3. Although no combustion reactions were described in the Procedure section, two combustion reactions did occur in the course of this experiment. The reactants were H_2 and CH_4 (natural gas), respectively. Write a balanced equation for the combustion of each of these substances.

_____

_____

4. Identify the combustion reaction in question 3 that is also a combination reaction.

_____

5. Describe in your own words the five types of chemical reactions listed in the Background section. Explain how to distinguish each of these types of reactions.

_____

_____

_____

_____

_____

_____

_____

_____

_____

_____

_____

_____

6. List the tests that were used to identify the three gases produced in this experiment.

_____

_____

_____

_____

_____

_____

_____

7. Which type(s) of reactions are characterized by:

   a. two products

   _____

   _____

   b. a single reactant

   _____

   _____

   c. two reactants

   _____

   _____

   d. a single product

   _____

   _____

GOING FURTHER

Develop a Hypothesis

Based on the results of this lab, develop a hypothesis about the type of chemical reaction (and the predicted chemical equation) that occurs when iron filings are added to 6M hydrochloric acid.

_____

_____

_____

Design an Experiment

Propose an experiment to test your hypothesis. If resources are available and you have your teacher's permission, perform the experiment.

_____

_____

_____

Chapter 11 • *Chemical Reactions*

15 REACTIVITY OF METALS

Text Reference
Section 11.2

PURPOSE

To measure the relative reactivities of selected metallic elements.

BACKGROUND

The chemical reactivity of a metal determines how the metal is used. For example, gold, which is commonly used in jewelry, is highly resistant to chemical reactions. Sodium, however, is not used in jewelry because it is so reactive it will explode if it contacts water. The chemistry of the metals is based on their ability to lose electrons. Differences in chemical reactivity among metals depend on the relative ease with which they give up electrons.

You can measure the relative reactivity of two metals by placing a small pure sample of one metal in a solution containing the ions of the other metal. If the small metal sample is more reactive than the metal whose ions are in solution, electrons will move from the solid metal sample into the solution. For example, a piece of iron placed in a solution containing copper(II) ions will corrode, while fine copper particles deposit on the iron. However, no reaction occurs when a strip of copper metal is placed in a solution of iron(II) ions.

In this experiment, you will test the reactivities of a variety of metals with different metal ions. You will then use the results of your tests to construct a scale of relative reactivities of the metals.

MATERIALS (PER PAIR)

safety goggles and apron
gloves
glass-marking pencil
8 medium test tubes

steel wool
test-tube rack
3 dropper pipets
tweezers

thin metal strips, 0.25 mm thick, approximately 2.00 cm × 0.50 cm:
   8 strips copper, Cu
   8 strips zinc, Zn
   8 strips magnesium, Mg $\boxed{F}$
solutions, 5% w/v, in dropper bottles:
   lead(II) nitrate, $Pb(NO_3)_2$ $\boxed{T}$ zinc chloride, $ZnCl_2$ $\boxed{T}$
   silver nitrate, $AgNO_3$ $\boxed{T}$ $\boxed{I}$ sodium chloride, NaCl
   copper(II) sulfate, $CuSO_4$ $\boxed{T}$ $\boxed{I}$ potassium chloride, KCl
   magnesium chloride, $MgCl_2$

SAFETY FIRST!

In this lab, observe all precautions, especially the ones listed below. If you see a safety icon beside a step in the Procedure, refer to the list below for its meaning.

 Caution: Wear your safety goggles. (All steps.)

 Caution: Wear your lab apron. (All steps.)

 Caution: Wear plastic gloves. (All steps.)

 Caution: Magnesium metal is flammable. Keep this material away from open flames. (Step 5.)

 Caution: Solutions of lead and copper ions are toxic. (Steps 3–6.)

Caution: Silver nitrate is toxic and will leave dark brown stains on skin and clothing. (Steps 3–6.)

 Note: Return or dispose of all materials according to the instructions of your teacher. (Step 6.)

PROCEDURE

As you perform this experiment, record your observations in Data Table 1.

 1. Polish metal strips of copper, zinc, and magnesium with steel wool until they are clean and shiny.

2. Using a glass-marking pencil, label eight test tubes with the numbers 1–8. Place the tubes in a test-tube rack.

 3. To tube 1, add 5 drops of $Pb(NO_3)_2$ solution. To tube 2, add 5 drops of $AgNO_3$ solution. Using tweezers, add one strip of copper metal to each tube. Record your observations.

4. Add 5 drops of solution to each tube as follows: tube 3, $CuSO_4$; tube 4, $Pb(NO_3)_2$; tube 5, $MgCl_2$. Add a strip of zinc metal to each tube. Record your observations.

 5. Add 5 drops of solution to each tube, as follows: tube 6, $ZnCl_2$; tube 7, NaCl; tube 8, KCl. Add a strip of polished magnesium metal to each tube. Record your observations.

 6. Follow your teacher's instructions for proper disposal of the materials.

Name _____ Date _____ Class _____

OBSERVATIONS

DATA TABLE 1: OBSERVATIONS OF METAL ACTIVITY			
Tube	Metal Ion	Metal	Observations
1			
2			
3			
4			
5			
6			
7			
8			

ANALYSES AND CONCLUSIONS

1. Why is it necessary to polish the metal strips before doing the experiment?

   _____

2. Write balanced chemical equations for those reactions that actually occurred.

   _____

   _____

   _____

3. In which of the five general classifications of chemical reactions do the reactions in your answer for question 2 belong?

   _____

4. Using your experimental data, list the metals in order of increasing activity. Explain how you arrived at your list.

_____

_____

_____

_____

_____

_____

_____

_____

_____

_____

_____

_____

_____

_____

5. Using the results of problem 4, do you think there would be a reaction if strips of copper or zinc were placed in solutions of KCl or NaCl? Explain.

_____

_____

GOING FURTHER

Develop a Hypothesis

Based on the results of this lab, develop a hypothesis about how the relative activities of the metals correspond to their arrangement in the periodic table.

_____

_____

Design an Experiment

Propose an experiment to test your hypothesis. If resources are available and you have your teacher's permission, perform the experiment.

_____

_____

16 IDENTIFICATION OF ANIONS AND CATIONS IN SOLUTION

Text Reference
Section 11.3

PURPOSE

To identify the ions in an unknown solution through the application of chemical tests.

BACKGROUND

Detectives in mystery novels often rush evidence from the crime scene to the lab for analysis. In this experiment, you will become a chemical detective. You will conduct laboratory analysis to determine the ionic composition of an unknown solution. The process of determining the composition of a sample of matter by conducting chemical tests is called *qualitative analysis*. Solutions of unknown ions can be subjected to chemical tests, and the results can be compared to the results given by known ions in the same tests. By conducting the appropriate tests and applying logic, the identities of the ions present in an unknown solution can be determined.

The analyses you perform are based upon the idea that no two ions produce the same set of chemical reactions. Each ion reacts in its own characteristic way. In this experiment, you will observe several types of chemical reactions commonly used as tests in qualitative analysis. These reactions include a color change, the production of a gas, and the formation of a precipitate—a solid product. As you do this experiment, remember that careful observation and logical reasoning are the keys to being a good detective. Who knows what ions lurk in your unknown solution?

MATERIALS (PER PAIR)

safety goggles and apron
250-mL beaker
gas burner
ring stand
ring support
wire gauze
crucible tongs
9 small test tubes
test-tube rack

25-mL graduated cylinder
dropper pipet
nichrome wire (10-cm length)
cobalt-blue glass
test-tube holder
forceps
plastic wash bottle
distilled water
red litmus paper, 1 cm × 10 cm

Part A. Anions

0.1*M* sodium chloride, NaCl
6*M* nitric acid, HNO₃ [C] [T]
0.1*M* silver nitrate, AgNO₃ [T] [I]
0.1*M* sodium sulfate, Na₂SO₄
6*M* hydrochloric acid,
    HCl [C] [T]
0.1*M* barium chloride, BaCl₂ [T]

0.1*M* sodium hydrogen
    carbonate, NaHCO₃
0.05*M* sodium phosphate,
    Na₃PO₄
0.1*M* ammonium molybdate,
    (NH₄)₂MoO₄
unknown solutions (anions) [T]

Part B. Cations

3*M* sulfuric acid,
    H₂SO₄ [C] [T]
0.1*M* iron(III) sulfate, Fe₂(SO₄)₃
0.1*M* potassium thiocyanate,
    KSCN [T]
0.1*M* sodium chloride, NaCl
6*M* hydrochloric acid,
    HCl [C] [T]

0.1*M* potassium chloride, KCl
0.1*M* calcium nitrate, Ca(NO₃)₂
0.1*M* sodium oxalate,
    Na₂C₂O₄ [T]
0.1*M* ammonium nitrate,
    NH₄NO₃
6*M* sodium hydroxide, NaOH [C] [T]
unknown solutions (cations)

SAFETY FIRST!

In this lab, observe all precautions, especially the ones listed below. If you see a safety icon beside a step in the Procedure, refer to the list below for its meaning.

 Caution: Wear your safety goggles. (All steps.)

 Caution: Nitric acid, hydrochloric acid, sulfuric acid, and sodium hydroxide are corrosive and can cause severe injury. Never cover the opening of a test tube with your finger when mixing chemicals in the tube. To mix the contents, "flick" the tube as demonstrated by your teacher. (Steps 3, 4, 5, 6, 9, 10, 11, 12, 13.)

 Caution: Silver, barium, and oxalate compounds are poisonous. Avoid contact with these chemicals. (Steps 3, 4, 12.)

Caution: Silver nitrate will stain skin and clothing. (Step 3.)

Caution: Never pick up a dropper bottle by its cap. Always hold a dropper with the tip lower than the rubber bulb so that the liquid does not run into the bulb.

 Caution: Exercise care when working with a hot water bath. (Steps 1, 6, 12.)

 Note: Return or dispose of all materials according to the instructions of your teacher. (Steps 7, 14.)

 Note: Wash your hands thoroughly after completing this experiment.

PROCEDURE

As you perform the experiment, record your observations in Data Table 1.

Procedure note: In testing for different ions in Steps 3–13, you will always begin with two test tubes. For each step, you must add 2 mL of the known solution to one test tube and 2 mL of your unknown solution to a second test tube. The name of the known solution is given in each step.

Note that 1 mL is approximately 20 drops. Count out 40 drops of water in a test tube and make note of the level of water in the tube. Throughout the experiment, fill a test tube to this same level whenever a 2-mL sample is called for. This practice will save you considerable time. Always clean the medicine dropper after each use.

Part A. Testing for Anions (Day 1)

1. Set up a boiling water bath for use in Step 6.

2. Thoroughly clean all the test tubes used in this experiment, rinsing them well with distilled water. Record the number of the unknown solution you will be testing.

3. Test for chloride ion, Cl^-. Known solution is sodium chloride. **CAUTION:** *Nitric acid is corrosive. Do not put your finger over the top of the tube to cover it.* Add 2 mL of 6M nitric acid to each tube and gently flick the tubes to mix. Add 10 drops of silver nitrate to each tube and flick to mix. Record your observations.

4. Test for sulfate ion, SO_4^{2-}. Known solution is sodium sulfate. **CAUTION:** *Hydrochloric acid is corrosive.* Add 2 mL of 6M hydrochloric acid to each tube and mix. Add 10 drops of barium chloride solution to each tube and mix. Record your observations.

5. Test for hydrogen carbonate ion, HCO_3^-. Known solution is sodium hydrogen carbonate. Carefully observe the test tubes as you add 2 mL of 6M hydrochloric acid to each tube. Record your observations.

6. Test for phosphate ion, PO_4^{3-}. Known solution is sodium phosphate. Add 1 mL of 6M nitric acid and 10 drops of ammonium molybdate solution to each tube and mix. Place the tubes in a boiling water bath and heat for 5 minutes. Allow tubes to cool in a test-tube rack for 10 minutes. Record your observations. (Retain the water bath for Part B, Step 12.)

7. Follow your teacher's instructions for proper disposal of the materials.

Part B. Testing For Cations (Day 2)

8. Review the general directions at the beginning of the Procedure section. Prepare your test tubes as in Part A, Step 2.

9. Test for iron(III) ion, Fe^{3+}. Known solution is iron (III) sulfate. **CAUTION:** *Sulfuric acid is corrosive.* Add 5 drops of 3M sulfuric acid and 5 drops of potassium thiocyanate solution to each tube. Flick gently to mix. Record your observations.

6M HCl

Figure 16.1

 10. Flame-test for sodium ion, Na⁺. Known solution is sodium chloride. Add 3 drops of 6M hydrochloric acid to each tube. Flick gently to mix.

Add 3–4 mL of 6M hydrochloric acid to a small test tube in a test-tube rack. Heat the end of a 10-cm length of nichrome wire in a hot burner flame, as shown in Figure 16.1. While it is still hot, dip the end of the wire into the hydrochloric acid in the test tube. Remove the wire from the acid and immediately reheat it in the burner flame. Repeat this acid cleaning of the wire until the flame remains unchanged when the wire is heated.

Dip the acid-cleaned wire into the sodium chloride solution. Immediately hold it in the hot burner flame. Observe the color of the flame. Acid-clean the wire and then test the unknown solution. Record the color of the flame. (A faintly colored flame is not considered a positive test for sodium.) Save the prepared unknown solution for the next test.

 11. Flame-test for potassium ion, K⁺. Known solution is potassium chloride. Add 3 drops of 6M hydrochloric acid to each tube and flick gently to mix. Acid-clean the nichrome wire. Flame-test the potassium chloride solution. Acid-clean the wire and test your unknown. If your unknown contains sodium, the color of the sodium flame will mask the color that is characteristic of potassium. You will be able to see the potassium color, if it is there, by looking at the flame through a piece of cobalt-blue glass. Record your results.

 12. Test for calcium ion, Ca²⁺. Known solution is calcium nitrate. To each tube, add 10 drops of sodium oxalate solution. Warm the tubes in the boiling water bath for a few minutes. Record your observations.

(Optional) You can also perform a flame test for calcium. Add 3 drops of 6*M* hydrochloric acid to fresh 2-mL samples of the calcium nitrate solution and the unknown solution. Perform flame tests as in Step 10. Record the color of the calcium flame and the results for your unknown.

 13. Test for ammonium ion, NH_4^+. Known solution is ammonium nitrate. **CAUTION:** *Sodium hydroxide can cause burns.* To each tube, add 3 drops of 6*M* sodium hydroxide. Hold the tube containing the ammonium nitrate solution with a test-tube holder. *Gently* warm the tube along its sides using a back-and-forth motion through a burner flame. Do not allow the solution to boil. **CAUTION:** *At all times, make sure that the opening of the tube is pointed away from other people.* Hold a moistened piece of red litmus paper near the mouth of the test tube, as shown in Figure 16.2. The test will be spoiled if the solution contacts the litmus paper. Record the changes you observe. Fan the vapors coming out of the tube toward your nose with your hand. Cautiously sniff the vapors. Record your observations. Repeat the procedure for your unknown solution.

Figure 16.2

14. Follow your teacher's instructions for proper disposal of the materials.

Name _____ Date _____ Class _____

OBSERVATIONS

DATA TABLE 1: OBSERVATIONS				
Ion	Test Reagents/ Test Procedure	Test Results for Solution with Ion	Test Results for Unknown Solution No.___	Is Ion Present in Unknown?
Cl^-				
SO_4^{2-}				
HCO_3^-				
PO_3^{4-}				
Fe^{3+}				
Na^+				
K^+				
Ca^{2+}				
NH_4^+				

ANALYSES AND CONCLUSIONS

1. List the anions present in your unknown.

_____

_____

2. List the cations present in your unknown.

_____

_____

3. Write the complete ionic equation and the net ionic equation for the reactions that occur in Steps 3, 4, 5, 12, and 13.

_____

_____

_____

_____

_____

_____

_____

_____

4. It is possible to get a false-positive or a false-negative result when testing for ions. Propose a situation that could lead to a false positive for a particular ion. Choose a different ion and show how a false negative could result. Which do you think is more likely to happen—a false-positive or a false-negative result? Explain your reasoning.

_____

_____

_____

_____

_____

GOING FURTHER

Develop a Hypothesis

In the test for the sulfate ion (Step 4), hydrochloric acid was added before the barium chloride solution was added. Propose a hypothesis to explain why the hydrochloric acid is needed.

_____

_____

_____

Design an Experiment

Propose an experiment to test your hypothesis. If resources are available and you have your teacher's permission, perform the experiment.

_____

_____

_____

17 PRECIPITATION REACTIONS

Text Reference
Section 11.3

PURPOSE

To determine which combinations of ions form water-insoluble precipitates.

BACKGROUND

Two colorless solutions, cadmium chloride ($CdCl_2$) and potassium sulfide (K_2S), are poured together. As the solutions mix, a bright yellow solid forms. This insoluble compound, cadmium sulfide (CdS), was once used as a yellow pigment for oil paint. The paint was called cadmium yellow.

An insoluble substance that "falls out" of a solution is called a *precipitate*. The formation of precipitates other than cadmium sulfide is often less dramatic. For example, the scum that forms a ring around the bathtub is, in part, a precipitate formed by the reaction of calcium ions in the bathwater with soap ions. Whenever you mix solutions containing ions, you may obtain new combinations of ions. If one or more of these new ion combinations happens to be insoluble in water, it falls out of the solution as a precipitate.

In this experiment, you will mix pairs of six different ionic solutions in all possible combinations to determine which pairs result in precipitate formation. Based upon your results, you will infer what reactions have occurred and write complete and net ionic equations for each reaction that has taken place.

MATERIALS (PER PAIR)

safety goggles   plastic wash bottle
spot plate or 15 small test tubes   6 dropper pipets
glass stirring rod   distilled water

Set 1

0.1*M* barium nitrate, $Ba(NO_3)_2$ [T] [C]
0.1*M* sodium sulfate, Na_2SO_4 0.1*M* magnesium chloride,
0.1*M* aluminum sulfate, $MgCl_2$ [T]
   $Al_2(SO_4)_3$ [T] [I]   0.1*M* aluminum chloride,
0.1*M* magnesium nitrate, $AlCl_3$ [T] [I]
   $Mg(NO_3)_2$

Set 2

0.1*M* potassium chloride, KCl   0.2*M* sodium hydroxide,
0.1*M* magnesium chloride,   NaOH [T] [C]
   $MgCl_2$ 0.1*M* barium chloride, $BaCl_2$ [T] [C]
0.1*M* sodium sulfate, Na_2SO_4 0.1*M* magnesium sulfate, $MgSO_4$

Set 3

0.1M barium chloride, BaCl₂ $\boxed{T}$ $\boxed{C}$ 0.2M aluminum sulfate,
0.1M magnesium nitrate,   Al₂(SO₄)₃ $\boxed{T}$
   Mg(NO₃)₂   0.2M potassium chromate,
0.2M sodium chromate,   K₂CrO₄ $\boxed{C}$ $\boxed{T}$
   Na₂CrO₄ $\boxed{T}$ 0.2M silver nitrate, AgNO₃ $\boxed{C}$ $\boxed{T}$

SAFETY FIRST!

In this lab, the solutions you use may contain harmful materials. Never touch any of the chemicals. In the event of a spill, inform your teacher immediately. Observe all precautions, especially the ones listed below. If you see a safety icon beside a step in the Procedure, refer to the list below for its meaning.

 Caution: Wear your safety goggles. (All steps.)

  Caution: Potassium chromate, sodium chromate, and sodium hydroxide are toxic, corrosive substances that can cause severe skin and eye injury. (Steps 1, 2.)

Caution: Aluminum chloride is an irritant. Avoid skin contact.

Caution: Silver and barium compounds are poisonous. Silver nitrate will stain skin and clothing. Avoid contact with these chemicals and wash your hands thoroughly after use.

 Note: Return or dispose of all materials according to the instructions of your teacher. (Step 3.)

 Note: Wash your hands thoroughly after completing this experiment.

PROCEDURES

As you perform this experiment, record your observations in Data Table 1.

 1. Obtain a spot plate and a set of chemicals in dropper bottles. (The tests may be done in small test tubes.)

 2. Using Data Table 1 as a guide, mix every possible pair of solutions in a set in a separate spot plate depression or test tube. Use two drops of each solution. Do not contaminate the individual droppers with different solutions. Mix the solutions with a stirring rod. Rinse the rod with distilled water after each mixing. Observe each mixture carefully for signs of a precipitate. (Some precipitates are light in color and hard to see.) Note the color of any precipitate formed. Record the results in Data Table 1.

 3. Follow your teacher's instructions for proper disposal of the materials.

Name _____ Date _____ Class _____

OBSERVATIONS

DATA TABLE 1: MIXING PAIRS OF IONIC SOLUTIONS TO TEST FOR PRECIPITATE FORMATION		
Solution A	**Solution B**	**Results of Mixing A and B**
Set 1:		
1 $Ba(NO_3)_2$	2 Na_2SO_4	
1 $Ba(NO_3)_2$	3 $Al_2(SO_4)_3$	
1 $Ba(NO_3)_2$	4 $Mg(NO_3)_2$	
1 $Ba(NO_3)_2$	5 $MgCl_2$	
1 $Ba(NO_3)_2$	6 $AlCl_3$	
2 Na_2SO_4	3 $Al_2(SO_4)_3$	
2 Na_2SO_4	4 $Mg(NO_3)_2$	
2 Na_2SO_4	5 $MgCl_2$	
2 Na_2SO_4	6 $AlCl_3$	
3 $Al_2(SO_4)_3$	4 $Mg(NO_3)_2$	
3 $Al_2(SO_4)_3$	5 $MgCl_2$	
3 $Al_2(SO_4)_3$	6 $AlCl_3$	
4 $Mg(NO_3)_2$	5 $MgCl_2$	
4 $Mg(NO_3)_2$	6 $AlCl_3$	
5 $MgCl_2$	6 $AlCl_3$	
Set 2:		
1 KCl	2 $MgCl_2$	
1 KCl	3 Na_2SO_4	
1 KCl	4 $NaOH$	
1 KCl	5 $BaCl_2$	
1 KCl	6 $MgSO_4$	
2 $MgCl_2$	3 Na_2SO_4	
2 $MgCl_2$	4 $NaOH$	
2 $MgCl_2$	5 $BaCl_2$	
2 $MgCl_2$	6 $MgSO_4$	
3 Na_2SO_4	4 $NaOH$	
3 Na_2SO_4	5 $BaCl_2$	
3 Na_2SO_4	6 $MgSO_4$	
4 $NaOH$	5 $BaCl_2$	
4 $NaOH$	6 $MgSO_4$	
5 $BaCl_2$	6 $MgSO_4$	
Set 3:		
1 $BaCl_2$	2 $Mg(NO_3)_2$	
1 $BaCl_2$	3 Na_2CrO_4	
1 $BaCl_2$	4 $Al_2(SO_4)_3$	
1 $BaCl_2$	5 K_2CrO_4	
1 $BaCl_2$	6 $AgNO_3$	
2 $Mg(NO_3)_2$	3 Na_2CrO_4	
2 $Mg(NO_3)_2$	4 $Al_2(SO_4)_3$	
2 $Mg(NO_3)_2$	5 K_2CrO_4	
2 $Mg(NO_3)_2$	6 $AgNO_3$	
3 Na_2CrO_4	4 $Al_2(SO_4)_3$	
3 Na_2CrO_4	5 K_2CrO_4	
3 Na_2CrO_4	6 $AgNO_3$	
4 $Al_2(SO_4)_3$	5 K_2CrO_4	
4 $Al_2(SO_4)_3$	6 $AgNO_3$	
5 K_2CrO_4	6 $AgNO_3$	

Name _____ Date _____ Class _____

ANALYSES AND CONCLUSIONS

1. For each combination of solutions that gave a precipitate, write correct formulas for the two new compounds that could form from the ions present. (Remember to balance the ionic charges!) Enter these formulas in Data Table 2.

DATA TABLE 2: PRECIPITATION RESULTS AND ANALYSIS		
Solution Pairs Yielding Precipitates	Formulas of Possible Precipitates (Circle Choice)	Reason for Choice
Set 1:		
Set 2:		
Set 3:		

2. For those combinations that produced a precipitate, decide which of the two new compounds is the precipitate by eliminating the other. Remember that all compounds in your sets are soluble, so they cannot be precipitates in any of the reactions. Also, a combination of ions will either always form a precipitate or never form one. Circle the formula of each compound you believe to be a precipitate, and record the reasons for your choices in Data Table 2.

3. Write complete ionic equations for the precipitation reactions that you observed. Show the reactants as ions, the precipitate as a solid, and the spectator ions as unchanged. Balance each equation for mass and charge. The total charge should be zero on each side of the equation.

_____

_____

_____

_____

_____

_____

_____

_____

_____

_____

_____

_____

_____

4. Write the net ionic equations for each reaction in the preceding question.

_____

_____

_____

_____

_____

_____

_____

_____

_____

_____

_____

_____

5. What is the function of spectator ions in a precipitation reaction?

_____

_____

6. Explain in your own words why a precipitate forms.

_____

_____

_____

7. How does a complete ionic equation differ from a net ionic equation?

_____

_____

_____

_____

_____

GOING FURTHER

Develop a Hypothesis

Suppose you are given three different solutions containing Na_3PO_4, $Ba(NO_3)_2$, and K_2CO_3, respectively. Based on the results of this lab, hypothesize about which combinations of these solutions will produce insoluble precipitates. (**Hint:** Use your observations of the behavior of the compounds studied in this lab to develop general statements about the solubility of ionic compounds containing Na^+, Ba^{2+}, K^+, NO_3^-, and CO_3^{2-}.)

_____

_____

_____

_____

Name _____ Date _____ Class _____

Design an Experiment

Propose an experiment to test your hypothesis. If resources are available and you have your teacher's permission, perform the experiment.

_____

_____

_____

_____

18 | QUALITATIVE ANALYSIS

Text Reference
Section 11.3

PURPOSE

To develop a systematic panel of chemical tests to identify an unknown solution.

BACKGROUND

In Experiment 16, you learned how to identify the presence of common ions by conducting chemical tests, a process called qualitative analysis. But how do you test a solution containing mixtures of ions with similar chemical behavior? For example, both calcium and barium ions react with oxalate ions $C_2O_4^{2-}$ to form white precipitates. If you add oxalate ions to an unknown solution and a white precipitate forms, you cannot say conclusively whether the solution contains only calcium ions, only barium ions, or a combination of both. Additional tests are required to identify the unknown solution.

In this experiment, you will observe the reactions that occur when four solutions are mixed with each of three different reagents. Using these reactions as a reference, you will develop a systematic set of tests to identify an unknown solution. The solutions and reagents are deliberately unlabeled; knowledge of the chemicals used is not important. Instead, focus your attention on making careful observations and developing a logical, systematic approach for identifying the unknown solution.

MATERIALS (PER PAIR)

safety goggles
spot plate or 3–12 small
   test tubes
paper towels
plastic wash bottle

distilled water
set of reagents: A, B, C [T] [I]
set of solutions: 1, 2, 3, 4 [T] [I]
unknown solutions

SAFETY FIRST!

In this lab, the solutions you use may contain harmful materials. Treat all unknown solutions as if they were hazardous. Observe all precautions, especially the ones listed below. If you see a safety icon beside a step in the Procedure, refer to the list below for its meaning.

 Caution: Wear your safety goggles. (All steps.)

 Caution: Some of the chemicals used in this experiment are poisonous. Treat all chemicals with care. Do not mix any chemicals except as directed in the Procedure section. Avoid skin contact with these chemicals. (Steps 1, 3, 4.)

Note: Return or dispose of all materials according to the instructions of your teacher. (Step 5.)

Note: Wash your hands thoroughly after completing this experiment.

PROCEDURE

As you perform the experiment, record your observations in Data Table 1.

1. Clean the spot plate or test tubes with distilled water. In separate depressions on the spot plate or in separate test tubes, mix solutions 1 through 4, one at a time, with each of the reagents. Use 1–2 drops of each solution. Record your observations.

2. Study your results and plan how to identify your unknown, using the fewest number of tests.

3. Obtain an unknown and identify it as solution 1, 2, 3, or 4 by testing it with the reagents. Record the tests done and the results obtained.

4. Repeat Step 3 with a second unknown solution. Record the tests done and the results obtained.

5. Follow your teacher's instructions for proper disposal of the materials.

Name _____ Date _____ Class _____

OBSERVATIONS

DATA TABLE 1: RESULTS OF MIXING SOLUTIONS AND REAGENTS				
		Reagent A	Reagent B	Reagent C
Solution 1				
Solution 2				
Solution 3				
Solution 4				
Unknown				
Unknown				

ANALYSES AND CONCLUSIONS

1. Without knowing the identity of the chemicals in the experiment, you identified an unknown solution. Explain how.

_____

_____

_____

_____

_____

2. Based on your experimental results, how would you distinguish between solutions 1 and 3? Between solutions 2 and 3?

_____

_____

_____

3. Suppose someone has randomly relabeled the solutions used in this experiment as I, II, III, and IV and the reagents as X, Y, and Z. Using the facts that follow, consult Data Table 1 and correctly identify the solutions and reagents by their original designations (1, 2, 3, 4, A, B, C).

When mixed:

I and Y produce a red precipitate.

II and Y produce no precipitate.

II and X produce a yellow precipitate.

III and Z produce a white precipitate.

_____

_____

GOING FURTHER

Design an Experiment

Based on the results of this lab, develop a scheme of analysis for an unknown solution that contains more than one chemical species. For example, would it be possible to characterize a mixture of solutions 1, 3, and 4 by using the test reagents?

If resources are available and you have your teacher's permission, perform the experiment.

_____

_____

_____

_____

_____

19 QUANTITATIVE ANALYSIS

Text Reference
Sections 12.1 and 12.2

PURPOSE

To determine the values for the coefficients used in a balanced chemical equation.

BACKGROUND

By now you are familiar with seeing and working with balanced chemical equations. But how do you know the coefficients in these equations are correct? Do the coefficients reflect how the chemical substances actually combine? In this experiment, you will determine the values for the coefficients used in the balanced chemical equation for the reaction of iron metal with a copper(II) chloride solution, which produces copper metal and an iron compound.

You will use the fact that the coefficients of the substances in a chemical equation represent the relative number of moles of each substance involved in the reaction. You will determine the relative numbers of moles of each reactant and product in the reaction you observe. From the mole ratios, you will derive the appropriate coefficients to be used in the chemical equation. If your experiment is successful, you should be able to determine the mole ratio of the *iron used* to the *copper produced*.

MATERIALS (PER PAIR)

safety goggles
gloves (optional)
glass-marking pencil
50-mL graduated cylinder
2 250-mL beakers
centigram balance
crucible tongs
plastic wash bottle
paper towels

glass stirring rod
drying oven or heat
  lamp
1*M* copper(II) chloride
  dihydrate, $CuCl_2 \cdot 2H_2O$ [T]
2 iron nails, Fe
steel wool
distilled water

SAFETY FIRST!

In this lab, observe all precautions, especially the ones listed below. If you see a safety icon beside a step in the Procedure, refer to the list below for its meaning.

 Caution: Wear your safety goggles. (All steps.)

 Caution: Copper(II) chloride solution is toxic. Avoid skin contact with this material. (Step 2.)

Name _____ Date _____ Class _____

PROCEDURE

As you perform the experiment, record your data in Data Table 1 and your observations in Data Table 2.

Day 1

 1. Using a glass-marking pencil, label a clean, dry 250-mL beaker with your name. Determine the mass of the beaker to the nearest 0.01 g, and record the measurement in Data Table 1.

 2. Add 50 mL of copper(II) chloride solution to the beaker.

3. Clean two iron nails with steel wool to remove any rust or protective coating. Determine the combined mass of the nails to the nearest 0.01 g and record the measurement.

4. Slide the nails carefully into the solution of copper(II) chloride. Let the beaker stand undisturbed for at least 20 minutes. Record any evidence of a chemical reaction in Data Table 2.

5. Using crucible tongs, remove one of the nails from the reaction solution. Hold the nail over the reaction beaker. Rinse the adherent reaction product off the nail and into the beaker, using a jet of distilled water from a wash bottle, as shown in Figure 19.1. Repeat this procedure for the second nail.

6. Allow the nails to dry on a paper towel in a safe place. (You will remeasure their mass later.)

Figure 19.1

Figure 19.2

7. Carefully decant the liquid portion of the reaction solution into another 250-mL beaker, as shown in Figure 19.2. Leave the solid reaction product in the original beaker. Dispose of the decanted solution by pouring it into the sink.

8. Use 25 mL of distilled water to wash the reaction product contained in the beaker. Decant the wash water into the collection container. Repeat the washing and decanting procedures two more times, being careful to avoid losing any reaction product. Pour the contents of the collection container into the sink.

9. Give the reaction beaker containing the solid product to your teacher to be dried.

Day 2

10. Determine the combined mass of the dry nails to the nearest 0.01 g and record the measurement.

11. Determine the mass of the beaker and the dry reaction product to the nearest 0.01 g and record the measurement. When you are finished, dispose of the nails and the solid product in a waste container.

Name _____ Date _____ Class _____

OBSERVATIONS

DATA TABLE 1: MASS DETERMINATIONS	
Items	Mass (g)
empty dry beaker	
iron nails (before reaction)	
iron nails (after reaction)	
beaker and dry product	

DATA TABLE 2: VISUAL EVIDENCE OF CHEMICAL REACTION	
Step	Observations

ANALYSES AND CONCLUSIONS

1. Determine the mass of iron lost by the nails.

2. Calculate the number of moles of iron used.

3. Determine the mass of the product.

Name _____ Date _____ Class _____

4. Assuming that one of the products is copper metal, calculate the number of moles of copper produced.

5. Calculate the mole ratio of iron used to copper produced. Express this ratio as a simple whole-number ratio.

6. Calculate the percent error in your value for the mole ratio. Your teacher will give you the accepted value.

$$\text{percent error} = \frac{|\text{experimental value} - \text{accepted value}|}{\text{accepted value}} \times 100\%$$

7. Assuming that one product is iron(II) chloride, write a balanced equation for the reaction. What type of reaction is this?

_____

_____

_____

_____

_____

8. Copper could be lost in this experiment during the washing and decanting steps. How would this effect the iron:copper mole ratio? Explain.

_____

_____

_____

_____

_____

_____

Name _____ Date _____ Class _____

9. What other factors might account for any error in your mole ratio?

_____

_____

_____

_____

_____

_____

10. Examine the data collected by other members of the class. Were the masses of iron and copper the same in all experiments? Were the mole ratios the same? Does the mole ratio of a substance in a chemical equation depend on the amounts of reactants used?

_____

_____

_____

_____

_____

_____

GOING FURTHER

Develop a Hypothesis

Based on the results of this lab, develop a hypothesis about other cations besides copper(II) ion that could be used in this experiment.

_____

_____

Design an Experiment

Propose an experiment to test your hypothesis. If resources are available and you have your teacher's permission, perform the experiment.

_____

_____

Chapter 12 • *Stoichiometry*   **EXPERIMENT**

20 BALANCED CHEMICAL EQUATIONS

Text Reference
Section 12.3

PURPOSE

To examine the relationship between amounts of reactants and products in a chemical reaction.

BACKGROUND

Like a gymnast on a beam, the amounts of material involved in a chemical reaction must be properly balanced. An unbalanced gymnast will fall off the beam; an unbalanced equation will waste chemical reactants. In this experiment, you will examine the stoichiometry—the relationship between amounts of materials—of the reaction between lead(II) nitrate and sodium iodide. The balanced equation is:

$$Pb(NO_3)_2(aq) + 2NaI(aq) \rightarrow PbI_2(s) + 2NaNO_3(aq)$$

You will also explore the concepts of limiting and excess reagents. A *limiting reagent* is completely used up in a reaction. The amount of product that can be formed depends on the quantity of limiting reagent present. An *excess reagent* is so called because, after the reaction is complete, there is still an amount left unreacted. Finally, you will estimate the actual yield of one product, lead(II) iodide, and compare it with the theoretical yield predicted from the balanced equation.

MATERIALS (PER PAIR)

safety goggles	6 rubber stoppers
6 large test tubes	centimeter ruler
test-tube rack	dropper pipet
2 50-mL burets	spot plate
twin buret clamp	plastic wash bottle
ring stand	0.5M lead(II) nitrate, Pb(NO$_3$)$_2$ T
glass-marking pencil	0.5M sodium iodide, NaI T
2 250-mL beakers	distilled water

SAFETY FIRST!

In this lab, observe all precautions, especially the ones listed below. If you see a safety icon beside a step in the Procedure, refer to the list below for its meaning.

 Caution: Wear your safety goggles. (All steps.)

 Caution: Lead(II) nitrate is toxic. Wash your hands thoroughly after use. (Step 3.)

 Note: Return or dispose of all materials according to the instructions of your teacher. (Step 12.)

Experiment 20 Balanced Chemical Equations **127**

PROCEDURE

As you perform the experiment, record your results in Data Tables 1 and 2.

Part A

1. Number, with the numerals 1–6, six large, clean, and dry test tubes.

2. Mount two 50-mL burets on a ring stand, using a twin buret clamp. Label one buret "NaI"; label the other "$Pb(NO_3)_2$."

3. Obtain, in separate labeled 250-mL beakers, about 50 mL of $0.5M$ $Pb(NO_3)_2$ and 75 mL of $0.5M$ NaI. Fill the labeled burets with these solutions.

4. Using the filled burets, add the solutions to the six test tubes, according to the following table. Place each tube in a test-tube rack.

	Tube 1	Tube 2	Tube 3	Tube 4	Tube 5	Tube 6
$0.5M$ $Pb(NO_3)_2$ (mL)	2.0	4.0	6.0	8.0	10.0	12.0
$0.5M$ NaI (mL)	16.0	14.0	12.0	10.0	8.0	6.0

Keep the remaining solutions in the burets for later use.

5. Seal each tube with a rubber stopper. Mix the contents by inverting each tube *three times*. Do not shake.

6. Leave the tubes undisturbed in the test-tube rack for at least 10 minutes.

7. Measure the height of the yellow precipitate [lead(II) iodide] in each tube to the nearest 0.1 cm and record the measurement.

Part B

8. **Testing the supernatant for excess reagent.** The liquid above a settled precipitate is called the *supernatant*. With a dropper pipet, remove a sample of supernatant from tube 1. Add *one* drop of supernatant to each of two adjacent depressions on a spot plate. Rinse the dropper with distilled water and repeat this procedure for tubes 2–6.

9. Add a drop of $0.5M$ $Pb(NO_3)_2$ to one set of samples from tubes 1–6.

10. Add a drop of $0.5M$ NaI to the other set of samples.

11. Record the results of these spot-plate tests in Data Table 2.

12. Follow your teacher's instructions for proper disposal of the materials.

Name _____ Date _____ Class _____

OBSERVATIONS

DATA TABLE 1: DATA FOR REACTION MIXTURES

Tube Number	$Pb(NO_3)_2$ (mL)	$Pb(NO_3)_2$ (mol)	NaI (mL)	NaI (mol)	Height Ppt. (cm)	Maximum Theoretical Yield Ppt. (mol)
1						
2						
3						
4						
5						
6						

DATA TABLE 2: SPOT TESTS OF SUPERNATANT SAMPLES FROM REACTION TUBES

Substance Added	Tube 1 Ppt.?	Tube 2 Ppt.?	Tube 3 Ppt.?	Tube 4 Ppt.?	Tube 5 Ppt.?	Tube 6 Ppt.?
$Pb(NO_3)_2$						
NaI						
reagent present in excess						

ANALYSES AND CONCLUSIONS

1. Calculate the number of moles of $Pb(NO_3)_2$ and NaI added to each tube. (**Hint:** Calculate how many moles would be in 1 mL and then multiply by the number of milliliters in the sample.) Enter your result in Data Table 1.

2. For the tube with the greatest amount of precipitate, calculate the mole ratio between $Pb(NO_3)_2$ and NaI.

3. Plot two *separate* bar graphs showing the height of lead(II) iodide (cm) versus tube number. One graph should show the height of lead(II) iodide actually obtained in each tube, and the other should show the maximum theoretical number of moles of lead(II) iodide in each tube. Number the tubes 1–6 from left to right.

4. In which tube was there little or no reaction of the supernatant with either $Pb(NO_3)_2$ or NaI? What is the mole ratio of the reactants in this tube?

5. How are your two graphs similar?

_____

_____

_____

_____

_____

6. a. Write a complete ionic equation for the reaction observed in this experiment.

_____

   b. Indicate which ions are spectator ions in this reaction.

_____

   c. Write a net ionic equation for this reaction.

_____

7. Examine the class data, especially for tube 3. Explain any inconsistency you observe in the results.

_____

_____

_____

_____

GOING FURTHER

Develop a Hypothesis

Based on the results of this lab, develop a hypothesis to explain how the stoichiometry could be determined for a reaction that forms a gas (for example, calcium carbonate + hydrochloric acid) instead of a precipitate.

_____

_____

_____

_____

Design an Experiment

Propose an experiment to test your hypothesis. If resources are available and you have your teacher's permission, perform the experiment.

_____

_____

_____

_____

21 ALLOTROPIC FORMS OF SULFUR

Text Reference
Section 13.3

PURPOSE

To observe and describe the allotropes of sulfur.

BACKGROUND

Some elements can have several different molecular forms while in the same physical state. These differing forms are called *allotropes*. Environmental conditions, such as temperature and pressure, determine which allotrope will form. Carbon is an element with several allotropes. The allotropes of carbon have very different physical properties. Diamond is hard, clear, and shiny. Graphite is black, with a slippery, greasy feel. Buckminsterfullerenes contain 60 carbon atoms arranged in a hollow sphere resembling a soccer ball. Sulfur is another element with several allotropes. Unlike carbon's allotropes, however, sulfur's allotropes can be easily produced in the lab.

In this experiment, you will observe the allotropes of sulfur.

MATERIALS

safety goggles
50-mL beaker
dropper pipet
2 watch glasses
100-mL beaker
250-mL beaker
medium test tube
test-tube holder
tweezers
magnifying glass or
 microscope

ring stand
ring support
wire gauze
gas burner
vegetable oil F
powdered sulfur, S F T
filter paper circles
distilled water
paper towels

SAFETY FIRST!

This lab is intended to be done as a teacher demonstration. Observe all precautions, especially the ones listed below. If you see a safety icon beside a step in the Procedure, refer to the list below for its meaning.

 Caution: Wear your safety goggles. (All steps.)

 Caution: This experiment must be conducted in a fume hood. Use a low flame to heat the sulfur. Sulfur is flammable and can be ignited. (Steps 3, 7, and 10.)

 Caution: Exercise care when working with an open flame. Tie back hair and loose clothing. (Steps 3, 7, 10.)

Caution: Avoid breathing fumes from heated sulfur. Individuals with asthma or allergies to sulfur compounds should not be present when this experiment is conducted. (Steps 3, 7, 10.)

Caution: Molten sulfur can cause severe burns. (Steps 8, 10.)

Note: Your teacher will properly dispose of the materials. (Step 12.)

PROCEDURE

Your teacher will conduct this experiment in a fume hood as a demonstration. During the demonstration, record your observations and draw sketches in Data Table 1. Note that the instructions in the Procedure are written for the teacher.

Part A. Orthorhombic Sulfur

1. Pour vegetable oil to a depth of about 0.5 cm into a 50-mL beaker.

2. Add a pea-sized sample of sulfur to the oil.

3. Using a gas burner, heat the oil-sulfur mixture over a low flame for a few seconds. **CAUTION:** *Excessive heating may cause the sulfur-oil mixture to ignite, producing toxic fumes.*

4. Using a dropper pipet, place a few drops of the warm oil-sulfur mixture on a watch glass. Put the watch glass and beaker aside. After about 20 minutes, examine the product under a magnifying glass or a microscope. Record your observations and sketch the shapes of any crystals that have formed.

Part B. Monoclinic Sulfur

5. Fold a circle of filter paper into the conical shape used for filtering, and place it in a 100-mL beaker for support, as shown in Figure 21.1.

6. Fill a medium test tube about one-third full with powdered sulfur.

7. Heat the test tube over a low flame. **CAUTION:** *Slow heating is recommended.* Continue heating until all the sulfur has melted to an orange-yellow liquid.

8. **CAUTION:** *Molten sulfur can cause painful burns.* Pour the liquid sulfur rapidly into the filter paper cone. As soon as the sulfur begins to solidify, carefully use tweezers to remove the filter paper from the beaker. Place the open filter paper on a watch glass. Examine the product with a magnifying glass or a microscope. Record your observations and sketch any crystals that have formed.

Figure 21.1

Part C. Plastic Sulfur

9. Add 150 mL of water to a 250-mL beaker. Fill the test tube used in Part B about one-third full with sulfur.

  10. Heat the test tube in a burner flame until the sulfur just begins to boil. The sulfur should be dark red at the boiling point. **CAUTION:** *Sulfur has a boiling point of 444°C!*

Figure 21.2

11. Rapidly pour the hot sulfur into the beaker of cold water, as shown in Figure 21.2. When the sulfur is cool, remove it from the water and place it on a paper towel to dry. Examine the dry sulfur, using a magnifying glass or microscope. Record your observations and sketch this form of the sulfur.

 12. Your teacher will properly dispose of the materials.

Name _____ Date _____ Class _____

OBSERVATIONS

DATA TABLE 1: OBSERVATIONS OF ALLOTROPIC SULFUR

Allotrope	Description	Drawing of sample
orthorhombic sulfur		
monoclinic sulfur		
plastic sulfur		

ANALYSES AND CONCLUSIONS

1. Which allotropes of sulfur are crystalline? Compare the structure of any crystals formed.

   _____

   _____

   _____

2. What happened to the plastic sulfur upon standing for a time? What does this suggest about the relative stabilities of the allotropes of sulfur?

   _____

   _____

   _____

   _____

   _____

   _____

3. Design an experiment to determine which of the crystalline forms of sulfur is the most stable at room temperature and 1 atm pressure.

_____

_____

_____

GOING FURTHER

Do Research

Sulfur is not the only element that can exist in more than one allotropic form. Do research on the allotropes of phosphorus. Describe their physical and chemical properties and any important industrial applications.

_____

_____

_____

_____

_____

_____

_____

_____

Chapter 13 • *States of Matter*   **EXPERIMENT**

22 CHANGES OF PHYSICAL STATE

Text Reference
Section 13.4

PURPOSE

To investigate the melting and freezing behavior of a compound.

BACKGROUND

If you have ever cooled a glass of water with ice cubes and watched water vapor condense on the outside of the glass, you know water can exist in distinct physical states—the solid state (ice), the liquid state (water), and the gaseous state (water vapor). In any pure substance, changes of physical state occur at constant, discrete temperatures that are uniquely characteristic of the substance. Changes in physical state include solids melting, liquids freezing or boiling, and gases condensing.

In this experiment, you will closely examine what happens when a substance undergoes a change in physical state. Specifically, you will investigate the melting and freezing behavior of a sample of an organic compound called lauric acid, $CH_3(CH_2)_{10}COOH$. You are chiefly concerned with two questions. First, does liquid lauric acid begin to freeze at the same temperature that solid lauric acid begins to melt? Second, what happens to the temperature of the lauric acid between the time freezing or melting begins and the time it is complete? You will also consider what happens to the energy that is put into or removed from the lauric acid system during melting or freezing.

MATERIALS (PER PAIR)

safety goggles
2 400-mL beakers
2 thermometers
rubber stopper
large test tube
2 wire gauzes
2 utility clamps
2 gas burners

2 ring stands
2 ring supports
pliers
beaker tongs or insulated glove
timer with second hand
tap water
lauric acid, $CH_3(CH_2)_{10}COOH$
20-cm copper wire, Cu

SAFETY FIRST!

In this lab, observe all precautions, especially the ones listed below. If you see a safety icon beside a step in the Procedure, refer to the list below for its meaning.

 Caution: Wear your safety goggles. (All steps.)

Caution: Exercise care when working with hot water baths to prevent a thermal burn. Do not touch the beaker containing hot water with your bare hands. (Steps 2, 4, 5.)

 Caution: Never use a thermometer as a stirrer. (Steps 3, 5, 6.)

Note: Return or dispose of all materials according to the instructions of your teacher. (Step 7.)

PROCEDURE

As you perform the experiment, record your data in Data Table 1.

Part A. The Change From Liquid to Solid

1. Heat about 250 mL of water in a 400-mL beaker to 30°C. Separately, heat 250 mL of water in another 400-mL beaker to 60°C.

2. Use a utility clamp to support a large test tube containing approximately 20 g of acid in the hot (60°C) water, as shown in Figure 22.1. Make sure that the lauric acid is totally beneath the water in the beaker and that the test tube does not touch the bottom of the beaker.

Rubber stopper

Thermometer

Copper wire stirrer

Utility clamp

Large test tube

400-mL beaker

Lauric acid

Ring stand

Figure 22.1

Figure 22.2

3. While the sample is heating, use the pliers to construct a stirrer from a piece of stiff copper wire, as shown in Figure 22.2. When the crystals have melted, slip the loop of the wire stirrer around a thermometer fitted with a rubber stopper. Referring to Figure 22.1, place the stirrer-thermometer assembly in the test tube so that the thermometer bulb is at the center of the molten lauric acid and the stirrer moves easily up and down. The bulb of the thermometer should not touch the bottom of the test tube. Make certain that the markings on the thermometer can be easily read.

4. Carefully replace the beaker containing the 60°C water with the beaker containing the 30°C water. Do this by removing the gas burner and lowering the ring support while holding the beaker with tongs or insulated gloves. Return the ring support to its previous position.

5. Gently stir the lauric acid. When its temperature has fallen to about 55°C, take a temperature reading every 30 seconds. Record the temperature to the nearest 0.1°C. Continue stirring the lauric acid and recording temperature readings until the temperature of the material has fallen to 40°C or lower. (**Note:** When most of the lauric acid has solidified, you will no longer be able to stir the contents. Continue taking temperature readings during this period.)

Part B. The Change From Solid to Liquid

6. Replace the beaker containing 30°C water with one that contains water at approximately 55°C. Begin to collect temperature data immediately. Record temperature measurements of the test-tube contents every 30 seconds until the lauric acid is completely melted. Begin stirring as soon as you are able to move the copper stirrer freely. **CAUTION:** *Do not force the stirrer.*

7. Carefully disassemble the apparatus and dispose of the lauric acid as directed by your teacher.

Name _____ Date _____ Class _____

OBSERVATIONS

<table>
<tr><td colspan="4">DATA TABLE 1: HEATING AND COOLING DATA</td></tr>
<tr><td colspan="2">Part A</td><td colspan="2">Part B</td></tr>
<tr><td>Time (min)</td><td>Temperature (°C)</td><td>Time (min)</td><td>Temperature (°C)</td></tr>
<tr><td></td><td></td><td></td><td></td></tr>
<tr><td></td><td></td><td></td><td></td></tr>
<tr><td></td><td></td><td></td><td></td></tr>
<tr><td></td><td></td><td></td><td></td></tr>
<tr><td></td><td></td><td></td><td></td></tr>
<tr><td></td><td></td><td></td><td></td></tr>
<tr><td></td><td></td><td></td><td></td></tr>
<tr><td></td><td></td><td></td><td></td></tr>
<tr><td></td><td></td><td></td><td></td></tr>
<tr><td></td><td></td><td></td><td></td></tr>
<tr><td></td><td></td><td></td><td></td></tr>
<tr><td></td><td></td><td></td><td></td></tr>
<tr><td></td><td></td><td></td><td></td></tr>
<tr><td></td><td></td><td></td><td></td></tr>
<tr><td></td><td></td><td></td><td></td></tr>
<tr><td></td><td></td><td></td><td></td></tr>
<tr><td></td><td></td><td></td><td></td></tr>
<tr><td></td><td></td><td></td><td></td></tr>
<tr><td></td><td></td><td></td><td></td></tr>
<tr><td></td><td></td><td></td><td></td></tr>
<tr><td></td><td></td><td></td><td></td></tr>
<tr><td></td><td></td><td></td><td></td></tr>
<tr><td></td><td></td><td></td><td></td></tr>
</table>

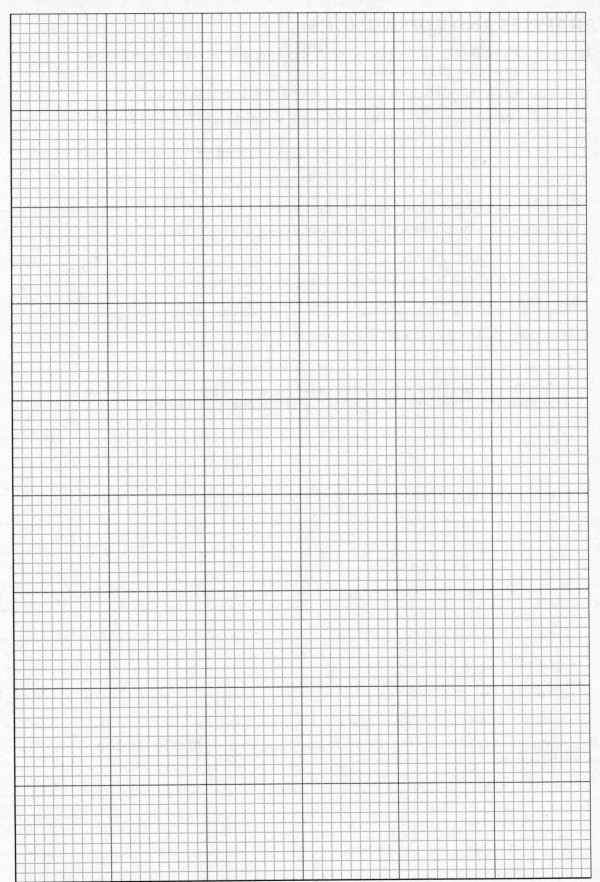

ANALYSES AND CONCLUSIONS

1. Construct a graph of your data from Part A. Plot temperature versus time. Draw a smooth curve through the points.

2. Plot the data from Part B on the same graph and draw a smooth curve.

3. Does the temperature of a substance vary while it is melting or freezing? Explain.

   _____

   _____

   _____

4. Using data from Part A, determine the freezing point of lauric acid.

   _____

5. Using data from Part B, determine the melting point of lauric acid.

   _____

6. Does lauric acid melt and freeze at the same temperature?

   _____

7. Explain the shape of the curves in terms of the energy changes that are occurring in the sample as it heats up and melts and as it cools down and freezes.

   _____

   _____

   _____

   _____

   _____

   _____

   _____

   _____

   _____

   _____

8. Explain how an increase in the amount of lauric acid used would affect the shape of the curves.

   _____

   _____

   _____

   _____

9. Explain in your own words what is going on at the molecular level as liquid lauric acid cools and freezes.

_____

_____

_____

_____

_____

_____

_____

_____

_____

_____

_____

_____

_____

GOING FURTHER

Develop a Hypothesis

Based on what you have learned about the melting behavior of lauric acid, develop a hypothesis about how the melting behavior of lauric acid would change if an impurity was introduced into the sample.

_____

_____

_____

_____

Do Research

If resources are available, read textbooks or articles about the melting behaviors of solids that will support or disprove your hypothesis.

_____

_____

23 PRESSURE–VOLUME RELATIONSHIPS FOR GASES

Text Reference
Section 14.2

PURPOSE

To investigate the relationship between the pressure and volume of a gas.

BACKGROUND

When you squeeze a tennis ball, the ball compresses easily at first. But as you squeeze harder, the ball becomes harder and harder to compress. You can explain these qualitative observations simply. For example, you know that the gas contained inside the tennis ball is being compressed into a smaller volume. As a result, the harder you squeeze, the smaller the volume and the greater the pressure exerted by the gas pushing outward against the ball. Therefore, the harder you squeeze the ball, the more resistance you encounter. This example suggests a relationship between the volume and pressure of a gas. In this experiment, you will measure the pressure of a gas sample as its volume is changed. You will then analyze your data to determine the relationship that exists between the volume and pressure of a gas.

MATERIALS (PER PAIR)

safety goggles
plastic tubing, 1-cm × 5-cm
    length
50-cm glass capillary tube,
    fire polished
500-mL filter flask
one-holed rubber stopper, to
    fit filter flask
30-mL plastic syringe
2 ring stands

2 utility clamps
centimeter ruler
50-mL graduated cylinder
glass-marking pencil
500-mL graduated cylinder
pinch clamp
barometer
dibutyl phthalate (DBP),
    $C_6H_4(CO_2C_4H_9)_2$ $\boxed{T}$
silicone grease

SAFETY FIRST!

In this lab, observe all precautions, especially the ones listed below. If you see a safety icon beside a step in the Procedure, refer to the list below for its meaning.

 Caution: Wear your safety goggles. (All steps.)

 Caution: Exercise care when handling the glass capillary tube. It is easy to break. (Step 3.)

Caution: Dibutyl phthalate (DBP) is toxic. Do not come in contact with this chemical. Contact your teacher immediately in the event of a spill. (Steps 4–12.)

 Note: Return or dispose of all materials according to the instructions of your teacher. (Step 12.)

PROCEDURE

As you perform the experiment, record your data in Data Tables 1 and 2.

 1. Your teacher will have a partial lab set up prepared for you. You need to carefully finish assembling the apparatus. Refer to Figure 23.1.

2. Fit a 5-cm length of plastic tubing over the sidearm of the flask.

 3. Take the capillary tube-stopper assembly out of the flask. Carefully measure the outside diameter of the capillary tube.

4. Carefully measure 50 mL of dibutyl phthalate (DBP) in a *dry* 50-mL graduated cylinder. Pour this volume into the *dry* flask. Replace the capillary tube-stopper assembly. The lower end of the capillary tube should be about 5 mm below the surface of the dibutyl phthalate.

5. Measure and record the length of the tube that is inside the flask and below the stopper.

6. Apply a *thin film* of silicone grease to the 30-mL syringe if the plunger does not operate smoothly. Depress the plunger to the 30-mL mark. Refer to Figure 23.1. Insert the end of the syringe into the plastic tubing attached to the sidearm of the flask. Use a utility clamp attached to a ring stand to support the syringe.

Figure 23.1

7. Make sure that all connections are tight and your setup matches Figure 23.1.

8. Make sure that the plunger reads 30 mL. Record this reading and the height of the DBP in the capillary tube.

9. Now depress the plunger to the 25-mL mark. Record this reading. Wait until the DBP comes to rest in the capillary tube. Then measure and record this height.

10. Repeat this process at 5-mL intervals until as much air as possible has been pushed out of the syringe and into the flask.

11. Remove the syringe from the plastic tubing. Set the plunger at the 30-mL mark and reattach the syringe to the flask. Repeat Steps 8–10 and record your data in Data Table 2.

 12. Mark the neck of the flask at the bottom of the rubber stopper. Remove the stopper assembly and the syringe, leaving the plastic tubing in place on the sidearm. Dispose of the DBP and rinse the flask as directed by your teacher.

13. Use a pinch clamp to close the end of the plastic tubing, as shown in Figure 23.2. Fill the flask with water to the mark on the neck. Pour this water into a 500-mL graduated cylinder. Record the volume to the nearest milliliter. This is the volume of your flask.

14. Record atmospheric pressure and room temperature in Data Table 1.

Figure 23.2

Name _____ Date _____ Class _____

OBSERVATIONS

DATA TABLE 1: PRELIMINARY MEASUREMENTS
diameter of capillary tube:
length of capillary tube in flask:
barometric pressure:
room temperature:
volume of flask:

DATA TABLE 2: SYRINGE VOLUME AND DBP HEIGHT READINGS			
Trial 1		**Trial 2**	
Syringe Volume (mL)	DBP Height (cm)	Syringe Volume (mL)	DBP Height (cm)

ANALYSES AND CONCLUSIONS

1. Calculate the volume of air present in your apparatus during the experiment. You must correct the value determined in Step 13 (the volume of the flask) to include the following volumes: the volume of the capillary tube in the flask, the volume of the DBP, and the volume of air in the syringe.

   First, calculate the volume occupied by the capillary tube, using your measurements for the diameter of the tube and for the length of that part of the tube that was within the flask.

   $$\text{volume of capillary tube} = \pi \times \text{radius}^2 \times \text{length}$$
   $$= 3.14 \times (\text{diameter}/2)^2 \times \text{length}$$

   Next, calculate the volume of air in the flask, without the capillary tube or the DBP.

   $$\text{volume of air} = \text{volume of flask} - \text{volume of DBP} - \text{volume of tube}$$

Finally, for each trial, calculate the total volume of the air in the apparatus by adding the volume of the air in the syringe to the volume of air in the flask. Record this volume in Data Table 3.

DATA TABLE 3: VOLUME AND PRESSURE CALCULATIONS FOR AIR ENCLOSED IN FLASK					
Trial 1			Trial 2		
P (mm Hg)	V (mL)	$P \times V$ (mm Hg $\times$ mL)	P (mm Hg)	V (mL)	$P \times V$ (mm Hg $\times$ mL)

2. For each trial, calculate the pressure exerted by the air enclosed within the flask. Use millimeters of mercury (mm Hg) as the units of pressure. You have already read the pressure directly in centimeters of DBP (cm DBP), but now you must convert this figure to millimeters of mercury (mm Hg). DBP has a density of 1.05 g/cm^3; the density of mercury is 13.6 g/cm^3. This means that a pressure that supports a 1-mm column of DBP will support a column of mercury (1.05/13.6 = 0.0772 mm) high.

Calculate the pressure of the volume of enclosed air in millimeters of mercury, using this equation:

$$\begin{matrix} \text{pressure} \\ \text{of enclosed} \\ \text{air in mm Hg} \end{matrix} = \left(\begin{matrix} \text{height of} \\ \text{DBP in mm} \end{matrix} \times \frac{0.077 \text{ mm Hg}}{\text{mm DBP}} \right) + \begin{matrix} \text{room pressure} \\ \text{in mm Hg} \end{matrix}$$

Record the pressure for each trial in Data Table 3.

3. Calculate the product of the pressure of the enclosed air (see problem 2) and the volume of the enclosed air (see problem 1) for each trial. Record the results in Data Table 3.

4. Make a graph of pressure versus volume. Draw a best-fit smooth line for your data points. Title and label your graph.

5. Based on your data, what relationship exists between the pressure and volume of a gas (assuming constant temperature)?

_____

_____

_____

6. Look up a statement of Boyle's law in your textbook. Are your results consistent with Boyle's law? Examine the class data. Is it consistent with the law? Explain.

_____

_____

_____

7. Would your results have been affected if the room temperature had changed during the experiment? Explain.

_____

_____

_____

8. How would your results have been affected if you had used a different gas in the

_____

_____

_____

GOING FURTHER

Develop a Hypothesis

Based on the results of this lab, develop a hypothesis to explain why weather balloons are only partially filled up before they are released into the atmosphere. (These balloons can reach altitudes of 40,000 feet.)

_____

_____

Design an Experiment

Propose an experiment to test your hypothesis.

_____

_____

Name _____ Date _____ Class _____

24 TEMPERATURE–VOLUME RELATIONSHIPS FOR GASES

Text Reference
Section 14.2

PURPOSE

To investigate the relationship of the volume of a gas and its temperature.

BACKGROUND

Have you noticed that the tires on automobiles appear to be a little flat on a cold winter's day or that a balloon inflated in a cold room will expand when taken to a warm room. These observations suggest that there is a relationship between the temperature and volume of a gas. If a gas is heated, its volume increases. If a gas is cooled, its volume decreases. In this experiment, you will measure the volume of a sample of air at different temperatures and analyze the data to determine the relationship between the temperature and the volume of a gas. You will also extrapolate from your experimental data to determine absolute zero—the temperature at a which a gas theoretically has no volume.

MATERIALS (PER PAIR)

safety goggles	small rubber band
glass capillary tube,	thermometer
2 mm × 20 cm	2 400-mL beakers
gas burner	forceps
dropper pipet	centimeter ruler
watch glass	dibutyl phthalate,
test-tube holder	$C_6H_4(CO_2C_4H_9)_2$ T
ring stand	ice and water
ring support	
2 utility clamps	
wire gauze	

SAFETY FIRST!

In this lab, observe all precautions, especially the ones listed below. If you see a safety icon beside a step in the Procedure, refer to the list below for its meaning.

 Caution: Wear your safety goggles. (All steps.)

 Caution: Dibutyl phthalate is toxic. Do not come in contact with this chemical. (All steps.)

Caution: Exercise care when working with an open flame. Tie back hair and loose clothing. Do not use the burner near flammable materials (Steps 1, 9.)

Caution: Exercise care when working with hot water. Hot glass tubing can cause burns. Make certain that any glass you use is cool before you handle it. Remember that hot glass looks the same as cold glass. If you should be burned, hold the burned area under cold running water until the burning sensation stops. Notify your teacher immediately. (Steps 1, 9.)

Note: Return or dispose of all materials according to the instructions of your teacher. (Step 10.)

PROCEDURE

As you perform the experiment, record your observations in Data Table 1.

1. Seal one end of the capillary tube by rotating it in a hot burner flame. Fire-polish the open end. **CAUTION:** *Place all hot glassware on a heat-resistant ceramic square to cool.*

2. Using a dropper pipet, place about 2 mL of dibutyl phthalate (DBP) on a clean, dry watch glass.

3. Grasp the capillary tube in a test-tube holder and pass it back and forth through the burner flame for about 5 seconds, as shown in Figure 24.1. Remove the tube from the heat and immediately insert the *open end* into the DBP on the watch glass. Allow a 1-cm length of DBP to be drawn up into the tube.

4. On a ring stand, clamp the tube vertically, with its *open end up*, and allow the tube to cool to room temperature. The column of trapped air should be between 5 and 10 cm long.

5. Push a small rubber band over the capillary tube until it is about halfway up the tube. This rubber band will serve as a distance marker.

6. Lower the clamped capillary tube, *open end up*, and a thermometer into ice water in a 400-mL beaker so that the entire column of trapped air is submerged. Refer to Figure 24.2. Wait several minutes. Without removing the tube from the ice water, use forceps to slide the rubber band to mark the top of the air column. Wait another minute and readjust the band if necessary.

Fanning the capillary tube in flame

DBP

Trapping a volume of air

Trapped air

1 cm

The DBP seal

Figure 24.1

7. Measure and record the height of the column of trapped air inside the capillary tube. Measure and record the temperature of the ice water bath to the nearest 0.1°C.

Capillary tube

Thermometer

DBP seal

Rubber band

Trapped air

Ice water

Wire gauze

Burner
(as required)

Ring stand

Figure 24.2

8. Repeat Steps 6 and 7, using a 400-mL beaker filled with water at room temperature.

 9. Use a gas burner to heat the water in the beaker to about 40°C. Measure and record the new water temperature and the length of the air column. Repeat this procedure at 20°C intervals, up to 100°C, time permitting.

 10. Save the DBP for reuse, or dispose of it as directed by your teacher.

Name _____ Date _____ Class _____

OBSERVATIONS

DATA TABLE 1: DATA AND CALCULATIONS

Temperature of Water Bath (°C)	Height of Air Column (relative volume) (cm)	Temperature (K)	V/T (cm/K)

ANALYSES AND CONCLUSIONS

1. Convert Celsius temperatures to Kelvin temperatures and record the results in Data Table 1.

2. The height of the air column is proportional to the volume of air contained in the capillary tube. Therefore, use the height of the air column as the value for the volume of the gas, and calculate the volume/temperature ratio for each trial. Enter your results in Data Table 1.

3. Plot a graph of relative volume (measured in centimeters) versus temperature (in kelvins). Draw a best-fit straight line through the data points. Should the point (0, 0) be on the line?

4. Plot a second graph using the same data, but using degrees Celsius as the unit of temperature. Begin the volume scale at 0 cm, but start the temperature scale at −300°C. Again, draw a best-fit straight line through the data points. Use dashes to extend the straight line from the lowest data point to the horizontal axis. According to your graph, what is the Celsius temperature at which the volume would be equal to 0? How does this value compare with the actual value for absolute zero, in degrees Celsius?

_____

_____

_____

_____

_____

_____

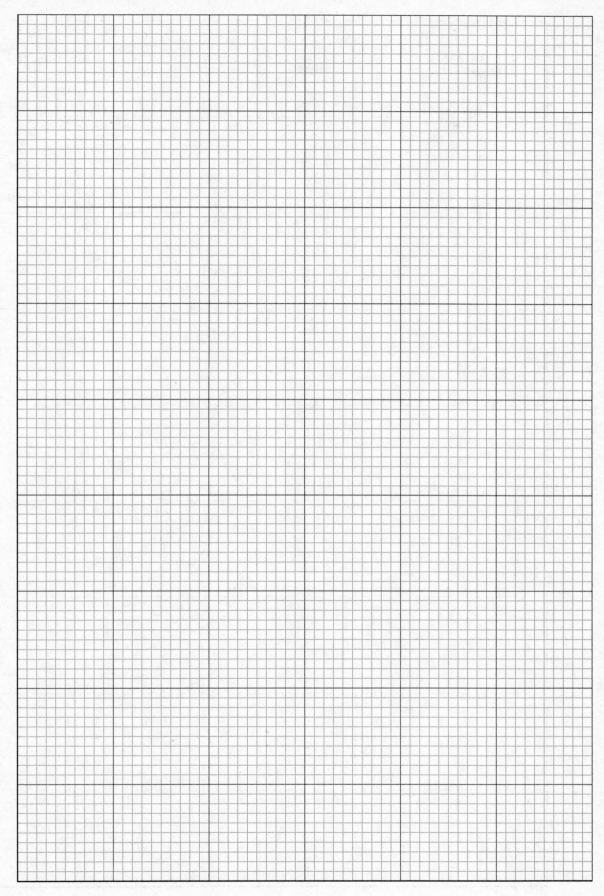

Name _____ Date _____ Class _____

5. Does your data show a volume-temperature relationship for a gas? Explain.

_____

_____

_____

6. The pressure did not vary during the experiment, because all trials were performed at constant room (atmospheric) pressure. If the pressure had varied, how would it have affected your results? Explain.

_____

_____

_____

7. What are some possible sources of error in this experiment?

_____

_____

_____

_____

8. How do the class results for the value of absolute zero compare with the actual value? What factors (besides those mentioned in problem 7) could be responsible for any error noted in the class results?

_____

_____

GOING FURTHER

Develop a Hypothesis

Interpret the results of this lab in terms of the kinetic theory of matter as it applies to gases.

_____

_____

_____

_____

Design an Experiment

To verify your ideas, do research on the kinetic theory of gases. What are some of the predictions made by this theory, and how has it been tested? What other types of experiments could be designed to test this theory?

_____

_____

25 DIFFUSION OF GASES

Text Reference
Section 14.4

PURPOSE

To verify Graham's law of diffusion.

BACKGROUND

Have you noticed that, if someone enters a room and sits near you, it can take several minutes before you are aware of his or her cologne? You become aware of the scent because molecules in the cologne diffuse through the surrounding air. *Diffusion* is the process in which particles in a system move from an area of high concentration to an area of low concentration. Diffusion continues until a uniform concentration of particles is reached throughout the system. The rate at which molecules of a gas diffuse, at constant temperature, decreases as the molar mass of the gas increases. In fact, the rate of gas diffusion at constant temperature is inversely proportional to the square root of the molar mass of the gas. This proportionality is called Graham's law of diffusion.

$$\text{rate of diffusion} \propto \frac{1}{\sqrt{\text{molar mass}}}$$

In this experiment, you will determine the relative rates of diffusion for two gases with significantly different molar masses. The gases that you will study are ammonia, NH_3, and hydrogen chloride, HCl.

MATERIALS

safety goggles and apron	timer, with second hand
2 ring stands	meter stick
2 utility clamps	tweezers
glass tube, 1 cm × 70 cm	concentrated hydrochloric acid,
cotton wads	12M HCl(*aq*) C T I
2 medicine droppers	concentrated ammonia,
2 rubber stoppers	15M NH$_3$(*aq*) C T I

SAFETY FIRST!

In this lab, observe all precautions, especially the ones listed below. If you see a safety icon beside a step in the Procedure, refer to the list below for its meaning.

 Caution: Wear your safety goggles. (All steps.)

 Caution: Concentrated hydrochloric acid is highly corrosive and can cause severe burns. (Step 2.)

Caution: Concentrated ammonia solution is corrosive. Avoid skin contact. Avoid the inhalation of ammonia fumes. Use a fume hood for this demonstration. (Step 2.)

 Note: Your teacher will dispose of all materials. (Step 4.)

PROCEDURE

Your teacher will perform this experiment in a fume hood as a teacher demonstration. The instructions in the Procedure are written for your teacher. During the demonstration, record your observations in Data Table 1.

 1. Use two ring stands and two utility clamps to hold a clean, dry glass tube in a level position, as shown in Figure 25.1. Fit a cotton plug snugly into each end of the tube.

 2. Use medicine droppers to simultaneously add 5 drops of concentrated HCl to the cotton plug at one end of the tube and 5 drops of concentrated NH_3 solution to the cotton plug at the other end. Close the ends with rubber stoppers. Note and record the start time in Data Table 1.

3. Record the time it takes to see a white deposit form in the tube. Measure the distances (in centimeters) from the inside end of each cotton plug to the center of the white deposit. Record these measurements in Data Table 1.

4. Your teacher will dispose of the materials.

Figure 25.1

Name _____ Date _____ Class _____

OBSERVATIONS

DATA TABLE 1: DATA AND CALCULATIONS
start time:
time when deposit forms:
elapsed time:
distance from HCl to product:
distance from NH_3 to product:
rate of diffusion HCl (distance/time):
rate of diffusion NH_3 (distance/time):
experimental ratio of rates (NH_3/HCl):
theoretical ratio of rates (NH_3/HCl):

ANALYSES AND CONCLUSIONS

1. Calculate the rate of diffusion for each gas by dividing the distance (centimeters) each gas traveled by the time (seconds) required for the appearance of the white deposit. Enter the calculated rates in Data Table 1.

$$\text{rate of diffusion} = \frac{\text{distance traveled by gas}}{\text{time required for product formation}}$$

2. Find the ratio of the rate of diffusion of NH_3 and the rate of diffusion of HCl. (Use the rates calculated in Step 1.) Record this ratio in Data Table 1.

3. Calculate the theoretical ratio of the rates of diffusion of these gases, using the following equation.

$$\frac{\text{diffusion rate of } NH_3}{\text{diffusion rate of HCl}} = \frac{\sqrt{\text{molar mass HCl}}}{\sqrt{\text{molar mass } NH_3}}$$

Enter the value for the theoretical ratio in Data Table 1.

4. Would a change in temperature affect the diffusion rates you calculated? Explain.

_____

_____

_____

5. Would a change in temperature affect the ratio of diffusion rates? Explain.

_____

_____

_____

6. Are the results of this experiment consistent with Graham's law of diffusion? Explain.

_____

_____

7. The white substance in the tube is ammonium chloride, NH_4Cl. It is the only product in the reaction. Write a balanced equation for this reaction. What type of chemical reaction is this?

_____

_____

8. Calculate the percent error in your experimentally determined value for the ratio of diffusion rates of NH_3 and HCl. Use the theoretical ratio calculated in problem 3 as the accepted value for the ratio.

$$\text{percent error} = \frac{|\text{experimental ratio} - \text{theoretical ratio}|}{\text{theoretical ratio}} \times 100\%$$

GOING FURTHER

Develop a Hypothesis

Suppose an opened bottle of vinegar containing acetic acid (CH_3COOH) was placed next to an opened bottle of pentylamine ($C_5H_{13}N$). Which would you smell first? What is the diffusion ratio?

_____

_____

Design an Experiment

Propose an experiment to test your hypothesis. If resources are available and you have your teacher's permission, perform the experiment.

_____

_____

Chapter 15 • *Water and Aqueous Systems*   **EXPERIMENT**

DISTILLATION

Text Reference
Section 15.2

PURPOSE

To investigate the use of distillation as a method for separating the volatile and nonvolatile components of a liquid solution.

BACKGROUND

Pure water is a valuable commodity, as anyone who has experienced flooding and a contaminated water supply knows. Because water is an excellent solvent, it never exists in its pure state in nature. Even water purified for drinking contains a number of dissolved substances. However, pure water can be obtained from aqueous solutions through a process called *distillation*. In distillation a solution is boiled, vaporizing the water and leaving behind any dissolved solid material. The vapor is directed through a condenser consisting of a straight glass tube encased by an outer glass jacket. Cold water circulates through the outer jacket, causing the water vapor in the inner tube to condense on the cold walls. The purified condensed liquid, called the *distillate*, can then be collected.

In this experiment, you will distill a solution of water that contains one volatile and one nonvolatile impurity. A volatile substance is one that easily evaporates from a solution.

MATERIALS (PER GROUP)

safety goggles and apron
condenser
2 utility clamps
ring stand
2 rubber hoses for condenser
thermometer
2 one-holed rubber stoppers
250-mL distillation flask
ring support
wire gauze
gas burner
250-mL beaker
2 100-mL beakers
spatula

100-mL graduated cylinder
long-stemmed funnel
3 medium test tubes
dropper pipet
towel
glycerin
sodium chloride, NaCl
distilled water
1% phenolphthalein solution ⬚I
6M ammonia, NH$_3$ ⬚T ⬚I
boiling chips
3M nitric acid, HNO$_3$ ⬚C ⬚T
0.1M silver nitrate, AgNO$_3$ ⬚T ⬚I

Name _____ Date _____ Class _____

SAFETY FIRST!

In this lab, observe all precautions, especially the ones listed below. If you see a safety icon beside a step in the Procedure, refer to the list below for its meaning.

 Caution: Wear your safety goggles. (All steps.)

 Caution: Nitric acid is corrosive and can cause severe burns. Silver nitrate can stain skin and clothing. (Step 6.)

 Caution: Ammonia is an irritant. Avoid inhaling the fumes of this chemical. (Step 2.)

 Caution: Be careful when putting glass tubing or a thermometer into a rubber stopper. Wrap the glassware in a towel to prevent cutting yourself in case of breakage. Grasp the thermometer close to the rubber stopper and twist gently when inserting. (Step 1.)

 Caution: Exercise care when working with an open flame. Tie back hair and loose clothing. Do not use the burner near flammable materials. (Step 4.)

 Note: Return or dispose of all materials according to the instructions of your teacher. (Step 9.)

PROCEDURE

As you perform the experiment, record your observations in Data Table 1.

1. Study the distillation apparatus shown in Figure 26.1. First, support the condenser with a utility clamp and ring stand. Connect a length of rubber hose from the cold water tap to the "Cold water in" connection on the condenser. Connect another length of rubber hose to the "Cold water out" connection on the condenser, and run the hose into the sink. Turn on the cold water and check for leaks. The water should flow steadily through the outer tube of the condenser and into the sink. Turn off the water.

Figure 26.1

CAUTION: *Use glycerin or water to lubricate the thermometer.* Insert the thermometer into a one-holed rubber stopper that securely fits the neck of the round-bottomed 250-mL flask. Insert the thermometer into the stopper by twisting the thermometer and stopper in opposite directions. Adjust the position of the thermometer so the thermometer bulb reaches just to the sidearm of the flask when the stopper is in position. *Wait until the entire distillation apparatus is assembled before inserting the stopper and thermometer into the flask.*

CAUTION: *Use glycerin or water to lubricate the sidearm.* Insert the sidearm of the flask into a one-holed rubber stopper that fits the neck of the condenser. The stopper should be positioned far enough in so that the sidearm extends into the straight portion of the inner condenser tube.

Finish assembling the distillation apparatus. Tighten the utility clamps on the condenser and the flask only enough to gently support the apparatus. **CAUTION:** *Do not tighten the clamp too tightly; otherwise, the glass will break.* The apparatus should be *secure*, but *not rigid*. Insert the rubber stopper and thermometer into the flask.

2. Dissolve about 1 g of NaCl in 100 mL of water in a 250-mL beaker. Add 2 drops of phenolphthalein solution and 2 drops of $6M$ NH$_3$ to the solution. Note the color of the solution. **CAUTION:** *Aqueous ammonia is an irritant. Do not inhale its vapors.*

3. Remove the thermometer and stopper from the flask and pour the colored solution through a long-stemmed funnel into the flask. Add three or four boiling chips to the solution.

4. Turn on the cold water. Add 2 drops of phenolphthalein solution to a clean 100-mL beaker and position it at the end of the condenser to catch the distillate. Use the gas burner to gently heat the contents of the flask. Record the temperature at which liquid begins to drip from the condenser. Adjust the burner flame to keep the solution boiling steadily. Note any color changes that occur during the distillation.

5. Continue the distillation until about 25 mL of distillate has been collected. Remove the collection beaker from under the condenser and replace it with another clean 100-mL beaker. Add 2 drops of phenolphthalein solution to this beaker and collect another 25 mL of distillate.

6. While waiting for the second distillate to accumulate, perform the following tests on the first distillate. Compare the color of the distillate to the color of the mixture in the flask. **CAUTION:** *HNO$_3$ is corrosive and can cause burns.* Add 3 mL of this distillate to a medium test tube and test for the presence of chloride ions by adding 10 drops of $3M$ HNO$_3$ and 5 drops of $0.1M$ AgNO$_3$. Test for the presence of ammonia in the distillate by using the technique described in Step 11 of Experiment 2 on page 28 to detect ammonia fumes. Record your results and observations in Data Table 1.

7. When the second 25 mL of distillate has been collected, turn off the gas burner. Repeat the procedure in Step 6 for the second distillate; record your results and observations in Data Table 1.

8. Allow the apparatus to cool completely before carefully taking it apart. If time permits, perform the tests in Step 6 on the solution that remains in the flask.

9. Discard the solutions as directed by your teacher. Save the boiling chips for future use.

Name _____ Date _____ Class _____

OBSERVATIONS

DATA TABLE 1: DISTILLATION DATA FOR AQUEOUS SOLUTION OF NaCl, NH₃, AND PHENOLPHTHALEIN					
Test	Solution Before Distillation	Solution After First Distillation	Solution After Second Distillation	First Distillate	Second Distillate
color					
Cl⁻					
NH₃ fumes					

ANALYSES AND CONCLUSIONS

1. For each of the solutes used in this experiment, state whether it is volatile or nonvolatile. Give evidence for your answer.

   _____

   _____

   _____

2. Should you have tested for sodium ion in the distillate? Explain.

   _____

   _____

   _____

GOING FURTHER

Develop a Hypothesis

Based on the results of this lab, propose a hypothesis about whether or not distillation could be used to separate a mixture of volatile liquids.

_____

_____

_____

Design an Experiment

Propose an experiment to test your hypothesis. If resources are available and you have your teacher's permission, perform the experiment.

_____

_____

_____

27 THE SOLVENT PROPERTIES OF WATER

Text Reference
Section 15.2

PURPOSE

To examine the relationship between a compound's polarity and its solubility in water.

BACKGROUND

"Oil and water don't mix!" You've probably heard this phrase before. Though this phrase is true, there are plenty of substances that do dissolve in water. The polar nature of the water molecule is largely responsible for its remarkable solvent action. Because of its polarity, water is able to dissolve ionic compounds, such as sodium chloride and copper sulfate, and polar covalent compounds, such as sugar and ammonia. Many chemical reactions and most biochemical reactions take place in water.

Similarly, many substances dissolve in oily, nonpolar solvents, such as gasoline and kerosene. In general, only nonpolar molecules will dissolve in nonpolar solvents.

In this experiment, you will examine the relationship between a compound's polarity and its solubility in water.

MATERIALS (PER PAIR)

safety goggles   sucrose, $C_{12}H_{22}O_{11}$
10 small test tubes   sodium thiosulfate, $Na_2S_2O_3$
test-tube rack   calcium carbonate, $CaCO_3$
plastic wash bottle   hexane, C_6H_{14} [F] [T]
spatula   potassium sulfate, K_2SO_4 [T]
dropper pipet   ethanol, C_2H_5OH [F] [T]
sodium chloride, NaCl   kerosene, C_{12}–C_{15} [F] [T]
glycerin, $C_3H_8O_3$ distilled water

SAFETY FIRST!

In this lab, observe all precautions, especially the ones listed below. If you see a safety icon beside a step in the Procedure, refer to the list below for its meaning.

 Caution: Wear your safety goggles. (All steps.)

 Caution: Ethanol, hexane, and kerosene are flammable. Do not use these substances near open flames. (All steps.)

Caution: Avoid skin contact with these chemicals. Many of them are toxic. (Step 2.)

Note: Return or dispose of all materials according to the instructions of your teacher. (Step 3.)

Note: Wash your hands thoroughly after completing this experiment.

PROCEDURE

As you perform the experiment, record your results and observations in Data Table 1.

 1. Record the chemical formula, physical state, and color of each of the substances in the Materials section, with the exception of distilled water.

 2. Test each of the substances for water solubility. Add 3–4 mL of distilled water to each small test tube. Add a very small quantity of the substance to be tested to an individual test tube. For solids, use a sample about the size of a match head. For liquids, use one drop. Be careful not to contaminate the chemicals with one another.

Flick the test tube gently and note what happens. If all of the substance dissolves, add another small quantity and flick gently. Repeat the process several more times if the material continues to dissolve. Describe each substance as insoluble, slightly soluble, or very soluble, based on its behavior. Record these descriptions in Data Table 1.

 3. Dispose of the hexane and kerosene samples as directed by your teacher. Dispose of all other samples by flushing them, with water, down the drain. Rinse the test tubes.

Name _____ Date _____ Class _____

OBSERVATIONS

DATA TABLE 1: RESULTS AND OBSERVATIONS			
Substance	Formula	Physical State	Solubility in Water
sodium chloride			
glycerin			
sucrose			
sodium thiosulfate			
calcium carbonate			
hexane			
potassium sulfate			
ethanol			
kerosene*			

*mixture of hydrocarbons

ANALYSES AND CONCLUSIONS

1. Polar and ionic substances generally dissolve in water; nonpolar substances do not. Explain.

_____

_____

_____

_____

_____

2. Based on the fact that calcium carbonate is an ionic compound, you may be puzzled by your experimental results for this compound. Propose an explanation for the solubility of calcium carbonate.

_____

_____

_____

3. What basis can you use to decide whether the liquids tested are polar or nonpolar? Which of the liquid substances tested are polar? Which are nonpolar?

_____

_____

_____

4. The structural formulas of the four liquids other than kerosene that were tested in this experiment are shown. Do these structural formulas support the solubility data obtained? Explain.

Glycerin

```
        H
        |
  H — C — O — H
        |
  H — C — O — H
        |
  H — C — O — H
        |
        H
```

Hexane

```
    H   H   H   H   H   H
    |   |   |   |   |   |
H — C — C — C — C — C — C — H
    |   |   |   |   |   |
    H   H   H   H   H   H
```

Ethanol

```
    H   H
    |   |
H — C — C — O — H
    |   |
    H   H
```

_____

_____

GOING FURTHER

Develop a Hypothesis

Based on the results of this lab, develop a hypothesis about how soaps and detergents are able to *emulsify* oils and greases in a solution of water.

_____

_____

Do Research

To test your hypothesis, look up the chemical structures of some soaps and detergents. What do they all have in common, and how are their emulsifying properties related to their chemical structures?

_____

_____

_____

_____

28 WATER OF HYDRATION

PURPOSE

To investigate the effect of heat on several hydrates.

BACKGROUND

Have you ever had your arm put in a plaster cast? If you have, then you already know something about hydrates. Plaster of Paris is the semihydrate of calcium sulfate, $CaSO_4 \cdot \frac{1}{2}H_2O$. When you add water to plaster of Paris and allow it to set, it is gradually transformed into a hard crystalline compound, calcium sulfate dihydrate, $CaSO_4 \cdot 2H_2O$. Water is an integral part of many ionic solids, and such ionic solids are called *hydrates*. The water in these solids is called *water of hydration*.

The water of hydration is more loosely bound in the hydrated crystal than the ions are. Thus, you can usually drive off the water by heating the crystals. The material that remains after the water is gone is called the *anhydrous salt*.

In this experiment, you will heat several hydrates and observe the appearance of the reactants and products involved. You will also heat a nonhydrated compound as a basis for comparison.

MATERIALS (PER PAIR)

safety goggles
glass-marking pencil
4 medium test tubes
spatula
test-tube holder
gas burner

copper(II) sulfate pentahydrate,
   $CuSO_4 \cdot 5H_2O$ [T] [I]
sodium chloride, NaCl
magnesium sulfate heptahydrate,
   $MgSO_4 \cdot 7H_2O$
sodium carbonate decahydrate,
   $Na_2CO_3 \cdot 10H_2O$ [I]

SAFETY FIRST!

In this lab, observe all precautions, especially the ones listed below. If you see a safety icon beside a step in the Procedure, refer to the list below for its meaning.

 Caution: Wear your safety goggles. (All steps.)

 Caution: Copper compounds are toxic. Avoid contact with copper(II) sulfate pentahydrate. (All steps.)

 Caution: Exercise care when heating a test tube over a flame. Use a test-tube holder. (Step 2.)

Caution: Exercise care when working with an open flame. Tie back hair and loose clothing. Do not use the burner near flammable materials. (Step 2.)

 Note: Return or dispose of all materials according to the instructions of your teacher. (Step 4.)

PROCEDURE

As you perform the experiment, record your observations in Data Table 1.

 1. Label four clean, dry test tubes with the numbers 1–4. To separate test tubes add about 1 g of each of the following substances.

tube 1	$CuSO_4{\cdot}5H_2O$
tube 2	$NaCl$
tube 3	$MgSO_4{\cdot}7H_2O$
tube 4	$Na_2CO_3{\cdot}10H_2O$

 2. Grasp tube 1 in a test-tube holder. Hold the tube almost horizontally and heat it *gently* in a burner flame, as shown in Figure 28.1. **CAUTION:** *Never point the mouth of the tube at yourself or anyone else.* Record what you observe near the mouth of the test tube, and note any change in the appearance of the crystals.

3. Repeat Step 2 for tubes 2, 3, and 4. Record your observations.

 4. Follow your teacher's instructions for proper disposal of the materials.

Figure 28.1

Name _____ Date _____ Class _____

OBSERVATIONS

Tube	Substance	Observations
DATA TABLE 1: OBSERVATIONS		
1		
2		
3		
4		

ANALYSES AND CONCLUSIONS

1. In which tubes did you observe a change near the test tube's mouth?

   _____

2. In which tubes did the appearance of the crystals change?

   _____

3. Write a general statement to describe what you would expect to observe when a hydrate is heated.

   _____

   _____

4. For any substance that was a hydrate, write a balanced equation for the change that took place when the substance was heated. In each case, assume that the anhydrous salt was formed.

_____

_____

_____

_____

5. Design and carry out an experiment for determining the number of moles of water per mole of anhydrous salt in a $BaSO_4$ hydrate.

GOING FURTHER

Do Research

Over time, a bottle of anhydrous salt gradually becomes hydrated from exposure to humidity in the air. As a result, the mass of a given quantity of the sample does not accurately reflect the amount of salt in the sample. To control for this "partial" hydration process, chemists often determine the amount of salt in a particular hydrated sample by dissolving it in a known volume of distilled water and measuring other physical properties. What other physical properties could be measured to determine the amount of salt in an aqueous solution?

_____

_____

29 ELECTROLYTES AND NONELECTROLYTES

PURPOSE

To investigate the electrical properties of aqueous solutions of ionic and molecular substances.

Text Reference
Section 15.2

BACKGROUND

If an electrical device accidentally falls into water in which you're standing, you could receive a severe or even fatal shock. This is possible because small amounts of dissolved ions in the water allow it to conduct electricity. Thus, in the case of an electrical device accidentally dropped into water, the electricity normally conducted to the device is instead conducted into you. Substances that dissolve in water to produce electrically conductive solutions are called *electrolytes*. If, when dissolved, the substance is a good conductor of electricity, it is called a *strong electrolyte*. In general, strong electrolytes are almost completely ionized when dissolved in solution. If, when dissolved, the substance is a poor conductor of electricity, it is called a *weak electrolyte*. In general, weak electrolytes are only slightly ionized when dissolved in solution. Substances that dissolve in water without ionizing will not conduct electricity and are called *nonelectrolytes*.

In this experiment, you will observe as your teacher tests several solutions for conductivity. You will classify the solute in each solution as a strong electrolyte, a weak electrolyte, or a nonelectrolyte.

MATERIALS

(Teacher Demonstration)
safety goggles and apron
conductivity apparatus,
    including light bulbs
100-mL beaker
plastic wash bottle
paper towels
5% sodium chloride solution,
    NaCl(aq)
sodium chloride , NaCl
5% sucrose solution,
    $C_{12}H_{22}O_{11}$(aq)

1M hydrochloric acid, HCl [T] [I]
glacial ethanoic acid, CH_3COOH
    [C] [T] [F]
ethanol, C_2H_5OH [F] [T]
kerosene, C_{12}–C_{15} [F] [T] [I]
1M sodium hydroxide,
    NaOH [C] [T]
6M ethanoic acid, CH_3COOH [C]
6M ammonia, NH_3(aq) [T] [I]
1M ammonia, NH_3(aq) [T] [I]
distilled water and tap water

SAFETY FIRST!

This lab should be done as a teacher demonstration. Observe all precautions, especially the ones listed below. If you see a safety icon beside a step in the Procedure, refer to the list below for its meaning.

 Caution: Wear your safety goggles. (All steps.)

Caution: Hydrochloric and ethanoic acids are irritating and corrosive and can cause severe injury, depending on concentration. Sodium hydroxide is corrosive and can cause severe burns. (Step 3.)

Caution: Ammonia is an irritant and has a choking smell. Avoid inhalation and skin contact with this chemical. (Step 3.)

Caution: Note that your teacher will always be sure that the switch is turned off and the plug is removed from the outlet before handling the conductivity apparatus. This is done to prevent electric shock. (Steps 1–4.)

Note: Properly dispose of all materials. (Step 4.)

PROCEDURE

As this demonstration is conducted by your teacher, record your observations in Data Table 1.

1. The apparatus commonly used in determining electrical conductivity is shown in Figure 29.1. **CAUTION:** *The plug of the conductivity apparatus should be removed from the outlet, and the switch should be turned off except when making a test.*

2. Your teacher will put about 20 mL of the 5% sodium chloride solution into a 100-mL beaker. The beaker will be positioned so that the electrodes are immersed to a depth of 0.5–1.0 cm in the solution. The apparatus will then be plugged in and the switch turned on. Record your observations in Data Table 1. The apparatus will then be turned off and unplugged.

3. Your teacher will clean and dry the electrodes and repeat Step 2, testing each of the substances listed in the Materials section. For liquids, a 20-mL sample will be used; for solids, a depth of 1 cm, in a *dry* beaker, will be used.

4. Your teacher will properly dispose of the materials.

Figure 29.1

40-W bulb

10-W bulb

Electrode supporters and electrical connections

Electrodes

Sample solution in 100-mL beaker

Movable support for sample container

Switch

Weighted base

110 V (AC)

Name _____ Date _____ Class _____

OBSERVATIONS

DATA TABLE 1: CONDUCTIVITY DATA		
Substance	Observation	Comments
5% NaCl solution		
distilled water		
tap water		
NaCl crystals		
5% sucrose solution		
kerosene		
1M HCl		
1M NaOH		
glacial CH_3COOH		
6M CH_3COOH		
6M NH_3		
1M NH_3		
ethanol, C_2H_5OH		

ANALYSES AND CONCLUSIONS

1. In Data Table 1, identify each substance tested as a strong electrolyte, a weak electrolyte, or a nonelectrolyte.

    _____

    _____

    _____

    _____

    _____

    _____

2. For each strong or weak electrolyte, write the formulas of the ions that are present in a solution of the substance.

    _____

    _____

    _____

    _____

    _____

    _____

3. Based on the type of bonding present in hydrochloric acid, the results of the conductivity test may have been unexpected. Explain.

    _____

    _____

    _____

    _____

    _____

4. Compare the conductivity of solid sodium chloride and a 5% solution of sodium chloride. Explain any difference.

    _____

    _____

    _____

    _____

    _____

5. Glacial ethanoic acid is ethanoic acid that is at least 99.8% pure—that is, it contains no more than 0.2% water. Compare the conductivity of glacial ethanoic acid with that of $6M$ ethanoic acid and explain the difference.

_____

_____

_____

_____

_____

_____

6. Compare the conductivity of $6M$ ammonia and $1M$ ammonia. Explain any difference.

_____

_____

_____

_____

_____

_____

7. What types of bonding do compounds that are electrolytes have?

_____

_____

GOING FURTHER

Develop a Hypothesis

Based on the results of this lab, propose a hypothesis about the electrical behavior of other molecular and ionic substances.

_____

_____

_____

Design an Experiment

Propose an experiment to test your idea(s). If resources are available and you have your teacher's permission, perform the experiment.

_____

_____

30 FACTORS AFFECTING SOLUTION FORMATION

Text Reference
Section 16.1

PURPOSE

To investigate factors that influence the rate of solution formation.

BACKGROUND

When you put a spoonful of sugar into a glass of iced tea, you probably begin to stir it up immediately. Why? If your reply is that the sugar will sink to the bottom and not easily dissolve if it is not stirred, you already understand an important fact about solution formation. Stirring is one factor that determines how fast a substance will dissolve, forming a solution.

A solution consists of a *solute*, the material that is dissolved, and a *solvent*, the material that the solute is dissolved in. In this experiment, you will investigate the effects of stirring, temperature, and particle size on the rate of dissolution.

MATERIALS (PER PAIR)

safety goggles	wire gauze
7 large test tubes	spatula
glass-marking pencil	thermometer
mortar and pestle	copper(II) sulfate pentahydrate,
test-tube rack	$CuSO_4 \cdot 5H_2O$ [T] [I]
2 100-mL beakers	weighing paper
50-mL graduated cylinder	distilled water
gas burner	crushed ice
ring stand	sodium chloride, NaCl
ring support	paper towels

SAFETY FIRST!

In this lab, observe all precautions, especially the ones listed below. If you see a safety icon beside a step in the Procedure, refer to the list below for its meaning.

 Caution: Wear your safety goggles. (All steps.)

 Caution: Do not touch hot equipment. (Step 8.)

 Caution: $CuSO_4 \cdot 5H_2O$ is toxic and irritating. Avoid contact with this material. (Steps 1, 2.)

Caution: Exercise care when working with an open flame. Tie back hair and loose clothing. Do not use the burner near flammable materials. (Step 5.)

 Wash your hands thoroughly with soap and water.

Note: Return or dispose of all materials according to the instructions of your teacher. (Steps 4, 9.)

PROCEDURE

As you perform the experiment, record your observations in Data Tables 1 and 2.

Part A. Effects of Particle Size and Mixing

1. Label four large test tubes with the numbers 1–4. Use a spatula to put four pea-sized crystals of copper(II) sulfate pentahydrate, $CuSO_4 \cdot 5H_2O$, on a piece of weighing paper.

2. Put one crystal of $CuSO_4 \cdot 5H_2O$ into tube 1 and another crystal into tube 2. Crush a third crystal with the mortar and pestle and pour the powder into tube 3. Crush the fourth crystal and pour the powder into tube 4.

3. Fill each of the four test tubes about one-third full of water. Place tubes 1 and 3 in the test-tube rack without shaking them. Flick tubes 2 and 4. Note how long it takes for the contents of each of the four tubes to dissolve. Record your observations in Data Table 1.

4. Follow your teacher's instructions for proper disposal of the materials. Be sure to wash your hands thoroughly after completing Part A.

Part B. Effect of Temperature

5. Add 50 mL of distilled water to a 100-mL beaker. Using a gas burner, heat the water until it is almost boiling. While the water is heating, proceed to Step 6.

6. Half-fill a 100-mL beaker with crushed ice and then add approximately 30 mL of distilled water to the beaker. While the water is chilling, proceed to Step 7.

7. Label three large test tubes with the numbers 1–3. Add 5 g of sodium chloride to each test tube. Place the tubes in a test-tube rack.

8. Fill tube 1 one-third full with ice-cold water (see Step 6). Fill tube 2 one-third full with distilled water at room temperature. Fill tube 3 one-third full with hot water (see Step 5). **CAUTION:** *Pour the hot water from the beaker, using a paper towel "handle," as shown in Figure 30.1.* Gently flick the contents of the test tubes. Note how long it takes for the contents of each tube to dissolve. Record your observations in Data Table 2.

9. Dispose of the contents of the three test tubes by pouring them down the drain.

Figure 30.1

Name _____ Date _____ Class _____

OBSERVATIONS

DATA TABLE 1: EFFECTS OF PARTICLE SIZE AND MIXING ON SOLUTION FORMATION				
Tube	Particle Size	Mixed?	Time to Dissolve	Observations
1				
2				
3				
4				

DATA TABLE 2: EFFECTS OF TEMPERATURE ON SOLUTION FORMATION			
Tube	Temperature	Time to Dissolve	Observations
1			
2			
3			

ANALYSES AND CONCLUSIONS

1. What effects does particle size appear to have on the rate at which a solute dissolves? Why should particle size make a difference in the rate of dissolving?

_____

_____

_____

2. Does shaking the test tube affect the rate at which a solute dissolves? Explain your results.

_____

_____

_____

3. Using kinetic theory, explain the effect of temperature on the dissolution rate of a solute.

_____

_____

_____

_____

_____

_____

GOING FURTHER

Develop a Hypothesis

Based on the results of this lab, develop a hypothesis concerning the effect of temperature on the amount of solute that will dissolve in a given volume of solvent.

_____

_____

_____

Design an Experiment

Propose an experiment to test your hypothesis. If resources are available and you have your teacher's permission, perform the experiment.

_____

_____

_____

31 SUPERSATURATION

PURPOSE

To prepare a supersaturated solution of a salt and observe the effect of adding a small seed crystal to it.

BACKGROUND

Perhaps you've made rock candy by placing a string in a sugar solution and letting the sugar crystallize on the string. But did you know this candy-making method will work only with a particular kind of sugar solution? Under certain conditions, a solution may contain more solute than is normally contained in a saturated solution at the same temperature. This type of solution is unstable and is called *supersaturated*. The addition of a single crystal of solute often causes the excess solute to crystallize. You must use a supersaturated solution when making rock candy. The addition of a string disturbs the unstable solution and begins the crystallization.

The solubility of most substances decreases as temperature decreases. This fact sometimes leads to the formation of supersaturated solutions. As the solution cools, the excess solute may or may not crystallize out. If the excess solute remains in the solution, the solution becomes supersaturated.

In this experiment, you will make a supersaturated solution and observe the effect of adding a seed crystal to it.

MATERIALS (PER PAIR)

safety goggles   test-tube rack
centigram balance   100-mL beaker
medium test tube   sodium sulfate decahydrate,
10-mL graduated cylinder $Na_2SO_4 \cdot 10H_2O$
test-tube holder   distilled water
gas burner   ice

SAFETY FIRST!

In this lab, observe all precautions, especially the ones listed below. If you see a safety icon beside a step in the Procedure, refer to the list below for its meaning.

 Caution: Wear your safety goggles. (All steps.)

 Caution: Do not touch hot equipment. (Step 2.)

Caution: Exercise care when working with an open flame. Tie back hair and loose clothing. Do not use burner near flammable materials. (Step 2.)

Caution: Never heat only the bottom of a test tube. Make sure to warm the bottom and sides of the tube evenly. (Step 2.)

Note: Return or dispose of all materials according to the instructions of your teacher. (Step 5.)

PROCEDURE

As you perform the experiment, record your observations in Data Table 1.

1. Place 5 g of $Na_2SO_4 \cdot 10H_2O$ in a clean medium-sized test tube. Add 10 mL of distilled water.

2. Hold the test tube in a test-tube holder and heat it in a burner flame, agitating the mixture gently until all of the solid has dissolved. **CAUTION:** *When heating a test tube, never point the mouth of the tube at yourself or anyone else.* Place the test tube in a test-tube rack. Add one more crystal of $Na_2SO_4 \cdot 10H_2O$ to the warmed solution and gently agitate it. Record your observations in Data Table 1.

3. Place the test tube and contents in a beaker of ice water to cool. Be careful not to disturb the test tube during the cooling process. If crystals begin to form as the tube is cooling, reheat the tube to redissolve the crystals and cool the tube again.

4. When the solution is cold, gently remove the tube from the ice water bath and put it in the test-tube rack. Add one small crystal of $Na_2SO_4 \cdot 10H_2O$. Describe what you see. Touch the bottom of the test tube to the palm of your hand. Record your observations in Data Table 1.

5. Follow your teacher's instructions for the proper disposal of the materials.

Name _____ Date _____ Class _____

OBSERVATIONS

DATA TABLE 1: OBSERVATIONS	
Step	Observations
2	
4	

ANALYSES AND CONCLUSIONS

1. Why is it necessary to heat the mixture in Step 2 of the Procedure?

   _____

   _____

   _____

2. Is the solution unsaturated, saturated, or supersaturated at the end of Step 2? Explain.

   _____

   _____

   _____

   _____

3. Is the solution unsaturated, saturated, or supersaturated at the end of Step 3? Give evidence for your answer.

   _____

   _____

   _____

   _____

4. At the end of Step 4, when crystallization is complete, is the solution unsaturated, saturated, or supersaturated? Explain.

_____

_____

_____

_____

_____

5. Describe a simple test to determine whether a solution is unsaturated, saturated, or supersaturated. Explain how to interpret the test.

_____

_____

_____

_____

_____

_____

GOING FURTHER

Develop a Hypothesis

Based on the results of this lab, develop a hypothesis concerning the effect of the rate of cooling of a supersaturated solution on its stability.

_____

_____

Design an Experiment

Propose an experiment to test your hypothesis. If resources are available and you have your teacher's permission, perform the experiment.

_____

_____

Chapter 16 • *Solutions*

32 INTRODUCTION TO CHROMATOGRAPHY

Text Reference
Section 16.2

PURPOSE

To separate food coloring dyes by paper chromatography.

BACKGROUND

You've probably seen different colors mixed together to form a new color. The mixing of paint is a common example: Red and yellow paints are mixed to make orange paint. Have you ever thought of how you might separate the orange paint to get the original colors back? Separations similar to this are often performed in chemistry. Chemical separations might be performed to determine the ingredients in a pill or to measure the amount of cholesterol in a sample of fat. *Chromatography* is a commonly used method for separating substances in a mixture. The name of the method is derived from the fact that chromatography was first applied to separating colored substances. (In Greek, *chromos* means "color.") Although the effectiveness of the separation is most easily detected if the components of the mixture are colored, the method is commonly applied to separating many kinds of mixtures.

In this experiment, you will separate the various food coloring dyes by paper chromatography.

MATERIALS (PER PAIR)

safety goggles
3 capillary tubes
pencil
3 large test tubes
3 cork stoppers
3 wire paper clips
test-tube rack

10-cm ruler
plastic wash bottle
filter paper strips,
   1 cm × 15 cm
yellow, blue, and green food
   coloring
distilled water

SAFETY FIRST!

In this lab, observe all precautions, especially the ones listed below. If you see a safety icon beside a step in the Procedure, refer to the list below for its meaning.

 Caution: Wear your safety goggles. (All steps.)

 Note: Return or dispose of all materials according to the instructions of your teacher. (Step 6.)

PROCEDURE

As you perform the experiment, record your data in Data Table 1.

1. Your teacher will show you how to use a capillary tube to apply dye (food coloring) to the filter paper strips. Use a pencil to mark a small circle, the size of the printed letter *o*, about 2 cm from one end of each of three filter paper strips. The penciled circle is the point of origin. Use a capillary tube to put one drop of dye at the point of origin on one of the filter strips. Repeat this procedure for the other dyes.

2. Fill each of three large test tubes with water to a depth of approximately 2 cm. Use a cork stopper to suspend each filter paper strip in a test tube, as shown in Figure 32.1. The end of the paper strip should be below the water level; the dye spot should be above the water level. Put each tube, as it is prepared, in the test-tube rack.

3. Permit the solvent in each tube to rise up the filter paper until it is about 2 cm from the top of the paper.

4. Remove the strips from the tubes. Using a pencil, mark on each strip the distance the water has traveled from the point of origin. Record these distances as D_f in the data table.

5. Measure on each paper strip the distance each dye spot has traveled. Record these distances as D_s. If the original dye spot has separated into several spots, measure and record the D_s for each spot.

6. Dispose of the water in the sink and the solids in the trash.

Figure 32.1

Name _____ Date _____ Class _____

OBSERVATIONS

DATA TABLE 1: PAPER CHROMATOGRAPHY OF FOOD DYES			
Dye	D_f Value (cm)	D_s Value (cm)	R_f Value (cm)
yellow			
blue			
green			

ANALYSES AND CONCLUSIONS

1. Calculate the R_f value for each substance that produces a spot in your paper chromatograms. The formula for R_f follows.

$$R_f = D_s/D_f$$

D_s is the distance traveled by the solute and D_f is the distance traveled by the solvent. Record the R_f values in Data Table 1.

2. Do the yellow and blue dyes appear to be composed of a single colored compound? Explain your reasoning.

_____

_____

_____

3. Does the green dye appear to be composed of a single colored compound?

_____

_____

_____

_____

4. Would it be a problem to use an ink pen or a marking pen instead of a pencil, as directed in Step 1 of the Procedure? Explain.

_____

_____

5. Consider the molecular interactions that might occur between the dye, the solvent, and the paper. Suggest an explanation for the different R_f values for different dyes.

_____

_____

_____

_____

6. Blue ink from two different pens appears to be the exact same color. Explain how to determine whether the inks are identical.

_____

_____

GOING FURTHER

Develop a Hypothesis

Chromatography on paper can be done using solvents other than water. Develop a hypothesis concerning what types of mixtures would be better separated using a different solvent than water.

_____

_____

_____

_____

Do Research

If resources are available, read articles and textbooks to collect information that may or may not support your hypothesis.

_____

_____

Chapter 16 • *Solutions*   **EXPERIMENT**

33 FREEZING POINT

Text Reference
Section 16.4

PURPOSE

To examine the effect of a solute on the freezing behavior of a solution.

BACKGROUND

If you live in an area that has cold winters, you know that salt is often applied to the roads when it snows. The salt causes corrosion problems for the vehicles that use the salted roads, so what is the reason for its use? From Experiment 22 you know that a pure liquid freezes to a solid at a constant temperature unique to that substance. But what happens to the freezing point if a solute is dissolved in the pure liquid? Will the solution freeze at a higher or lower temperature than the pure liquid? Will the temperature remain constant throughout the freezing process?

In this experiment, you will investigate the effect of a solute on the freezing behavior of a solution. When you are done, you should understand why salt is used on roads in the winter.

MATERIALS (PER PAIR)

safety goggles
centigram balance
spatula
large test tube
ring stand and utility clamp
thermometer
copper wire stirrer
3-pronged jaw clamp

gas burner
timer with a second hand
benzoic acid, C_6H_5COOH [T] [I] [F]
one of the following solutes:
   camphor, $C_{10}H_{16}O$ [F] [T] [I]
   urea, $CO(NH_2)_2$ [I] [T] [C]
potassium ethanoate,
   CH_3COOK [I]

SAFETY FIRST!

In this lab, observe all precautions, especially the ones listed below. If you see a safety icon beside a step in the Procedure, refer to the list below for its meaning.

 Caution: Wear your safety goggles. (All steps.)

 Caution: Benzoic acid is an irritant and mildly toxic. (Steps 1–6.)

 Caution: Avoid inhaling benzoic acid vapors. (Step 3.)

Caution: Exercise care when working with an open flame. Tie back hair and loose clothing. Do not use the burner near flammable materials. (Steps 3–5.)

Caution: Never use a thermometer as a stirrer. (Step 4.)

Note: Return or dispose of all materials according to the instructions of your teacher. (Step 12.)

Figure 33.1

PROCEDURE

As you perform the experiment, record your observations in Data Table 1.

Part A. The Freezing Point of Pure Benzoic Acid

1. Measure 10.0 grams of benzoic acid, to the nearest 0.1 g. Place the benzoic acid in a large, clean, dry test tube.

2. Secure the test tube in a utility clamp attached to a ring stand. Place the stirrer around the thermometer. With a three-pronged clamp, clamp the thermometer above the test tube so it rests on the solid benzoic acid.

3. **CAUTION:** *Do not heat the benzoic acid above 140°C. Above 140°C, benzoic acid gives off toxic fumes.* Gently heat the benzoic acid to melting, using the gas burner.

4. Lower the thermometer into the molten benzoic acid so that the bulb is immersed and the stirrer surrounds the thermometer, as shown in Figure 33.1. Secure the thermometer clamp.

5. Stir the molten benzoic acid. When the temperature of the benzoic acid reaches 140°C, discontinue heating and turn off the gas burner.

6. As the benzoic acid cools, take temperature readings every 30 seconds for the first 3 minutes and then every minute. Record all temperatures to the nearest 0.5°C. Stir for as long as possible, but do not force the stirrer. Collect data until the temperature drops to about 100°C.

Part B. The Freezing Point with 0.0050 Mole of Solute

7. Calculate the mass of 0.0050 mole of the solute assigned to you by your teacher. Record its name in the data table. Measure out this calculated mass to the nearest 0.01 g and record the measurement.

8. Transfer the solute to the test tube of benzoic acid used in Part A. Carefully reheat the mixture, stirring constantly as it melts and the solute dissolves. Heat the mixture to about 140°C.

9. Turn off the burner and repeat Step 6 for this mixture.

Part C. The Freezing Point with 0.010 Mole of Solute

10. Using the mixture from Part B, repeat Step 7 (add another 0.0050 mole of the same solute). The solution now contains 0.010 moles of solute.

11. Remelt the mixture and heat it to 140°C. When all of the solute has dissolved, turn off the burner and repeat Step 6.

 12. Follow your teacher's instructions for the proper disposal of the materials.

Name _____ Date _____ Class _____

OBSERVATIONS

Time (m)	Temperature (°C) of Benzoic acid	Temperature (°C) of Benzoic Acid Plus 0.0050 mol Solute	Temperature (°C) of Benzoic Acid Plus 0.010 mol Solute
0			
0.5			
1			
1.5			
2			
2.5			
3			
4			
5			
6			
7			
8			
9			
10			
11			

DATA TABLE 1: COOLING OF BENZOIC ACID AND BENZOIC ACID PLUS SOLUTE

ANALYSES AND CONCLUSIONS

1. Plot a graph of temperature (°C) versus time (minutes) for all three freezing-point determinations. Plot and label all three curves on the same graph, connecting the points for each determination in a smooth curve. If your graph shows a dip similar to the one in Figure 33.2, it is likely that your solution supercooled. The true freezing point of the solution can be found by disregarding the dip and extrapolating from the highest point of the horizontal portion of the graph to the vertical axis.

Figure 33.2

2. From your graph, determine the freezing point of the benzoic acid and of the two solutions.

3. What was the magnitude of the freezing-point depression, ΔT_1, caused by the addition of the first 0.0050 mole of solute?

4. What was the magnitude of the freezing-point depression, ΔT_2, of benzoic acid, caused by the addition of 0.010 mole of solute?

5. Average all the ΔT_1 values obtained in the class for camphor. Do the same for ΔT_2. Repeat these calculations for each solute used. Record the results in Data Table 2.

DATA TABLE 2: CLASS AVERAGES FOR FREEZING-POINT DEPRESSIONS		
Solute	Average ΔT_1(°C)	Average ΔT_2(°C)
camphor		
urea		
potassium ethanoate		

6. Compare ΔT_1 to ΔT_2 for each solute in this experiment. What general statement can you make concerning the relationship between the number of moles of solute and the magnitude of the freezing-point depression?

_____

_____

_____

7. Compare the freezing-point depression caused by urea to that caused by camphor. Does your data support the idea that the freezing-point depression depends only on the number of moles of particles in the solution? Explain.

_____

_____

_____

_____

_____

8. The freezing-point depression of potassium ethanoate is greater than that of the other two solutes when an equal number of moles of each is used. Explain.

_____

_____

_____

_____

_____

_____

_____

_____

9. The freezing point of benzoic acid remains relatively constant throughout the freezing process. Is the same true for the freezing point of a solution? Explain any

_____

_____

_____

_____

GOING FURTHER

Develop a Hypothesis

Based on the results of this lab, develop a hypothesis concerning how the *boiling* point of a solution compares to that of the pure solvent.

_____

_____

Design an Experiment

Propose an experiment to test your hypothesis. If resources are available and you have your teacher's permission, perform the experiment.

_____

_____

THE SPECIFIC HEAT OF A METAL

34

Text Reference
Sections 17.1 and 17.2

PURPOSE

To determine the specific heat of a substance.

BACKGROUND

On a sunny day, the water in a swimming pool may warm up a degree or two while the concrete around the pool may become too hot to walk on in your bare feet. This may seem strange because both the concrete and the water are being heated by the same source—the sun. This evidence suggests it takes more heat to raise the temperature of some substances than others. This, in fact, is true: The amount of heat that is required to raise the temperature of 1 g of a substance by 1°C is the called the *specific heat capacity,* or simply the *specific heat,* of that substance. Water, for example, has a specific heat of 1.0 cal/(g°C). This value is high in comparison with the specific heats for other materials, such as concrete. In this experiment, you will use a simple calorimeter and your knowledge of the specific heat of water to determine the specific heat of lead.

MATERIALS (PER PAIR)

safety goggles	utility clamp
400-mL beaker	100-mL graduated cylinder
ring stand	plastic-foam cup
ring support	250-mL beaker
wire gauze	thermometer
gas burner	glass stirring rod
50-mL beaker	lead shot, Pb [T]
centigram balance	distilled water
large test tube	unknown metal [T]

SAFETY FIRST!

In this lab, observe all precautions, especially the ones listed below. If you see a safety icon beside a step in the Procedure, refer to the list below for its meaning.

 Caution: Wear your safety goggles. (All steps.)

 Caution: Lead is a toxic metal. Wash your hands thoroughly after use. (Step 2.)

 Caution: Do not touch hot equipment. (Steps 1, 3, 6.)

Caution: If you should break a thermometer, immediately report the incident to your teacher. Never use a thermometer as a stirrer. (Step 6.)

Note: Return or dispose of all materials according to the instructions of your teacher. (Step 7.)

PROCEDURE

As you perform the experiment, record your data in Data Table 1.

1. Heat 250 mL of water in a 400-mL beaker until it is boiling gently.

2. While the water is heating, determine and record the mass of a clean, dry 50-mL beaker to the nearest 0.01 g. Add between 80 g and 120 g of lead shot to the beaker. Measure the combined mass of the beaker and lead to the nearest 0.01 g and record the measurement.

3. Transfer the lead shot to a large, dry test tube. Use the utility clamp to suspend the test tube in the boiling water, as shown in Figure 34.1. The lead shot should be below the level of the water in the beaker. Leave the test tube in the boiling water bath for at least 10 minutes.

Utility clamp
Large test tube
Ring stand
400-mL beaker
Metal
Wire gauze
Ring support

Figure 34.1

Plastic-foam cup

250-mL beaker

100 g water

Figure 34.2

4. While the lead shot is heating, measure 100 mL of distilled water in a graduated cylinder. Pour the water into a plastic-foam cup and place the cup in a 250-mL beaker for support, as shown in Figure 34.2.

5. Measure and record the temperature of the water in the plastic-foam cup and of the water in the boiling bath.

6. Remove the test tube from the boiling water and quickly pour the lead shot into the water-filled, plastic-foam cup. Place a thermometer and a glass stirring rod into the cup. Use the stirring rod to gently stir the lead shot. *Do not stir the lead shot with the thermometer.* Note the temperature frequently and record the maximum temperature reached.

7. Pour the water off and return the lead shot to your teacher.

8. (Optional) Follow the same procedure to determine the specific heat of an unknown metal.

OBSERVATIONS

DATA TABLE 1: MEASUREMENTS OF MASS AND TEMPERATURE		
	Trial 1	Trial 2
mass of 50-mL beaker		
mass of 50-mL beaker + lead shot		
mass of lead shot		
initial temperature of water in cup		
initial temperature of lead shot (temperature of boiling water)		
maximum temperature of lead + water		
mass of water		

ANALYSES AND CONCLUSIONS

1. Determine the changes in temperature of the water (ΔT_{water}) and of the lead shot (ΔT_{lead}) for each trial.

2. Calculate the heat gained by the water in each trial.

3. Remembering that the heat gained by the water is equal to, but has the opposite sign of, the heat lost by the lead, calculate the specific heat of lead for each trial.

4. Calculate the average value for the specific heat of lead in your experiment.

5. If you tested an unknown, repeat these calculations to determine the specific heat of the unknown metal.

6. Calculate the percent error in the specific heat value that you determined experimentally. Use the accepted value given by your teacher.

$$\text{percent error} = \frac{|\text{experimental value} - \text{accepted value}|}{\text{accepted value}} \times 100\%$$

7. You assumed that the initial temperature of the lead shot was the same as that of the boiling water. If the lead shot was actually at a lower temperature than the water, how would your value for the specific heat be affected?

_____

_____

8. Identify other possible sources of error in this experiment.

_____

_____

_____

9. Compare your value for the specific heat of lead to the values obtained by your classmates. Can specific heat be used to identify substances? Explain.

_____

_____

_____

_____

GOING FURTHER

Develop a Hypothesis

Based on the results of this lab, develop a hypothesis about how the measured specific heat of lead would differ if the hot lead was added to water in vessels made of different materials.

_____

_____

Design an Experiment

Propose an experiment to test your hypothesis. If resources are available and you have your teacher's permission, perform the experiment.

_____

_____

_____

Name _____ Date _____ Class _____

35 HEATS OF REACTION

Text Reference
Sections 17.2 and 17.4

PURPOSE

To measure the heats of reaction for three related exothermic reactions and to verify Hess's law of heat summation.

BACKGROUND

Energy changes occur in all chemical reactions; energy is either absorbed or released. If energy is released in the form of heat, the reaction is called *exothermic*. If energy is absorbed, the reaction is called *endothermic*. In this experiment, you will measure the amounts of heat released in these three related exothermic reactions:

(1) $NaOH(s) \rightarrow Na^+(aq) + OH^-(aq) + x_1$ kcal

(2) $NaOH(s) + H^+(aq) + Cl^-(aq) \rightarrow$
$$H_2O + Na^+(aq) + Cl^-(aq) + x_2 \text{ kcal}$$

(3) $Na^+(aq) + OH^-(aq) + H^+(aq) + Cl^-(aq) \rightarrow$
$$H_2O + Na^+(aq) + Cl^-(aq) + x_3 \text{ kcal}$$

After determining the heats of reaction, you will analyze your data and verify the additive nature of heats of reaction.

MATERIALS (PER PAIR)

safety goggles and apron	wire stirrer
plastic-foam cup	distilled water
100-mL graduated cylinder	sodium hydroxide pellets,
400-mL beaker	NaOH C T
thermometer	0.5*M* hydrochloric acid,
50-mL beaker	HCl T I
centigram balance	1.0*M* hydrochloric acid, HCl T I
spatula	1.0*M* sodium hydroxide,
	NaOH C T

SAFETY FIRST!

In this lab, observe all precautions, especially the ones listed below. If you see a safety icon beside a step in the Procedure, refer to the list below for its meaning.

 Caution: Wear your safety goggles. (All steps.)

 Caution: 0.5*M* and 1.0*M* hydrochloric acid are eye and skin irritants. (Steps 4, 7.)

Caution: Sodium hydroxide is a very corrosive material that can cause severe skin burns and permanent eye damage. Under no circumstances, handle solid sodium hydroxide with your fingers. Sodium hydroxide pellets absorb water from the air and can eventually be mistaken for a puddle of water. Never leave the sodium hydroxide container uncovered; never leave pellets on the balance or on the laboratory bench. (Steps 2, 5, 7.)

 Caution: If you should break a thermometer, immediately report the incident to your teacher. Never use a thermometer as a stirrer. (Steps 3, 8.)

 Note: Return or dispose of all materials according to the instructions of your teacher. (Steps 3, 6, 9.)

PROCEDURE

As you perform the experiment, record your data in Data Table 1.

Procedure note: After each reaction, dispose of the solution as directed by your teacher and rinse the cup and thermometer with water.

Reaction 1

 1. Measure 100 mL of distilled water into a plastic-foam cup. Place the cup inside a 400-mL beaker for support. This assembly, together with a thermometer, will serve as your calorimeter.

 2. Measure and record the mass of a 50-mL beaker to the nearest 0.01 g. **CAUTION:** *NaOH is extremely corrosive.* Using a spatula, add as close to 2.00 g as possible of sodium hydroxide pellets to the beaker. Measure and record the combined mass of the beaker and sodium hydroxide to the nearest 0.01 g. (Do this operation as quickly as possible to avoid error due to absorption of water by the NaOH.)

 3. Measure and record the temperature of the water in the foam cup to the nearest 0.5°C. Add the NaOH pellets to the water in the calorimeter. Stir the mixture gently with a wire stirrer until all the solid has dissolved. **CAUTION:** *Hold the thermometer with your hand at all times.* Record the highest temperature reached during the reaction.

Reaction 2

 4. **CAUTION:** *Low-concentration hydrochloric acid can irritate your skin.* Measure 100 mL of 0.5*M* HCl into the plastic-foam cup and place the cup inside a 400-mL beaker.

 5. Using a spatula, measure out 2.00 g of solid NaOH pellets. **CAUTION:** *NaOH is extremely corrosive.*

6. Measure and record the temperature of the HCl solution in the foam cup. Add the NaOH pellets to the acid solution and stir *gently* until the solid is dissolved. Measure and record the highest temperature reached by the solution during the reaction.

Reaction 3

7. Place the plastic-foam cup inside a 400-mL beaker. Measure 50 mL of 1.0*M* HCl into the cup. Rinse the graduated cylinder and fill with 50 mL of 1.0*M* NaOH.

8. Measure and record the temperature of the HCl solution (in the cup) and the NaOH solution (in the cylinder) to the nearest 0.5°C. Rinse the thermometer between measurements.

9. Pour the NaOH solution into the foam cup. Stirring the mixture gently, measure and record the highest temperature reached.

Name _____ Date _____ Class _____

OBSERVATIONS

DATA TABLE 1: EXPERIMENTAL DATA				
Parameter	Reaction 1	Reaction 2	Parameter	Reaction 3
mass (beaker)			initial temperature (HCl solution)	
mass (beaker + NaOH)			initial temperature (NaOH solution)	
mass (NaOH)			average initial temperature	
initial temperature			final temperature	
final temperature				

ANALYSES AND CONCLUSIONS

1. Determine the change in temperature, ΔT, for each reaction. Record your results in Data Table 2.

2. Calculate the mass of the reaction mixture in each reaction. (To do this, first determine the total volume of the solution. Then calculate the mass of the solution, based on the assumption that the density of the solution is the same as that of pure water, 1.0 g/mL.) Record your results in Data Table 2.

3. Calculate the total heat released in each reaction, assuming that the specific heat of the solution is the same as that of pure water, 1.0 cal/(g°C). Remember:

$$\text{heat of reaction} = \text{mass} \times \text{specific heat} \times \Delta T$$

Record your results in Data Table 2.

Name _____ Date _____ Class _____

4. Calculate the number of moles of NaOH used in reactions 1 and 2, and record the results in Data Table 2.

5. In reaction 3, the number of moles of NaOH can be calculated from the concentration of the solution (1.0M, or 1.0 mole of NaOH per liter of solution) and the volume used. The calculation is shown below.

$$50.0 \text{ mL NaOH} \times \frac{1 \text{ mol NaOH}}{1000 \text{ mL NaOH}} = 0.050 \text{ mol NaOH}$$

Enter this result in Data Table 2.

6. Calculate the energy released per mole of NaOH for each reaction and enter your results in Data Table 2.

DATA TABLE 2: RESULTS OF CALCULATIONS

Reaction Number	Mass of Reaction Mixture	ΔT	Total Heat Released	mol NaOH Consumed	Heat Released per mol NaOH
1					
2					
3					

7. Show that the equations for reactions 1 and 3, which are given in the Background section, add up to give the equation for reaction 2. Include the energy released per mole of NaOH in each equation.

8. Examine all the class data. Does the sum of the energy released per mole of NaOH for reactions 1 and 3 equal the energy released per mole of NaOH in reaction 2? What factors might account for any difference?

_____

_____

_____

_____

_____

_____

_____

9. Calculate the percent difference between the heat given off in reaction 2 and the sum of the heats given off in reactions 1 and 3. Assume that the heat given off in reaction 2 is correct.

$$\text{percent difference (in evolved heat)} = \frac{|(\text{heat}_1 + \text{heat}_3) - \text{heat}_2|}{\text{heat}_2} \times 100\%$$

10. Would changing the amount of NaOH used in reaction 1 affect the value obtained for the energy given off per mole of NaOH? Explain.

_____

_____

_____

_____

11. State in your own words what is meant by the additive nature of heats of reaction.

_____

_____

_____

_____

_____

_____

_____

12. Taking into account your answer to problem 4, explain why you were asked to use exactly 2.00 g of NaOH in reactions 1 and 2, and an equivalent number of moles of NaOH in reaction 3.

_____

_____

_____

GOING FURTHER

Develop a Hypothesis

Suppose nitric acid (HNO_3) was substituted for HCl in reactions 2 and 3. Propose a hypothesis about how the heat change for reaction 2 would be affected.

_____

_____

_____

Design an Experiment

Propose an experiment to test your hypothesis. If resources are available and you have your teacher's permission, perform the experiment.

_____

_____

_____

36 FACTORS AFFECTING REACTION RATES

Text reference
Section 18.1

PURPOSE

To investigate the factors that can speed up or slow down chemical reactions.

BACKGROUND

You may have noticed that chemical reactions occur at different speeds. The explosion of fireworks is instantaneous; the rusting of an iron gate is relatively slow. In most situations, you would like to make the rusting of iron proceed as slowly as possible. On the other hand, a chemical company might want to speed up the reactions that produce the chemicals they sell. In order to understand how the rates of chemical reactions can be controlled, it is necessary to understand the factors that influence the rates of chemical reaction.

In this experiment, you will study the effect that temperature, reactant concentration, particle size, catalysts, and surface area have on chemical reaction rates.

MATERIALS (PER PAIR)

safety goggles
gloves (optional)
10-mL graduated cylinder
16 medium test tubes
2 250-mL beakers
ring stand
ring support
wire gauze
thermometer
gas burner
test-tube rack
watch or timer
aluminum foil
crucible tongs
100-mL graduated cylinder
250-mL plastic bottle
tape, for label
dropper pipet
metal cutter
centigram balance
paper towels
6M hydrochloric acid, HCl C T
ice

zinc strips, Zn, 0.25 mm ×
  0.50 cm × 2.00 cm
steel wool
wood splints
matches
distilled water
3% hydrogen peroxide, H_2O_2
0.1M iron(III) chloride,
  $FeCl_3$ T I C
0.1M sodium chloride, NaCl
0.1M iron(III) nitrate,
  $Fe(NO_3)_3$ T
0.1M calcium chloride, $CaCl_2$ T
0.1M potassium nitrate, KNO_3
0.1M manganese chloride,
  $MnCl_2$ T
0.1M hydrochloric acid,
  HCl T I
1M hydrochloric acid, HCl T I
3M hydrochloric acid, HCl C T
powdered zinc, Zn F T

SAFETY FIRST!

In this lab, observe all precautions, especially the ones listed below. If you see a safety icon beside a step in the Procedure, refer to the list below for its meaning.

 Caution: Wear your safety goggles. (All steps.)

 Caution: Concentrated hydrochloric acid is highly corrosive and can cause severe burns. (Steps 1, 6, 7.)

 Caution: Powdered zinc is flammable; keep it away from open flames. (Step 10.)

 Caution: Iron(III) chloride is an irritant. (Step 6.)

 Note: Return or dispose of all materials according to the instructions of your teacher. (Step 12.)

PROCEDURE

As you perform the experiment, record your data and observations in Data Tables 1, 2, 3, and 4.

Part A. Effect of Temperature on Reaction Rate

The reaction of zinc metal with hydrochloric acid will be examined.

 1. Pour 5.0 mL of 6M hydrochloric acid into each of three clean test tubes. Place one of the tubes in an ice water bath (ice-water mixture in 250-mL beaker). Place another in a hot water bath maintained at 50°C. (Heat the water in a 250-mL beaker over a gas burner.) Place the third tube in a test-tube rack at room temperature. Allow about 10 minutes for the tubes to reach the temperature of their surroundings.

2. Clean a zinc strip with steel wool. Cut three small pieces of zinc to the same size. Each piece should be approximately 0.5 cm × 2.0 cm. Save the remainder of the strip for Step 8.

3. Note the time in Data Table 1. Then drop one piece of zinc into each of the three test tubes containing hydrochloric acid. Cover each tube loosely with a piece of aluminum foil and wait for 2 minutes. Test for the identity of the gas produced by using tongs to hold a burning splint near the mouth of each of the tubes. Note the time at which each reaction ceases.

Part B. Effect of a Catalyst on Reaction Rate

The decomposition of hydrogen peroxide will be studied.

4. Measure 90 mL of distilled water into a clean 250-mL plastic bottle and add 10 mL of 3% hydrogen peroxide solution. Label the mixture as 0.3% hydrogen peroxide. This will be your test solution.

5. Rinse seven clean test tubes and a 10-mL graduated cylinder with the 0.3% hydrogen peroxide. Discard the rinses. Measure 5 mL of 0.3% hydrogen peroxide into each of the seven test tubes. Place the test tubes in a rack.

 6. Add 5 drops of each of the following solutions to separate test tubes of the hydrogen peroxide: 6M hydrochloric acid, 0.1M iron(III) chloride, 0.1M sodium chloride, 0.1M iron(III) nitrate, 0.1M calcium chloride, 0.1M potassium nitrate, and 0.1M manganese chloride. Flick each tube to mix its contents. Observe each solution and report the rate of gas production from each. Use the terms *fast*, *slow*, *very slow*, or *none* to describe the rate of gas production. Describe the catalytic activity as *high*, *low*, or *none*. Record your observations in Data Table 2.

Part C. Effect of Concentration on Reaction Rate, at Constant Temperature

The reactions of zinc metal with hydrochloric acid solutions of varying concentrations will be examined.

 7. Pour 5 mL of each of the following hydrochloric acid solutions into separate clean test tubes: 0.1M, 1M, 3M, and 6M.

8. Cut four small pieces (1 cm × 1 cm) from the zinc strip you cleaned in Part A. (Save the remainder of the zinc strip for use in Part D.) Drop one piece of zinc into each of the acid solutions. Record the start time and the end time of each reaction. Record your observations in Data Table 3.

Part D. Effect of Particle Size or Surface Area on Reaction Rate

The reaction of zinc metal with hydrochloric acid will be used to study the effect of particle size and surface area on the rate of reaction.

9. Cut a piece of zinc (0.5 cm × 2.0 cm) from a clean strip of the metal. Determine the mass of the piece of zinc to the nearest 0.01 g. Place the piece of zinc in a clean, dry test tube.

 10. Measure an equal quantity of powdered zinc into a second clean, dry test tube.

11. Place both test tubes in a rack; then add 5 mL of 1M hydrochloric acid to each. Observe the reactions for several minutes and record your observations in Data Table 4.

 12. Follow your teacher's instructions for proper disposal of the materials.

Name _____ Date _____ Class _____

OBSERVATIONS

DATA TABLE 1: EFFECT OF TEMPERATURE ON REACTION RATE

Reaction Condition	Time Reaction Started	Time Reaction Ended	Reaction Duration	Burning Splint Test Result
ice water 0°C				
room temp.				
hot water 50°C				

DATA TABLE 2: EFFECT OF CATALYSTS ON REACTION RATE

Test	HCl 6M	FeCl$_3$ 0.1M	NaCl 0.1M	Fe(NO$_3$)$_3$ 0.1M	CaCl$_2$ 0.1M	KNO$_3$ 0.1M	MnCl$_2$ 0.1M
oxygen production							
catalytic activity							

DATA TABLE 3: EFFECT OF CONCENTRATION ON REACTION RATE

Reaction Condition	Time Reaction Started	Time Reaction Ended	Reaction Duration	Observations
0.1M HCl				
1M HCl				
3M HCl				
6M HCl				

DATA TABLE 4: EFFECT OF PARTICLE SIZE OR SURFACE AREA ON REACTION RATE

Substance Tested	Observations
sheet zinc	
powdered zinc	

ANALYSES AND CONCLUSIONS

1. Write a balanced chemical equation for the reaction between hydrochloric acid and zinc metal.

2. Write a balanced chemical equation for the decomposition of hydrogen peroxide.

3. Which ionic compounds used in Part B were effective catalysts?

   _____

   _____

   _____

   _____

4. Examine the data in Data Table 2 and identify the ion responsible for the catalytic activity.

   _____

   _____

5. Many reaction rates approximately double for every 10°C increase in temperature. Are the results you obtained in Part A consistent with this general statement?

   _____

   _____

6. How does the surface area of a substance change as it is broken into smaller pieces?

   _____

7. Describe in your own words the effect of temperature on the rate of a reaction. Explain this effect in terms of the collision theory of reactions.

   _____

   _____

   _____

8. Describe in your own words the effect of concentration on the rate of a reaction. Explain this effect in terms of the collision theory of reactions.

   _____

   _____

   _____

9. Describe in your own words the effect of particle size or surface area on the rate of a reaction. Explain this effect in terms of the collision theory of reactions.

_____

_____

10. Describe in your own words the effect of a catalyst on the rate of a reaction. Explain this effect in terms of the collision theory of reactions.

_____

_____

_____

GOING FURTHER

Develop a Hypothesis

Based on the results of this lab, develop a hypothesis concerning the effect of changing the temperature on the rate of production of gas from an Alka-Seltzer tablet dropped in water.

_____

_____

_____

Design an Experiment

Propose an experiment to test your hypothesis. If resources are available and you have your teacher's permission, perform the experiment.

_____

_____

_____

37 THE CLOCK REACTION

Text Reference
Section 18.1

PURPOSE

To determine how the concentration of reactants affects reaction rates.

BACKGROUND

Suppose you work in a chemical plant that produces a valuable compound. The compound is produced at specific conditions, but now your company has asked you to increase the speed of the reaction. Can you change the conditions to make the reaction faster? In order to speed up the reaction, you must know something about the factors that influence reaction rates. To test the influence of these factors on the rate of your reaction, you must be able to find out how long it takes to produce a certain amount of the product, or how long it takes to use up a certain amount of one of the reactants.

The time it takes for a reaction to go to completion is easy to measure if a color change signals when one of the reactants is used up. This kind of reaction is called a *clock reaction*. To tell how long a clock reaction takes, all you need to do is time the reaction from the moment the reactants are mixed to the moment that the color appears.

In this experiment, you will conduct a quantitative study of the effect of concentration on the rate of a clock reaction.

MATERIALS (PER PAIR)

safety goggles
3 35-mL graduated cylinders
safety labels
100-mL beaker
dropper pipet
stirring rod
stopwatch
thermometer
plastic wash bottle

solution A: 0.20M potassium iodide, KI $\boxed{T}$
solution B: 0.0050M sodium thiosulfate, $Na_2S_2O_3$
solution C: 0.10M ammonium peroxydisulfate, $(NH_4)_2S_2O_8$ $\boxed{I}$
soluble starch
distilled water

SAFETY FIRST!

In this lab, observe all precautions, especially the ones listed below. If you see a safety icon beside a step in the Procedure, refer to the list below for its meaning.

 Caution: Wear your safety goggles. (All steps.)

Caution: If you should break a thermometer, immediately report the incident to your teacher. Never use a thermometer as a stirrer. (Step 2.)

Note: Return or dispose of all materials according to the instructions of your teacher. (Step 3.)

PROCEDURE

As you perform the experiment, record your data and observations in Data Table 2.

Procedure Note: Seven mixtures of solutions A, B, and C will be used in this experiment. The compositions of the mixtures are given in Data Table 1. Mixture 1 has the maximum concentration of each reactant. In mixtures 2, 3, and 4, solution A is diluted to vary the concentration of the iodide ion. In mixtures 5, 6, and 7, solution C is diluted to vary the concentration of the peroxydisulfate ion. All the solutions should be at room temperature.

1. Label three clean, dry graduated cylinders with the letters A, B, and C. Pour the solutions given for mixture 1 into these cylinders. Measure all volumes to the nearest 0.5 mL.

2. Pour the 10.0 mL of solution B into a clean 100-mL beaker. Add 5 drops of starch solution, using a dropper pipet. One person should be ready to signal the other person when to pour solutions A and C into the beaker. At the signal, the other person should pour the solutions into the beaker and stir the mixture occasionally until a blue color appears. Note the exact time that the solutions were poured together and the exact time that blue appears. Record in Data Table 2 the temperature of the solution and the time required, in seconds, for blue to appear.

DATA TABLE 1: PROPORTIONS FOR MIXTURES			
Mixture	Solution A (I^-)	Solution B ($S_2O_3^{2-}$)	Solution C ($S_2O_8^{2-}$)
1	20.0 mL	10.0 mL	20.0 mL
2	15.0 mL + 5.0 mL water	10.0 mL	20.0 mL
3	10.0 mL + 10.0 mL water	10.0 mL	20.0 mL
4	5.0 mL + 15.0 mL water	10.0 mL	20.0 mL
5	20.0 mL	10.0 mL	15.0 mL + 5.0 mL water
6	20.0 mL	10.0 mL	10.0 mL + 10.0 mL water
7	20.0 mL	10.0 mL	5.0 mL + 15.0 mL water

3. Discard the solution as directed by your teacher. Wash the beaker and rinse it well with distilled water. Shake it as dry as possible. Repeat the reaction with mixture 1 until you can obtain two approximately equal reaction times (trial 1, trial 2).

4. Repeat the experiment, using any mixture assigned by your teacher. Try to predict the outcome of each trial before you do it.

OBSERVATIONS

DATA TABLE 2: REACTION TIMES				
Mixture	Temperature (°C)	Time for Color to Appear (s) Trial 1	Trial 2	Average Time of Reaction (s)
1				
2				
3				
4				
5				
6				
7				

ANALYSES AND CONCLUSIONS

Class Data on the Effect of Concentration

1. Use class data to complete Data Table 2. If more than one trial was done for a mixture, compute the average of the reaction times.

2. Calculate the number of moles of iodide ion and peroxydisulfate ion in each of the seven mixtures studied. Enter these results in Data Table 3.

DATA TABLE 3: CALCULATIONS				
Mixture	mol I^-	Initial Concentration I^- (mol/L)	Mol $S_2O_8^{2-}$	Initial Concentration $S_2O_8^{2-}$ (mol/L)
1				
2				
3				
4				
5				
6				
7				

3. For each of the mixtures used, the total volume was 50.0 mL. Using this volume and the number of moles calculated in problem 2, determine the initial concentration of iodide and peroxydisulfate ions in each reaction mixture. Enter these initial concentrations in Data Table 3.

4. Plot a graph of iodide ion concentration versus reaction time. Use the data and calculated concentrations for mixtures 1, 2, 3, and 4. Connect the plotted points with a smooth curve.

5. On the same graph that you made for problem 4, plot a curve representing the concentration of peroxydisulfate versus time. Use the data and calculated concentration for mixtures 1, 5, 6, and 7.

6. Describe the relationship between reaction concentration and reaction rate.

_____

_____

_____

GOING FURTHER

Develop a Hypothesis

Based on the results of this lab, develop a hypothesis about how the concentration of thiosulfate ions will affect the rate of this reaction.

_____

_____

Design an Experiment

Propose an experiment to test your hypothesis. If resources are available and you have your teacher's permission, perform the experiment.

_____

_____

_____

Name _____ Date _____ Class _____

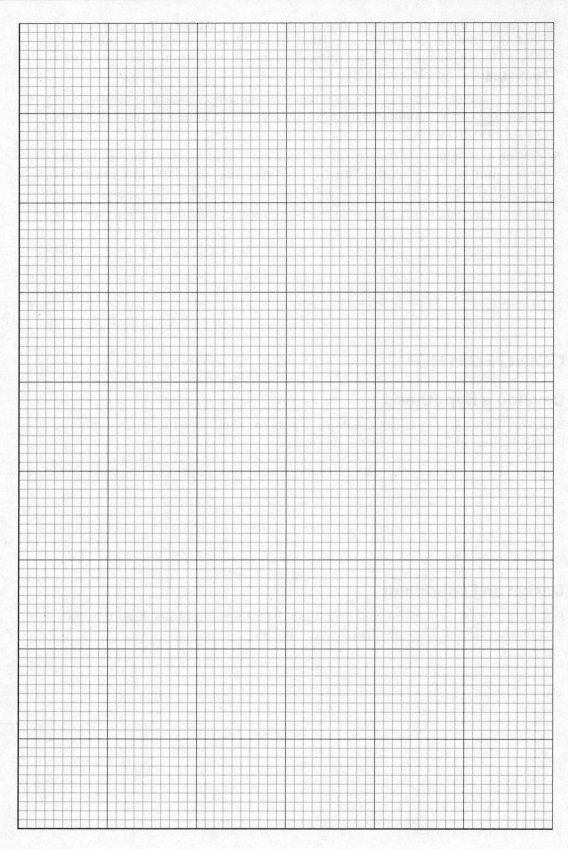

38 DISTURBING EQUILIBRIUM

Text Reference
Section 18.2

PURPOSE

To determine how equilibrium systems respond to stresses.

BACKGROUND

Imagine you are starting a terrarium. You add dirt, plants, and water, then seal the container. Some of the water in the terrarium will vaporize. Soon the air in the terrarium will hold as much water as possible. At this point, some of the vapor will begin to condense. Eventually, as much water is condensing as is vaporizing; the liquid water and its vapor are in *equilibrium*. What happens to the equilibrium if the conditions change? A change of conditions in the system is called a stress. For example, if the terrarium gets colder (undergoes a stress), some of the water vapor will condense. In response to the stress, a new equilibrium will be established. The new equilibrium will have less water vapor and more liquid water than the old equilibrium.

Are there any rules to help predict what happens when a stress is applied to physical and chemical systems in equilibrium? Yes, Le Châtelier's principle applies to systems in equilibrium. It states that, if a stress is placed on a system at equilibrium, the system will change in a way that relieves the stress.

In this experiment, you will impose stresses on physical and chemical systems at equilibrium to see how the systems change in response to the stresses.

MATERIALS (PER PAIR)

safety goggles	saturated potassium nitrate
dropper pipet	solution, KNO_3 [T]
5 medium test tubes	potassium chloride crystals, KCl
spatula	ice
250-mL beaker	distilled water
test-tube rack	0.1M potassium thiocyanate,
50-mL graduated cylinder	KSCN [T]
50-mL graduated cylinder	potassium nitrate crystals,
100-mL beaker	KNO_3 [T]
glass-marking pencil	0.1M iron(III) chloride, $FeCl_3$ [I] [T]
white card, 3 in. × 5 in.	

Figure 38.1

SAFETY FIRST!

In this lab, observe all precautions, especially the ones listed below. If you see a safety icon beside a step in the Procedure, refer to the list below for its meaning.

 Caution: Wear your safety goggles. (All steps.)

 Caution: Aqueous iron(III) chloride is an irritant. Avoid skin contact with this chemical. (Steps 4, 6.)

 Note: Return or dispose of all materials according to the instructions of your teacher. (Step 7.)

PROCEDURE

As you perform the experiment, record your observations in Data Table 1.

Part A. Effect of Temperature on a Physical Equilibrium

1. Add 2–3 mL of saturated potassium nitrate solution to a clean test tube. Using a spatula, add one crystal of potassium nitrate to the solution to act as a seed crystal.

2. Cool the test tube in a 250-mL beaker of ice water for 10 minutes. Record the results.

3. Remove the tube from the ice water and place it in the test-tube rack. Record what happens as the solution warms to room temperature.

Part B. Common Ion Effect on a Chemical Equilibrium

4. Use a graduated cylinder to add 50 mL of distilled water to a 100-mL beaker. Add 1 mL of 0.1M iron(III) chloride and 1 mL of 0.1M potassium thiocyanate to the water; stir. The color that appears is due to the presence of ferrothiocyanate ions, $FeSCN^{2+}$. Your teacher will write on the board the reaction that is observed. Record your observations.

5. Label four identical clean, dry test tubes with the numbers 1–4. Pour 5 mL of the mixture from Step 4 into each. Hold the tubes over a white background and look down into them, as shown in Figure 38.1. The solutions should appear equally dark.

6. Tube 1 is the control in this experiment. To tube 2, add 20 drops of 0.1M iron(III) chloride. To tube 3, add 20 drops of 0.1M potassium thiocyanate. Flick each tube to mix the solutions. To tube 4, add 1 g of potassium chloride crystals. Flick the tube to dissolve the crystals. Compare the colors of the solutions in tubes 2, 3, and 4 with the color of the solution in the control tube (tube 1). Record your observations.

7. Discard the solutions as directed by your teacher.

OBSERVATIONS

DATA TABLE 1: OBSERVATIONS

System	Observations
KNO_3 (saturated) (cooled)	
KNO_3 (saturated) (warmed)	
Fe^{3+}/SCN^- reaction	
Fe^{3+}/SCN^- mixture + additional Fe^{3+}	
Fe^{3+}/SCN^- mixture + additional SCN^-	
Fe^{3+}/SCN^- mixture + KCl(s)	

ANALYSES AND CONCLUSIONS

1. Write a balanced equation for the equilibrium that exists before the saturated potassium nitrate was cooled.

2. Did lowering the temperature (Step 2) affect the equilibrium? Explain your answer.

   _____

   _____

   _____

   _____

3. Did increasing the temperature (Step 3) disturb the equilibrium? What evidence do you have for your answer?

   _____

   _____

   _____

   _____

Name _____ Date _____ Class _____

4. Explain what happened in the potassium nitrate system in terms of Le Châtelier's principle.

   _____

   _____

   _____

   _____

5. Write a balanced equation for the equilibrium that existed after the ferric and thiocyanate ions were combined in the beaker.

6. What evidence was there that the equilibrium shifted when iron(III) chloride was added? In which direction did it shift?

   _____

   _____

   _____

7. What evidence was there that the equilibrium shifted when potassium thiocyanate was added? In which direction did it shift?

   _____

   _____

   _____

8. Explain the effect of adding potassium chloride to the system.

   _____

   _____

   _____

9. Explain the changes observed in the ferrothiocyanate ion system in terms of Le Châtelier's principle.

   _____

   _____

   _____

   _____

   _____

   _____

   _____

GOING FURTHER

Develop a Hypothesis

Based on the results of this experiment, develop a hypothesis concerning the effect of a catalyst on the relative amounts of reactants and products of a chemical reaction at equilibrium.

_____

_____

_____

_____

Design an Experiment

Propose an experiment to test your hypothesis. If resources are available and you have your teacher's permission, perform the experiment.

_____

_____

_____

_____

39 A SOLUBILITY PRODUCT CONSTANT

Text Reference
Section 18.3

PURPOSE

To determine the solubility product constant (K_{sp}) of lead(II) chloride.

BACKGROUND

From everyday experiences, you are familiar with several substances that are soluble in water. Table sugar (sucrose) and table salt (NaCl) are examples of soluble compounds. Many other substances, such as limestone ($CaCO_3$) and gasoline, are insoluble in water. *Solubility* and *insolubility* are relative terms, however. Almost all substances have at least a slight solubility in water. If you put a slightly soluble substance in water, a dynamic equilibrium is established between the dissolved substance and its solid form. In this equilibrium, the rate of dissolution of ions from the solid equals the rate of precipitation of the ions from the solution. How can you express in numerical terms the fraction of dissolved substance in the solution? One way is to use the K_{sp}, the solubility product constant.

In this experiment, you will find the K_{sp} of a slightly soluble salt, lead(II) chloride ($PbCl_2$). You will precipitate Pb^{2+} ions as lead(II) chromate ($PbCrO_4$) from a saturated solution of lead(II) chloride. The amount of lead chromate precipitated will tell you the concentration of Pb^{2+} ions in the saturated solution. When you know the concentration of lead ions, you can calculate the concentration of chloride ions and compute the K_{sp} for lead(II) chloride.

MATERIALS (PER PAIR)

safety goggles
2 250-mL beakers
centigram balance
100-mL graduated cylinder
ring stand
ring support
wire gauze
gas burner
glass stirring rod

filter funnel
plastic wash bottle
drying oven/heat lamp
filter paper
saturated lead(II) chloride
solution, $PbCl_2(aq)$ [T]
0.5*M* potassium chromate,
    K_2CrO_4 [T]
distilled water

SAFETY FIRST!

In this lab, observe all precautions, especially the ones listed below. If you see a safety icon beside a step in the Procedure, refer to the list below for its meaning.

 Caution: Wear your safety goggles. (All steps.)

Caution: Lead compounds and chromate compounds are toxic. (Steps 2–9.)

  Caution: Exercise extreme care when working with a hot water bath and an open flame. Before beginning, ensure that there is no danger that the beaker will be capsized. Remember that cold equipment looks the same as hot equipment. Do not touch the beaker with your bare hands. (Step 3.)

 Note: Return or dispose of all materials according to the instructions of your teacher. (Step 9.)

 Note: Wash your hands thoroughly after completing the experiment. (Step 9.)

PROCEDURE

As you perform the experiment, record your data in Data Table 1.

 1. Place a filter paper in a clean, dry 250-mL beaker. Determine the combined mass to the nearest 0.01 g and record the measurement in Data Table 1. Remove the filter paper from the beaker.

2. Slowly, to avoid disturbing the crystals, decant 100 mL of clear supernatant from the saturated $PbCl_2$ solution into the beaker. Add 20 mL of $0.5M$ K_2CrO_4 to the solution in the beaker.

3. Using a gas burner, heat the mixture in the beaker to the boiling point while occasionally stirring. Allow the mixture to cool, undisturbed, for 5 minutes.

4. Using the filter paper from Step 1, assemble a filtration setup (refer to Figure 2.2 on p. 27).

5. Decant the liquid from the beaker into the filter funnel. Avoid transferring the precipitate to the filter paper. Wash the precipitate in the beaker by adding 30 mL of distilled water and swirling the mixture gently. Again decant the liquid into the filter funnel. Repeat the washing procedure once more.

6. Place the filter paper and any solid material retained on it in the beaker that contains the washed precipitate.

7. The contents of the beaker will now be dried according to your teacher's instructions.

8. Determine the combined mass of the beaker and its dry contents to the nearest 0.01 g and record the measurement.

9. Dispose of the filtrate and precipitate as instructed by your teacher. Be sure to wash your hands thoroughly after completing this experiment.

OBSERVATIONS

DATA TABLE 1: DETERMINATION OF THE MASS OF LEAD(II) CHROMATE	
mass of beaker + filter paper	
mass of beaker + filter paper + precipitate	
mass of precipitate ($PbCrO_4$)	
volume of saturated $PbCl_2$ solution used	
molar mass $PbCrO_4$	
molar mass $PbCl_2$	

ANALYSES AND CONCLUSIONS

1. In a saturated aqueous solution of lead(II) chloride, an equilibrium is established between the solid lead(II) chloride and its ions. Write the balanced chemical equation that describes this equilibrium.

   _____

2. Write a balanced equation for the reaction of Pb^{2+} ions and CrO_4^{2-} ions.

   _____

3. Calculate the number of moles of $PbCrO_4$ you obtained in the experiment.

4. Determine the concentration (mol/L) of Pb^{2+} ions in the saturated $PbCl_2$ solution.

5. Find the Cl^- concentration (mol/L) in the saturated solution.

6. Set up the solubility product expression and calculate the K_{sp} for $PbCl_2$.

7. Calculate the percent error in your results. Use a chemistry handbook to look up the accepted K_{sp} values for $PbCl_2$ and $PbCrO_4$.

8. Suggest likely sources of error in this experiment.

_____

_____

_____

_____

9. Barium ions are extremely toxic. Yet patients in hospitals are required to drink a suspension of barium sulfate in order to have their stomachs and intestinal tracts X-rayed. Find the K_{sp} value for barium sulfate and explain why patients are not at risk with this treatment.

_____

_____

_____

GOING FURTHER

Develop a Hypothesis

Based on the results of this lab, develop a hypothesis about how other factors such as temperature, pH, and the presence of other dissolved ions and gases would affect the solubility constants of various salts, including lead(II) chloride.

_____

_____

_____

Design an Experiment

Propose an experiment to test your hypothesis. If resources are available and you have your teacher's permission, perform the experiment.

_____

_____

_____

Chapter 19 • *Acids, Bases, and Salts*   **EXPERIMENT**

ESTIMATION OF pH

Text Reference
Section 19.2

PURPOSE

To estimate the pH of solutions by using acid–base indicators.

BACKGROUND

If you are interested in gardening, you may know that plants such as azaleas and rhododendrons prefer acidic soils. A part of soil testing consists of the measurement of the pH of the soil. pH is important for many other applications in the home and in industry. For example, maintenance of the proper pH of water is important in caring for swimming pools. There are several ways to test pH. One of the most important ways is by means of acid–base indicators such as phenolphthalein. In neutral and acidic solutions, phenolphthalein is colorless. In alkaline solutions, it is pink. By adding a few drops of a weak solution of the indicator to a solution to be tested, you can tell immediately whether the test solution is alkaline. Other acid–base indicators change colors at different pH values. By systematically testing a solution with a series of indicators, you can often arrive at a good estimate of the pH of a solution.

In this experiment, you will estimate the pH of several solutions by using acid–base indicators. You will then use the same indicators to test the pH of several common household chemicals.

MATERIALS (PER PAIR)

safety goggles
dropper pipet
5 small test tubes
test-tube rack
10-mL graduated cylinder
stirring rod
plastic wash bottle
pH meter (optional)
0.1M hydrochloric acid, HCl $\boxed{\text{I}}$
0.1M ethanoic acid, CH_3COOH
household chemicals such as:
  lemon juice
  vinegar
  bleach
  baking soda
  carbonated beverage

0.1M ammonia, NH_3 $\boxed{\text{T}}$
0.1M sodium hydroxide,
  NaOH $\boxed{\text{I}}$
distilled water
methyl red solution
litmus solution (or litmus paper)
bromthymol blue solution
phenolphthalein solution

shampoo
cold tea
aspirin
milk
liquid antacid

SAFETY FIRST!

In this lab, observe all precautions, especially the ones listed below. If you see a safety icon beside a step in the Procedure, refer to the list below for its meaning.

 Caution: Wear your safety goggles. (All steps.)

 Caution: Hydrochloric acid and sodium hydroxide are irritants at the concentrations used in this experiment. (Step 1.)

 Caution: Ammonia is an irritant. Do not inhale ammonia fumes. (Step 1.)

 Caution: Return or dispose of all materials according to the instructions of your teacher. (Step 6.)

PROCEDURE

As you perform the experiment, record your observations in Data Tables 2 and 3.

 1. Add 1–2 mL of the following to five separate, clean test tubes: 0.1M hydrochloric acid, 0.1M ethanoic acid, 0.1M ammonia, 0.1M sodium hydroxide, and distilled water.

2. Add 2 drops of methyl red indicator solution to each tube. Flick to mix the contents. Record the final color in Data Table 2 and estimate the pH of the solution by referring to Data Table 1.

3. Using fresh samples of the solutions, repeat the procedure for each of the other indicators named in Data Table 1. If you are using paper indicator strips, use a glass rod to transfer a drop of the solution to the indicator strip. Record the results of all the tests in Data Table 2.

4. Test the common household chemicals that are available to you. Test liquids directly. Solids should be dissolved or suspended in water before testing. Record your results in Data Table 3.

5. If a pH meter is available, use it to determine the pH of the household chemicals.

 6. Follow your teacher's instructions for proper disposal of the materials.

Name _____ Date _____ Class _____

OBSERVATIONS

DATA TABLE 1: COMMON ACID–BASE INDICATORS

Indicator	Color in Acid (HIn form)	Color in Base (In⁻ form)	pH Range
litmus	red	blue	5.2–7.5
bromthymol blue	yellow	blue	6.0–7.6
phenolphthalein	colorless	pink	8.2–10.0

DATA TABLE 2: INDICATOR REACTIONS WITH STANDARD SOLUTIONS

Solution	Methyl Red	Litmus	Bromthymol Blue	Phenolphthalein	Estimated pH
0.1M HCl					
0.1M ethanoic acid					
distilled water					
0.1M ammonia					
0.1M NaOH					

DATA TABLE 3: INDICATOR REACTIONS WITH HOUSEHOLD CHEMICALS

Substance	Methyl Red	Litmus	Bromthymol Blue	Phenolphthalein	Estimated pH	Measured pH

ANALYSES AND CONCLUSIONS

1. Compare the pH of $0.1M$ ethanoic acid with that of $0.1M$ hydrochloric acid. Compare the pH of $0.1M$ ammonia with that of $0.1M$ sodium hydroxide. Explain any differences.

_____

_____

_____

_____

_____

_____

_____

_____

2. Which of the indicators used in this experiment could most accurately identify a neutral solution? Explain.

_____

_____

_____

3. Are the household chemicals you tested acidic, basic, or neutral?

_____

GOING FURTHER

Develop a Hypothesis

Based on the results of this lab, develop a hypothesis about how acid–base indicators change colors at different pH's.

_____

_____

_____

Do Research

If resources are available, read articles or books to collect information about the chemical structures of acid–base indicators under different conditions of pH that may or may not support your hypothesis.

_____

_____

41 REACTIONS OF ACIDS

Text Reference
Section 19.4

PURPOSE

To investigate common reactions of acids.

BACKGROUND

Because of its usefulness in many industrial processes, sulfuric acid is one of the most important bulk chemicals produced. The uses of acids are not limited to industry, however. Artists pull beautiful prints from metal lithographic plates that have been etched with hydrochloric acid. Hydrofluoric acid is used to etch designs on glass. You encounter natural acids when you pour vinegar (which contains ethanoic acid) on a salad or eat a tart apple (which contains malic acid). Acids can also cause problems. Acid precipitation can corrode metal; dissolve marble and limestone statues; and even damage buildings.

In this experiment, you will investigate some common reactions of acids. These characteristic reactions are often used to test for certain ions or metals.

MATERIALS (PER PAIR)

safety goggles
glass-marking pencil
6 small test tubes
test-tube rack
dropper pipet
forceps
2 spatulas
test-tube holder
gas burner
6M hydrochloric acid, HCl C T

paper
iron wire or small nails, Fe
copper wire, Cu
magnesium ribbon, Mg F
zinc strips, Zn,
    0.25 mm × 0.5 cm × 2.00 cm
sodium hydrogen carbonate,
    NaHCO$_3$
calcium carbonate, CaCO$_3$
wood splints
matches

SAFETY FIRST!

In this lab, observe all precautions, especially the ones listed below. If you see a safety icon beside a step in the Procedure, refer to the list below for its meaning.

 Caution: Wear your safety goggles. (All steps.)

 Caution: Concentrated hydrochloric acid is highly corrosive and can cause severe burns. (All steps.)

 Caution: Magnesium is flammable. Keep it away from open flames. (Step 2.)

Note: Return or dispose of all materials according to the instructions of your teacher. (Step 4.)

PROCEDURE

As you perform the experiment, record your observations in Data Table 1.

1. Label six small test tubes with the numbers 1–6. Place the tubes in a test-tube rack. **CAUTION:** *Hydrochloric acid is corrosive, especially at the 6M concentration.* Add 2 mL of 6*M* hydrochloric acid to each tube.

2. Obtain the items indicated below and place them on labeled pieces of paper. Using forceps, carefully transfer the materials to the numbered test tubes, as the following list indicates.

   tube 1   2-cm length of clean iron wire or a small nail
   tube 2   2-cm length of copper wire
   tube 3   2-cm length of magnesium ribbon
   tube 4   small strip of zinc

   Using a spatula, transfer the following materials to the numbered test tubes as indicated.

   tube 5   pea-sized quantity of sodium hydrogen carbonate
   tube 6   pea-sized piece of calcium carbonate

3. Observe the tubes for several minutes to determine if a gas is produced. Attempt to identify any gas produced by holding a burning wood splint at the mouth of the test tube. If it appears no gas is being produced, place the test tube in a holder and warm the tube gently, *without boiling*, in a burner flame. **CAUTION:** *Do not point the mouth of the tube toward yourself or anyone else.* Remove the tube from the flame and test for the presence of gas production. Record your observations.

4. Follow your teacher's instructions for proper disposal of the materials.

Name _____ Date _____ Class _____

OBSERVATIONS

DATA TABLE 1: REACTIONS WITH HYDROCHLORIC ACID	
Substance	Observations
iron	
copper	
magnesium	
zinc	
sodium hydrogen carbonate	
calcium carbonate	

ANALYSES AND CONCLUSIONS

1. List the four metals tested in order of increasing reactivity with hydrochloric acid. List any nonreactive metals first, then the least reactive, and so on, up to the most reactive.

   _____

   _____

   _____

   _____

2. Was the same gas produced when all the metals reacted with hydrochloric acid? What was the gas? How did you identify the gas?

   _____

   _____

   _____

   _____

3. Write a balanced equation for the reaction of the two metals that reacted most vigorously with hydrochloric acid.

_____

_____

4. Was the same gas produced when sodium hydrogen carbonate and calcium carbonate reacted with hydrochloric acid? What was the gas? How did you identify this gas?

_____

_____

_____

5. Write balanced equations for the reactions of sodium hydrogen carbonate and calcium carbonate with hydrochloric acid.

_____

_____

GOING FURTHER

Develop a Hypothesis

Based on the results of this lab, develop a hypothesis about how the relative strength of the acid used would affect the rate of the reaction with metals and carbonates.

_____

_____

_____

Design an Experiment

Propose an experiment to test your hypothesis. If resources are available and you have your teacher's permission, perform the experiment.

_____

_____

_____

42 NEUTRALIZATION REACTIONS

Text Reference
Section 19.4

PURPOSE

To produce and isolate a salt by neutralizing a base with an acid.

BACKGROUND

Early chemists discovered that sour acids and bitter bases combine to form relatively bland-tasting (neutral) salts. (**CAUTION:** *Never taste any chemical in the laboratory.*) For example, equivalent amounts of hydrochloric acid and sodium hydroxide combine to form neutral water and neutral sodium chloride, common table salt.

$$HCl(aq) + NaOH(aq) \rightarrow NaCl(aq) + H_2O(l)$$

In this reaction, the H^+ and OH^- ions—which are responsible for the properties of the acid and base, respectively—combine to produce water. The products of the reaction do not have the properties of an acid or a base. The reaction is, therefore, called a *neutralization reaction*.

In this experiment, you will use a neutralization reaction between a strong acid and a strong base to make a salt.

MATERIALS (PER PAIR)

safety goggles
250-mL beaker
ring stand
ring clamp
wire gauze
gas burner
10-mL graduated cylinder
50-mL beaker

glass stirring rod
dropper pipet
evaporating dish
crucible tongs
1*M* sodium hydroxide,
  NaOH [C] [T]
phenolphthalein solution
1*M* hydrochloric acid, HCl [T] [I]

SAFETY FIRST!

In this lab, observe all precautions, especially the ones listed below. If you see a safety icon beside a step in the Procedure, refer to the list below for its meaning.

 Caution: Wear your safety goggles. (All steps.)

 Caution: Hydrochloric acid is an irritant at the concentration used in this experiment. Sodium hydroxide is corrosive and can cause severe burns. (Steps 2, 3.)

 Caution: Do not touch or taste any of the chemicals. (Step 5.)

Caution: Exercise care when working with hot water baths. The steam can cause severe burns. Use tongs to handle the evaporating dish. (Steps 4, 5.)

Caution: Exercise care when working with an open flame. Tie back hair and loose clothing. Do not use the burner near flammable materials. (Step 1.)

Note: Return or dispose of all materials according to the instructions of your teacher. (Step 6.)

PROCEDURE

As you perform the experiment, record your observations in Data Table 1.

1. Fill a 250-mL beaker three-fourths full with water and set up a boiling water bath. While the water is heating, proceed to the next step.

2. Pour 5.0 mL of 1M sodium hydroxide solution into a 50-mL beaker. Add 1 or 2 drops of phenolphthalein indicator solution to the sodium hydroxide.

3. Add, drop by drop, 1M hydrochloric acid to the beaker, using a dropper pipet. Stir constantly while adding the acid. Continue adding acid until the color of the solution just disappears.

4. Transfer about 5 mL of the neutralized solution to a clean evaporating dish. Place the evaporating dish over the boiling water bath, as shown in Figure 42.1. Evaporate the solution to dryness. **CAUTION:** *Be careful not to be burned by the steam coming from the water bath.*

5. Turn off the gas burner and remove the evaporating dish from the beaker, using tongs. Examine the residue in the evaporating dish. **CAUTION:** *Do not touch or taste the residue.*

6. Follow your teacher's instructions for proper disposal of the materials.

Figure 42.1

Name _____ Date _____ Class _____

OBSERVATIONS

DATA TABLE 1: OBSERVATIONS

Step	Observation
2	
3	
5	

ANALYSES AND CONCLUSIONS

1. Write a balanced equation for the neutralization reaction that took place in this experiment.

_____

2. How does the product that was prepared in this experiment compare with the same product as it is prepared commercially?

_____

_____

_____

_____

3. Why should you not taste the residue from this reaction, even though you known the salt produced is commonly used in food?

_____

_____

_____

4. How could you determine whether the phenolphthalein remains in the residue of the reaction?

_____

_____

_____

_____

5. Design an experiment in which you produce and examine the products of several other neutralization reactions. Include in your procedure a step in which you determine whether the product is truly free of all traces of acid or base.

_____

_____

_____

_____

_____

_____

_____

_____

_____

_____

GOING FURTHER

Develop a Hypothesis

Research the most common antacids to determine the active ingredients used to neutralize stomach acid. Based on the results of this lab, develop a hypothesis about the effectiveness of various antacid products in neutralizing acid.

_____

_____

_____

Design an Experiment

Propose an experiment to test your hypothesis. If resources are available and you have your teacher's permission, perform the experiment.

_____

_____

_____

_____

Chapter 19 • *Acids, Bases, and Salts*

EXPERIMENT

43 ACID–BASE TITRATIONS

PURPOSE

To measure the normality of ethanoic acid in vinegar, using a standardized solution of sodium hydroxide.

Text Reference
Section 19.4

BACKGROUND

Every day, scientists in many fields conduct experiments designed to answer one question: How much acid or base does this solution contain? The chemical reactions used to answer this question are, for the main part, neutralization reactions, and *titration* is the method generally used.

You can neutralize an acid with a base very precisely by using the technique of titration. During a titration, a solution of known acidity (a standard solution) is gradually added to a solution of unknown basicity. At the point of neutralization, the number of equivalents of acid must be equal to the number of equivalents of base. Thus, titration tells you the equivalents of base in your unknown solution. The neutralization, or equivalence point, of the reaction is estimated by the color change of an acid–base indicator or by a neutral reading (pH 7.0) on a pH meter. You can also reverse the titration procedure so a standard base solution is used to titrate an unknown acidic solution.

In this experiment, you will prepare a standard solution of an acidic compound, potassium hydrogen sulfate ($KHSO_4$). You will then use this solution to make a standard solution of sodium hydroxide by titration. Finally, you will use your standardized sodium hydroxide solution to titrate vinegar, a dilute solution of ethanoic acid, CH_3COOH.

MATERIALS (PER PAIR)

safety goggles
centigram balance
weighing bottle
filter funnel
spatula
100-mL graduated cylinder
250-mL volumetric flask
2 rubber stoppers, for
    volumetric flasks
3 250-mL plastic bottles
labels
10-mL graduated cylinder
2 50-mL burets
double buret clamp
ring stand
2 sheets white paper,
    25 cm × 25 cm

100-mL beaker
2 250-mL Erlenmeyer flasks
10-mL pipet
25-mL pipet
pipet suction bulb
100-mL volumetric flask
plastic wash bottle
potassium hydrogen sulfate,
    $KHSO_4$ [T]
distilled water
6M sodium hydroxide,
    NaOH [C] [T]
phenolphthalein solution
vinegar, dilute ethanoic acid,
    CH_3COOH

Figure 43.1

SAFETY FIRST!

In this lab, observe all precautions, especially the ones listed below. If you see a safety icon beside a step in the Procedure, refer to the list below for its meaning.

 Caution: Wear your safety goggles. (All steps.)

 Caution: Sodium hydroxide is corrosive and can cause severe burns. (Steps 4–16.)

 Caution: Potassium hydrogen sulfate is a toxic substance. (Steps 1–13.)

 Note: Return or dispose of all materials according to the instructions of your teacher. (Steps 6, 12, 16.)

PROCEDURE

As you perform the experiment, record your data and observations in Data Tables 1, 2, and 3.

Part A. Preparation of a Standard Solution of Potassium Hydrogen Sulfate

 1. Determine the mass of a sample of potassium hydrogen sulfate (the *acid*) in a weighing bottle, using the most accurate balance available to you. Using a funnel and a spatula, transfer 3–4 g of the acid to a clean 250-mL volumetric flask. Remeasure the mass of the weighing bottle and remaining sample. The difference between the two mass values is the mass of the acid in the flask.

2. Add about 100 mL of distilled water to the flask, washing into the flask any acid crystals clinging to the funnel. Remove the funnel and gently swirl the flask to dissolve the acid. When the acid is completely dissolved, fill the flask to the 250-mL mark with distilled water.

3. Stopper and mix the contents thoroughly by inverting the flask and swirling the mixture. Transfer the solution to a clean, dry 250-mL plastic bottle labeled "approximately 0.1N KHSO$_4$" and mark the label with your initials.

Part B. Standardization of a Solution of Sodium Hydroxide

 4. **CAUTION:** *Sodium hydroxide is corrosive.* Using a 10-mL graduated cylinder, measure out 5 mL of 6M sodium hydroxide. Transfer this solution to a clean, dry 250-mL plastic bottle labeled "approximately 0.1N NaOH" and mark the label with your initials. Add 250 mL of distilled water to the bottle, cap it, and shake it to mix the contents.

5. Clean and mount two 50-mL burets, as shown in Figure 43.1. Place a white sheet of paper or a white plastic base beneath each buret. Label the left buret "acid" and the right buret "base."

6. Rinse the "acid" buret with three 5-mL portions of the standard solution of potassium hydrogen sulfate. Let each portion drain out of the buret before adding the next rinse. Discard these rinses. Fill the buret with the potassium hydrogen sulfate solution. Before beginning the titration, remove any bubbles trapped in the tip of the buret and the stopcock.

7. Using the sodium hydroxide solution, rinse and fill the "base" buret. Use a wash bottle of distilled water to rinse off the tip of each buret; catch the runoff in a 100-mL beaker. Record the initial volume in each buret to the nearest 0.01 mL.

8. Add 10–12 mL of the acid solution to a clean 250-mL Erlenmeyer flask. Use the wash bottle to rinse the last drop of acid from the tip of the buret into the flask. Add 50 mL of distilled water and 1–2 drops of phenolphthalein to the flask.

9. Now, slowly add sodium hydroxide solution from the "base" buret to the flask. As you add the base, gently swirl the solution in the flask. A pink color will appear and quickly disappear as the solutions are mixed. As more and more base is added, the pink color will persist for a longer time before disappearing. This is a sign that you are nearing the equivalence point, also called the end point. Wash down the sides of the flask and the tip of the buret with distilled water from the wash bottle. Continue to add sodium hydroxide more slowly, until a single drop of base turns the solution a pale pink color that persists for 15–30 seconds.

10. If you overshoot the end point—that is, if you add too much base so the solution turns bright pink—simply add a few drops of acid from the acid buret to turn the solution colorless again. Approach the end point again, adding base drop by drop, until one drop causes the color change to pale pink.

11. When you are sure that you have achieved the end point, record the final volume reading of each buret. **Note:** Do not allow the level of the solution in either buret to go below the 50-mL mark. If you do, you will have to discard your sample and begin again.

12. Discard the solution in the Erlenmeyer flask as directed by your teacher, and rinse the flask well with distilled water. Refill both burets if necessary. Read the initial volume in each buret and do another titration, as described in Steps 8–11.

13. Before proceeding, calculate the normality of the sodium hydroxide solution for each titration, as described in Analyses and Conclusions, problems 1–6. If the normalities obtained from the two titrations do not agree within 1%, perform a third titration.

Part C. Determination of the Normality of Ethanoic Acid in Vinegar

14. Using a clean, dry 10-mL pipet and suction bulb, transfer 10 mL of commercial vinegar into a clean 100-mL volumetric flask. Fill the flask to the 100-mL mark with distilled water. Stopper the flask and mix the solution by inverting the flask 20–30 times. Transfer this solution to a clean, dry 250-mL plastic bottle. Label the bottle "10% vinegar" and mark the label with your initials.

15. Using a clean, dry 25-mL pipet, transfer a 20-mL sample of the diluted vinegar to a clean 250-mL Erlenmeyer flask. Add 50 mL of distilled water and 1–2 drops of phenolphthalein to the flask. Titrate the vinegar with the sodium hydroxide solution that you standardized in Part B. **Note:** If you overshoot the end point in these titrations, you will have to discard the sample and begin again. Do at least two titrations that agree to within 1%.

16. Follow your teacher's instructions for proper disposal of the materials.

Name _____ Date _____ Class _____

OBSERVATIONS

DATA TABLE 1: NORMALITY OF POTASSIUM HYDROGEN SULFATE

initial mass of weighing bottle and $KHSO_4$	
final mass of weighing bottle and $KHSO_4$	
mass of $KHSO_4$ used	
gram equivalent mass of $KHSO_4$	
equivalents of $KHSO_4$ used in 250 mL	
normality of $KHSO_4$	

DATA TABLE 2: NORMALITY OF SODIUM HYDROXIDE

	Trial 1		Trial 2		Trial 3	
	Acid	Base	Acid	Base	Acid	Base
final volume						
initial volume						
volume used						
normality of NaOH						
average normality of NaOH						

DATA TABLE 3: NORMALITY OF VINEGAR

	Trial 1		Trial 2		Trial 3	
	Vinegar	Base	Vinegar	Base	Vinegar	Base
final volume						
initial volume						
volume used						
normality of vinegar						
average normality of 10% vinegar						

Name _____ Date _____ Class _____

ANALYSES AND CONCLUSIONS

As you do the following calculations, enter the results in Data Tables 1, 2, or 3.

1. Determine the mass of potassium hydrogen sulfate used.

2. Find the gram equivalent mass of potassium hydrogen sulfate.

$$\text{gram equivalent mass} = \frac{\text{molar mass}}{\text{number of equivalents per mole}}$$

3. Calculate the number of equivalents of potassium hydrogen sulfate used.

$$\text{number of equivalents} = \frac{\text{mass}}{\text{gram equivalent mass}}$$

4. Determine the normality of your standard solution of potassium hydrogen sulfate. Be sure to use units properly in your calculation.

$$\text{normality} = \frac{\text{number of equivalents}}{\text{volume}}$$

5. Determine the volumes of acid and base used in each titration performed in Part B.

6. The normality of the sodium hydroxide solution is calculated with this equation:

$$\text{normality}_{base} = \text{normality}_{acid} \times \frac{\text{volume}_{acid}}{\text{volume}_{base}}$$

Calculate the normality of your sodium hydroxide solution for each titration. Record the value obtained for each trial, as well as the average value for all trials.

7. Determine the volume of 10% vinegar and sodium hydroxide solutions used in each titration.

8. Using the average normality of sodium hydroxide that was calculated in problem 6, determine the normality of your 10% vinegar solution (ethanoic acid).

$$\text{normality}_{acid} = \text{normality}_{base} \times \frac{\text{volume}_{base}}{\text{volume}_{acid}}$$

Record the value for each trial and the average value.

9. Examine the class results for the normality of vinegar. Account for any difference among these values.

_____

_____

_____

_____

_____

_____

_____

10. Explain why the plastic bottles into which you transferred your potassium hydrogen sulfate and vinegar solutions had to be dry, but you could add distilled water to the titration flask at any time and not affect your results.

_____

_____

_____

_____

_____

_____

_____

11. Why are the burets rinsed with the acid and base solutions before filling?

_____

_____

_____

12. Use your data from this experiment to calculate the percent by mass of ethanoic acid present in commercial, undiluted vinegar.

13. Explain why you cannot prepare a standard sodium hydroxide solution by determining the mass of the solid and dissolving it in a measured amount of water, as you did with the potassium hydrogen sulfate.

_____

_____

_____

GOING FURTHER

Develop a Hypothesis

Based on the results of this lab, develop a hypothesis about how the pH of the 10% solution of vinegar changes during the titration with NaOH. In what ways would the pH curves for the titration of ethanoic acid (vinegar), ascorbic acid (vitamin C), and citric acid (lemon juice) be the same? Different?

_____

_____

_____

Design an Experiment

Propose an experiment to test your hypothesis. If resources are available and you have your teacher's permission, perform the experiment.

_____

_____

_____

44 SALT HYDROLYSIS

Text Reference
Section 19.5

PURPOSE

To investigate the formation of nonneutral salt solutions.

BACKGROUND

Solutions of many salts are neutral, but some are acidic and others are basic. Neutralization of strong acids by strong bases produces neutral salts, such as NaBr and KNO_3. However, salts formed when weak acids neutralize strong bases or when strong acids neutralize weak bases are not neutral; these reactions produce hydrolyzing salts. The name *hydrolyzing salts* is given to those salts that are able to react with water to form hydronium ions or hydroxide ions, a process called *hydrolysis*.

In this experiment, you will measure the pH of solutions of various salts. You will analyze your results to determine if one of the ions produced in solution can react with water to produce hydronium ions or hydroxide ions.

MATERIALS (PER PAIR)

safety goggles
7 small or medium test tubes
test-tube rack
spatula
10-mL graduated cylinder
dropper pipet
freshly boiled distilled water
sodium chloride, NaCl
sodium ethanoate, CH_3COONa [I]

ammonium chloride,
  NH_4Cl [T] [I] [C]
sodium carbonate, Na_2CO_3
sodium hydrogen carbonate,
  $NaHCO_3$
sodium phosphate, Na_3PO_4 [I]
wide-range indicator solution or
  wide-range pH test paper
  (pH 1–14)

SAFETY FIRST!

In this lab, observe all precautions, especially the ones listed below. If you see a safety icon beside a step in the Procedure, refer to the list below for its meaning.

 Caution: Wear your safety goggles. (All steps.)

 Caution: Avoid skin contact with these chemicals. Some of them are toxic. (All steps.)

 Note: Return or dispose of all materials according to the instructions of your teacher. (Step 6.)

PROCEDURE

As you perform the experiment, record the results of your pH measurements in Data Table 1.

1. Place small quantities (less than pea size) of sodium chloride, sodium ethanoate, ammonium chloride, sodium carbonate, sodium hydrogen carbonate, and sodium phosphate into separate labeled test tubes. Place the tubes in a test-tube rack.

2. Add about 5 mL of cool, previously boiled distilled water to each tube. Flick each tube gently to dissolve the sample.

3. Add 2 drops of wide-range indicator solution to each tube, or dip a small piece of wide-range pH test paper into each tube.

4. Determine the pH of the solution in each tube by comparing the color of the solutions or test papers to a standard chart of indicator reactions.

5. Determine the pH of the boiled distilled water.

6. Dispose of the liquid wastes down the drain.

Name _____ Date _____ Class _____

OBSERVATIONS

DATA TABLE 1: MEASUREMENT OF pH OF SALT SOLUTIONS		
Aqueous Solution	Chemical Formula	Approximate pH
sodium chloride		
sodium ethanoate		
ammonium chloride		
sodium carbonate		
sodium hydrogen carbonate		
sodium phosphate		
boiled distilled water (control)		

ANALYSES AND CONCLUSIONS

1. Which salts produce neutral aqueous solutions?

   _____

2. Which salts produce acidic aqueous solutions?

   _____

3. Which salts produce basic aqueous solutions?

   _____

   _____

4. Why is it important to know the pH of the boiled distilled water?

   _____

5. For each salt, write a balanced equation to show how it ionizes in solution.

   _____

   _____

   _____

   _____

   _____

6. For each salt whose solution is acidic, write an additional equation to show which ion in solution reacts with water to produce the hydronium ion.

_____

7. For each salt whose solution is basic, write an additional equation to show which ion in solution reacts with water to produce the hydroxide ion.

_____

_____

_____

_____

8. What do all the acids of the anions identified in problem 7 have in common?

_____

9. Would you expect a sodium salt to produce an acidic solution? Explain.

_____

GOING FURTHER

Develop a Hypothesis

Based on the results of this lab, develop a hypothesis about whether solutions of other salts, such as sodium nitrate, sodium sulfate, ammonium sulfate, potassium sulfate, and $FeCl_3$, would be acidic or basic.

_____

_____

_____

_____

Design an Experiment

Propose an experiment to test your hypothesis. If resources are available and you have your teacher's permission, perform the experiment.

_____

_____

45 BUFFERS

Text Reference
Section 19.5

PURPOSE

To investigate the capacity of buffered solutions to withstand addition of acid and base without undergoing a significant change in pH.

BACKGROUND

Your blood must be maintained at pH 7.35–7.45 for you to stay healthy. However, chemical reactions taking place in your body are continuously pumping a stream of hydrogen ions into your blood. Your body maintains the proper blood pH, in spite of the hydrogen ions, due to blood buffers. *Buffered solutions* maintain a relatively constant pH when limited amounts of acid or base are added to them.

What are buffers? They usually consist of solutions of a weak acid and its salt or of a weak base and its salt. For example, a solution containing ethanoic acid (CH_3COOH) and its salt, sodium ethanoate (CH_3COONa), is a buffer. A solution containing ammonia (NH_3) and its salt, ammonium chloride (NH_4Cl), is also a buffer. Sodium ethanoate is formed by the neutralization of ethanoic acid by sodium hydroxide. Ammonium chloride is formed by the neutralization of ammonia by hydrochloric acid. In other words, a buffer can be created by the partial neutralization of a weak acid by a strong base or by partial neutralization of a weak base by a strong acid.

In this experiment, you will examine the effectiveness of different buffering systems in resisting changes in pH.

MATERIALS (PER PAIR)

safety goggles and apron
glass-marking pencil
7 medium test tubes
test-tube rack
10-mL graduated cylinder
2 50-mL beakers
2 dropper pipets
0.1M sodium carbonate, Na_2CO_3
0.1M sodium hydrogen
    carbonate, $NaHCO_3$

0.1M disodium hydrogen
    phosphate, Na_2HPO_4 ⟦I⟧
0.1M sodium dihydrogen
    phosphate, NaH_2PO_4 ⟦I⟧
boiled distilled water
wide-range indicator solution
    (pH 1–14) or wide-range pH
    paper (pH 1–14)
1M hydrochloric acid, HCl ⟦I⟧⟦T⟧⟦C⟧
1M sodium hydroxide, NaOH
    ⟦I⟧⟦C⟧⟦T⟧

Name _____ Date _____ Class _____

SAFETY FIRST!

In this lab, observe all precautions, especially the ones listed below. If you see a safety icon beside a step in the Procedure, refer to the list below for its meaning.

 Caution: Wear your safety goggles. (All steps.)

 Caution: Aqueous sodium hydroxide is an irritant at the concentration used in this experiment. It is corrosive and can cause severe burns. (Step 7.)

Caution: Never pick up a dropper bottle by its cap. Always hold a dropper with the lip lower than the rubber bulb so that the liquid does not run into the bulb. (Steps 5–8.)

 Note: Return or dispose of all materials according to the instructions of your teacher. (Step 9.)

PROCEDURE

As you perform the experiment, record your results in Data Table 1.

1. Label seven medium test tubes with the numbers 1–7.

2. Mix 5 mL of $0.1M$ Na_2CO_3 and 5 mL of $0.1M$ $NaHCO_3$ in a 50-mL beaker. This is a carbonate/hydrogen carbonate (CO_3^{2-}/HCO_3^-) buffer. Divide this buffer solution equally between test tubes 1 and 2.

3. In another 50-mL beaker, mix 5 mL of $0.1M$ Na_2HPO_4 and 5 mL of $0.1M$ NaH_2PO_4. This is a monohydrogen phosphate/dihydrogen phosphate (HPO_4^{2-}/$H_2PO_4^-$) buffer. Divide this buffer solution equally between test tubes 3 and 4.

4. Put 5 mL of $0.1M$ $NaHCO_3$ in test tube 5, 5 mL of $0.1M$ Na_2HPO_4 in test tube 6, and 5 mL of cool, previously boiled distilled water in test tube 7.

5. Use a dropper to add 3 drops of wide-range indicator to each test tube. Estimate the pH of each solution by comparing your results with those in the color chart supplied with the indicator. Record the results in Data Table 1.

6. Use a dropper to add 1 drop of $1M$ HCl to tubes 1, 3, 5, 6, and 7. Flick the test tubes to mix, note the color changes, and record the results.

7. Use a dropper to add 2 drops of $1M$ NaOH to tubes 1, 3, 5, 6, and 7—the tubes that received the HCl solution. Flick the test tubes to mix and note the color changes. Estimate and record the pH.

8. (Optional) Add hydrochloric acid, drop by drop, to tubes 2 and 4. Flick the test tubes to mix until the pH drops to about 2. Record the number of drops required for this to occur.

9. Follow your teacher's instructions for proper disposal of the materials.

Name _____ Date _____ Class _____

OBSERVATIONS

	DATA TABLE 1: EFFECTS OF ACID AND BASE ON BUFFERED AND UNBUFFERED SOLUTIONS				
Tube	Contents of Tube	Initial pH	pH After Adding 1 Drop HCl	pH After Adding 2 Drops NaOH	Number of Drops HCl Added (Optional)
1	CO_3^{2-}/HCO_3^-				
2	CO_3^{2-}/HCO_3^-				
3	$HPO_4^{2-}/H_2PO_4^-$				
4	$HPO_4^{2-}/H_2PO_4^-$				
5	$0.1M$ NaHCO$_3$				
6	$0.1M$ NaH$_2$PO$_4$				
7	Boiled distilled water				

ANALYSES AND CONCLUSIONS

1. Based upon your experimental evidence, how effective are the CO_3^{2-}/HCO_3^- and $HPO_4^{2-}/H_2PO_4^-$ buffer systems? Explain your answer.

_____

_____

_____

_____

_____

2. Do $0.1M$ NaHCO$_3$ and $0.1M$ NaH$_2$PO$_4$ solutions buffer as effectively as the CO_3^{2-}/HCO_3^- and $HPO_4^{2-}/H_2PO_4^-$ systems? Explain your answer.

_____

_____

_____

_____

_____

3. Write equations for the reaction of the $HPO_4{}^{2-}/H_2PO_4{}^-$ buffer system with an acid and a base.

_____

_____

4. Write equations for the reaction of the $CO_3{}^{2-}/HCO_3{}^-$ buffer system with an acid and a base.

_____

_____

5. Do all buffers maintain the pH in the same range? In a chemistry handbook, look up the pH range of buffers in the list that follows. Prepare and measure the pH of each buffer solution. How do your experimental results compare to the published values? Which of these buffer systems would be effective at pH 5.0?

Buffer System	pH Range
monohydrogen phosphate/dihydrogen phosphate	
ethanoate/ethanoic acid	
carbonate/hydrogen carbonate	
phosphate/monohydrogen phosphate	

_____

_____

GOING FURTHER

Develop a Hypothesis

The carbonate buffer system plays an important role in maintaining proper blood pH. However, under certain conditions, the buffering capacity of blood may be overwhelmed. For example, pH can be affected by irregular breathing patterns that alter the balance of gases, such as CO_2, in the blood. Inhaled air contains 0.04% CO_2; exhaled air contains 4% CO_2. Based on the results of this lab, develop a hypothesis about how the concentration of dissolved CO_2 in an aqueous solution affects the pH of the solution.

_____

_____

Design an Experiment

Propose an experiment to test your hypothesis. If resources are available and you have your teacher's permission, perform the experiment.

_____

_____

46 OXIDATION–REDUCTION REACTIONS

Text Reference
Section 20.1

PURPOSE

To investigate and compare the relative reduction potentials of copper, lead, and zinc.

BACKGROUND

The rusting of iron and the combustion of gasoline are common examples of oxidation–reduction reactions. Oxidation reactions are also thought to be partly responsible for the aging of the human body. Every oxidation reaction involves a transfer of electrons from the substance oxidized to the substance reduced. A substance undergoing oxidation gives up, or loses, electrons; a substance undergoing reduction gains electrons. The ease with which a substance oxidizes depends on the substance. For example, iron oxidizes more easily than either silver or gold.

In this experiment, you will study some oxidation–reduction reactions that occur between metals and metal ions. On the basis of your experiments, you will organize these substances into a series according to their relative ease of oxidation.

MATERIALS (PER PAIR)

safety goggles
glass-marking pencil
9 small test tubes
10-mL graduated cylinder
test-tube rack
plastic wash bottle
3 strips of copper, Cu, each
    0.25 mm × 0.50 cm × 2.00 cm
3 strips of lead, Pb, each
    0.25 mm × 0.50 cm × 2.00 cm

3 strips of zinc, Zn, each
    0.25 mm × 0.50 cm × 2.00 cm
steel wool
0.1M copper(II) nitrate,
    $Cu(NO_3)_2$ $\boxed{\text{T}}$
0.1M lead(II) nitrate,
    $Pb(NO_3)_2$ $\boxed{\text{T}}$
0.1M zinc nitrate, $Zn(NO_3)_2$ $\boxed{\text{I}}$
distilled water

SAFETY FIRST!

In this lab, observe all precautions, especially the ones listed below. If you see a safety icon beside a step in the Procedure, refer to the list below for its meaning.

 Caution: Wear your safety goggles. (All steps.)

Caution: Use a piece of paper or gloves to hold the steel wool to avoid getting metal slivers in your hand. (Steps 1, 2.)

Caution: Copper and lead compounds are toxic. (Steps 2, 3.)

 Note: Return or dispose of all materials according to the instructions of your teacher. (Step 6.)

PROCEDURE

As you perform the experiment, record your observations in Data Table 1.

 1. Polish the small metal strips of copper, lead, and zinc with steel wool.

 2. Label three test tubes "0.1M Cu(NO$_3$)$_2$." Add 3 mL of 0.1M copper(II) nitrate to each test tube. In one tube, place a strip of copper. In another, place a strip of lead. In the third, place a strip of zinc. Put the tubes in a test-tube rack.

 3. Repeat Step 2, labeling the tubes "0.1M Pb(NO$_3$)$_2$" and using 0.1M lead(II) nitrate in place of copper(II) nitrate.

4. Repeat Step 2, labeling the tubes "0.1M Zn(NO$_3$)$_2$" and using 0.1M zinc nitrate in place of copper(II) nitrate.

5. Allow the test tubes to stand undisturbed for 5–10 minutes. Record your observations in Data Table 1, briefly describing evidence of any reaction.

 6. Return the metal strips for reuse and dispose of the solutions as instructed by your teacher.

Name _____ Date _____ Class _____

OBSERVATIONS

DATA TABLE 1: REACTIONS OF METALS AND METAL IONS			
	Cu^{2+}	Pb^{2+}	Zn^{2+}
Cu(s)			
Pb(s)			
Zn(s)			

ANALYSES AND CONCLUSIONS

1. Write balanced equations for any reactions that you observed between solid metals and metal ions.

   _____

   _____

   _____

   _____

   _____

2. Which metal was oxidized by both of the other two metals?

   _____

3. Which metal was oxidized by only one of the other two metals?

   _____

4. Which metal was oxidized by neither of the other metals?

   _____

5. Write balanced *half-reactions* for the *reduction* of each of the three metal ions used in this experiment. Write the equations so that the metal ions are shown as reactants and the solid metals are shown as products. List these half-reactions so that the most easily oxidized metal is given last.

   _____

   _____

   _____

6. The relative ease of oxidation of the halogens is in this order: chlorine, bromine, iodine, with iodine the most easily oxidized. Design an experiment that would allow you to determine if the halogens are less easily or more easily oxidized than the metals used in this experiment.

_____

_____

_____

_____

_____

_____

_____

_____

_____

GOING FURTHER

Develop a Hypothesis

Many metals, including the ones examined in this lab, are oxidized by aqueous solutions of acids to produce hydrogen gas and metal ions. Based on the results of this lab, propose a hypothesis about the relative ease with which lead, copper, and zinc would be oxidized by an acid. Extend your hypothesis to include other metals such as iron, tin, and aluminum and discuss any periodic trends in oxidation by acids that would exist for the various metals.

_____

_____

Design an Experiment

Propose an experiment to test your hypothesis. If resources are available and you have your teacher's permission, perform the experiment.

_____

_____

_____

CORROSION

Text Reference
Sections 21.1 and 21.2

PURPOSE

To investigate various physical and chemical conditions that may affect the corrosion of iron.

BACKGROUND

Each year, the corrosion of metals does untold damage to cars, homes, and factories. *Corrosion* is a complex reduction–oxidation (redox) reaction in which metals are changed to their oxides or other compounds. In a corrosion reaction, electrons flow from the anode to the cathode. The anode and the cathode may be two different parts of the metal being corroded, or the cathode may be a different object that is in electrical contact with the metal being corroded.

In this experiment, you will study a variety of factors involved in the corrosion of iron.

MATERIALS (PER PAIR)

safety goggles	9 uncoated iron nails, Fe
gloves (optional)	steel wool
6 small test tubes	litmus paper or Hydrion paper
test-tube rack	agar, powdered
250-mL beaker	0.1M potassium ferricyanide,
ring stand	$K_3Fe(CN)_6$ ☐T
ring support	phenolphthalein solution
wire gauze	thin zinc strip, Zn (0.25 mm thick,
gas burner	0.2 cm × 5.0 cm)
glass stirring rod	copper wire, Cu (1.5 mm diameter,
dropper pipet	10 cm long)
pliers	0.1M iron(II) sulfate, $FeSO_4$ ☐T
2 petri dishes, with lids	distilled water

Solution Set 1

0.1M sodium hydroxide,	0.1M sodium chloride, NaCl
NaOH ☐I	0.1M hydrochloric acid, HCl ☐I
0.1M sodium dichromate,	
$Na_2Cr_2O_7$ ☐T ☐I	

Solution Set 2

0.1M potassium hydroxide,	0.1M potassium nitrate, KNO_3 ☐I
KOH ☐C ☐T	0.1M nitric acid, HNO_3 ☐C ☐T
0.1M sodium carbonate, Na_2CO_3	

Solution Set 3

0.1M sodium phosphate, NaPO$_4$ [I]

0.1M sodium oxalate, Na$_2$C$_2$O$_4$ [T]

0.1M sodium thiocyanate, NaSCN [T]

0.1M sulfuric acid, H$_2$SO$_4$ [C]

SAFETY FIRST!

In this lab, observe all precautions, especially the ones listed below. If you see a safety icon beside a step in the Procedure, refer to the list below for its meaning.

 Caution: Wear your safety goggles. (All steps.)

 Caution: Nitric, hydrochloric, and sulfuric acids are irritating and corrosive. (Step 2.)

 Caution: Sodium oxalate and sodium dichromate are toxic. Avoid contact with these chemicals. (Step 2.)

Caution: Never pick up a dropper bottle by its cap. (All steps.)

 Caution: Potassium ferricyanide can react with acids and chromates to produce toxic fumes. (Steps 6, 11, 12.)

Caution: Read all labels carefully and mix chemicals only according to directions. (All steps.)

 Caution: Exercise care when working with hot agar. It can cause severe burns to the skin. (Step 5.)

 Note: Return or dispose of all materials according to the instructions of your teacher. (Step 14.)

PROCEDURE

As you perform the experiment, record your observations in Data Table 1.

Part A. Reaction of Iron with Aqueous Solutions (Day 1)

 1. Clean five iron nails with steel wool. Place each nail in a separate small test tube.

 2. Your teacher will assign you one of the three sets of chemicals listed in the Materials section. Fill each of four test tubes with a different solution from the set until each nail is just covered. Fill the fifth tube with distilled water. Put the tubes in a test-tube rack.

3. Use litmus or Hydrion paper to determine whether each solution is acidic, basic, or neutral. Record the results in Data Table 1.

4. Allow the test tubes to stand overnight. You will study them tomorrow, when you begin with Step 10.

Part B. Effects of Stress, and Protection by Other Metals (Day 1)

 5. Heat 100 mL of distilled water to boiling in a 250-mL beaker. Remove the gas burner. **CAUTION:** *Hot agar causes severe burns to the skin.* Add, while stirring, 1 g of powdered agar. Replace the burner; heat and stir the mixture until the agar forms a suspension. Be careful not to burn the agar. Stop heating and turn off the gas burner.

 6. Add 5 drops of 0.1*M* potassium ferricyanide and 3 drops of phenolphthalein to the agar suspension. Stir to mix thoroughly. Allow the agar to cool, but not set, while you proceed to the next step.

7. Clean four irons nails with steel wool. Place one nail in a petri dish. Use pliers to bend a second nail into a right angle. Place the bent nail beside, but not touching, the straight nail (see Figure 47.1). Tightly wrap a 10-cm piece of copper wire around a third nail. Wrap the fourth nail tightly with a thin strip of zinc metal. Place these two metal-wrapped nails in a second petri dish. Be sure that the nails do not touch (see Figure 47.1).

Agar suspension

Copper wire

Zinc strip

Figure 47.1

8. Pour the warm agar suspension into the petri dishes. The nails and attached pieces of metal should be covered by agar to a depth of at least 2 mm.

9. View the dishes against a white background and make observations at the end of the class period. Cover the dishes and keep them undisturbed overnight. You will observe them again tomorrow.

Part C (Day 2)

10. Observe, against a white background, the test tubes that have stood overnight. In Data Table 1, record any evidence of reaction.

11. Test for the presence of ferrous ions, Fe^{2+}. In a separate small test tube, add one drop of $0.1M$ potassium ferricyanide to 1 mL of $0.1M$ iron(II) sulfate. Record your observations.

12. Now, test each of the five test tubes containing the nails for the presence of ferrous ions by adding 1 or 2 drops of $0.1M$ potassium ferricyanide. Record your observations. The presence of ferrous ions in the test tubes is evidence that corrosion has occurred.

13. Observe the dishes against a white background. Record your observations by sketching the dishes in Figure 47.2 on page 284. Show the location and color of any reaction products.

14. Follow your teacher's instructions for proper disposal of the materials.

Name _____ Date _____ Class _____

OBSERVATIONS

DATA TABLE 1: OBSERVATIONS				
Test Solution	pH	Initial Observations	Observations after 24 hours	*Test with $Fe(CN)_6^{3-}$
Set 1 NaOH				
$Na_2Cr_2O_7$				
NaCl				
HCl				
Set 2 KOH				
Na_2CO_3				
KNO_3				
HNO_3				
Set 3 Na_3PO_4				
$Na_2C_2O_4$				
NaSCN				
H_2SO_4				
Controls H_2O				
$FeSO_4$	reference test for presence of Fe^{2+} ions			

*Positive: production of blue color indicates the presence of Fe^{2+} ions in solution. Negative: no blue color

Name _____ Date _____ Class _____

 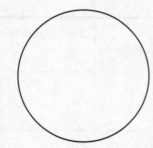

Figure 47.2

ANALYSES AND CONCLUSIONS

1. Obtain class data for the two sets of chemicals that you did not use in Part A. Enter this data in Data Table 1.

2. List the chemicals used in Part A for which there was no evidence of corrosion.

   _____

   _____

3. List the chemicals used in Part A for which there was evidence of corrosion.

   _____

   _____

   _____

   _____

   _____

   _____

   _____

   _____

   _____

   _____

   _____

   _____

_____

_____

_____

_____

_____

_____

4. Did either copper or zinc appear to protect the iron nail against corrosion? Explain.

_____

_____

5. Explain how the colors that developed in the petri dishes identify the anode and cathode for each reaction.

_____

_____

_____

_____

_____

6. What were the usual sites where corrosion took place for the nails embedded in the agar?

_____

_____

_____

7. Examine the data for Part A. Are there any ions that seem to inhibit corrosion or to promote it? Try to explain these effects.

_____

_____

_____

_____

8. Explain the results obtained in distilled water.

_____

_____

9. Consider your answer to problem 6. What effect does bending seem to have on the tendency of iron to corrode?

_____

_____

10. Explain the effects caused by wrapping the nails with zinc or copper. Discuss the relative ease of oxidation of iron, zinc, and copper in your answer.

_____

_____

_____

_____

_____

_____

_____

11. Is it correct to say that corrosion did not take place in the nail wrapped with zinc? Explain.

_____

_____

GOING FURTHER

Develop a Hypothesis

Based on the results of this lab, propose a hypothesis about other ways of preventing or retarding the corrosion of iron-based materials.

_____

_____

_____

_____

Design an Experiment

Propose an experiment to test your idea(s). If resources are available and you have your teacher's permission, perform the experiment.

_____

_____

ELECTROCHEMISTRY

48

Text Reference
Section 21.3

PURPOSE

To investigate the use of electrolytic cells to cause chemical changes.

BACKGROUND

It is common for manufactured products to be coated with a very thin layer of metal. For example, maybe you've eaten with silver-plated tableware. Your watchband, belt buckle, or jewelry may be gold-plated. All these plated items were produced using the electroplating process. *Electroplating* consists of depositing a thin layer of metal on another metal, either to protect the surface from corrosion or for a decorative effect. An electrolytic cell set up to electroplate a fork with a silver coating is shown in Figure 48.1. When the fork is being silver-plated, the anode metal is silver, the electrolytic solution is aqueous silver nitrate, and the cathode is the fork. The fork becomes silver-plated as a result of the reduction of Ag^+ ions, from the solution, at the cathode.

$$Ag^+(aq) + e^- \rightarrow Ag(s) \quad \text{reduction}$$

At the same time, the silver ions are replenished by oxidation of silver atoms at the anode.

$$Ag^+(s) \rightarrow Ag^+(aq) + e^- \quad \text{oxidation}$$

In this experiment, you will electroplate a metal object using a typical electrolytic cell. You will then remove the plating by reversing the direction of flow of electrons in the electrolytic cell.

Figure 48.1

MATERIALS (PER PAIR)

safety goggles
gloves (optional)
4 alligator clips
250-mL beaker
100-mL graduated cylinder
6-volt battery

silver coin
steel wool
2 copper wire lengths
copper strip, Cu, 0.25 mm thick,
    1 cm × 5 cm
1M copper(II) sulfate, $CuSO_4$ [T]
paper towels

SAFETY FIRST!

In this lab, observe all precautions, especially the ones listed below. If you see a safety icon beside a step in the Procedure, refer to the list below for its meaning.

 Caution: Wear your safety goggles. (All steps.)

Caution: Use a piece of paper or gloves to hold the steel wool to avoid getting metal slivers in your hand. (Steps 1, 2.)

 Note: Return or dispose of all materials according to the instructions of your teacher. (Step 6.)

PROCEDURE

As you perform the experiment, record your observations in Data Table 1.

1. Thoroughly clean a small silver object, such as a coin, with steel wool. Securely attach, with an alligator clip, a 25-cm length of copper wire to the object.

2. Polish a 1-cm × 5-cm strip of copper with steel wool. Use an alligator clip to attach a 25-cm length of copper wire to the strip.

3. Add 100 mL of 1M $CuSO_4$ to a 250-mL beaker and set up a system similar to that shown in Figure 48.2.

4. Use an alligator clip to connect the wire attached to the object to the negative terminal of a 6-volt battery. Use another alligator clip to connect the wire attached to the copper strip to the positive terminal. The object and the copper strip should not touch. Record your observations after 5 minutes have elapsed.

5. Reverse the connections and record your observations after 5 and 10 minutes.

6. Follow your teacher's instructions for proper disposal of the materials.

Figure 48.2

OBSERVATIONS

DATA TABLE 1: OBSERVATIONS OF ELECTROPLATING	
Time of Observation	Condition of Coin
after 5 minutes of current flow	
5 minutes after reversal of current flow	
10 minutes after reversal of current flow	

ANALYSES AND CONCLUSIONS

1. Write equations for the reactions that occur at the anode and at the cathode during electroplating.

   _____

   _____

   _____

2. What is oxidized in this experiment? At which electrode does oxidation occur?

   _____

   _____

3. What is reduced in this experiment? At which electrode does reduction take place?

   _____

   _____

   _____

4. To which battery terminal must an object be attached for it to become electroplated?

   _____

   _____

5. Sketch your electrochemical cell. Show the direction of ion movement and electron flow.

6. The dry cell or battery used in this experiment is an example of a voltaic cell. Explain the construction of a voltaic cell. Explain how a voltaic cell produces an electric current. What conditions can result in a "dead" battery? How does a car battery differ from the battery used in a flashlight?

_____

_____

_____

_____

_____

_____

_____

_____

_____

_____

_____

GOING FURTHER

Develop a Hypothesis

In this lab, you used a dry cell, or voltaic cell, to bring about a chemical reaction. Develop a hypothesis about how a photovoltaic cell could be used to drive a chemical process. For example, how can solar energy be used to drive a chemical process? How might solar energy be converted into a form of chemical energy that could be stored and used later?

_____

_____

Design an Experiment

Propose an experiment to test your idea(s). If resources are available and you have your teacher's permission, perform the experiment.

_____

_____

49 HYDROCARBONS: A STRUCTURAL STUDY

Text Reference
Section 22.4

PURPOSE

To investigate the three-dimensional shapes of hydrocarbon molecules by building molecular models.

BACKGROUND

The physical, chemical, and biological properties of molecules are determined, to a large extent, by their three-dimensional shapes. Often, a molecular compound in which the molecules are packed closely together forms large, dramatic crystals. When the molecules are not packed closely together, a molecular compound may remain a liquid, even at low temperatures. An understanding of molecular shapes is particularly important in organic chemistry and biochemistry. For example, many prescription and over-the-counter drugs are effective because their shapes resemble those of molecules produced by cells in the body.

Most people find it easier to think in three dimensions when they use three-dimensional models. By working with molecular models, you can learn to visualize and understand molecular shapes. In this experiment, you will use ball-and-stick models to study the shapes of hydrocarbon molecules.

MATERIALS (PER GROUP)

safety goggles
ball-and-stick molecular
    model kit

SAFETY FIRST!

In this lab, observe the precaution listed below.

 Caution: Wear your safety goggles. (All steps.)

PROCEDURE

Refer to Data Table 1 for the color code of the atoms. As you construct each model, complete Data Tables 2A and 2B.

DATA TABLE 1: COLOR CODE FOR MODELS	
Color	**Atom Represented**
black	carbon
yellow	hydrogen
red	oxygen
blue	nitrogen
green	chlorine
purple	iodine
orange	bromine

Part A. Continuous-Chain and Branched-Chain Alkanes

1. Make a model of methane, CH_4. Are all the angles formed by any two C—H bonds the same?

   _____

   _____

2. Make a model of ethane, C_2H_6. What happens when you hold one carbon and its attached hydrogens in a fixed position and rotate the other carbon and its attached hydrogens?

   _____

   _____

3. Make a model of propane, C_3H_8. Can this model be rearranged to form a different molecule? Explain.

   _____

   _____

4. Make a model of butane, C_4H_{10}. Can this model be rearranged to form a molecule that has the same molecular formula but a different structural formula? If so, name the structures. Molecules that have the same molecular formula, but different structural formulas, are called *structural isomers*.

   _____

   _____

5. Make a model of pentane, C_5H_{12}. Construct as many structural isomers of pentane as you can. For each structural isomer, list the name of the compound here and draw a sketch in Data Table 2A.

_____

_____

Part B. Cycloalkanes

6. Construct a model of hexane, C_6H_{14}. Remove two hydrogen atoms from the model so that the carbon atoms of the end of the chain can join together to form a ring. This ring structure is cyclohexane C_6H_{12}.

Manipulate your cyclohexane molecule so that two carbons directly across the ring from each other are above the plane of the other four carbons. This is called the *boat conformation*. Now manipulate the molecule so that one of these carbons is above, and the other below, the plane of the remaining four carbons. This is called the *chair conformation*. In Data Table 2A, draw these two conformations.

Is there free rotation about a C—C bond in cyclohexane?

_____

Part C. Alkenes and Geometric Isomers

7. Make a model of ethene, C_2H_4. What happens when you try to rotate the carbons about the double bond?

_____

8. Remove one hydrogen from each carbon in ethene and replace it with a chlorine. The name of the resulting compound is 1,2-dichloroethene, $C_2H_2Cl_2$. There are two structures possible for this compound. They are called *geometric isomers*, and are distinguished by the prefix *cis-* or the prefix *trans-*. In the *cis* configuration, the chlorines are on the same side of the double bond. In the *trans* configuration, the chlorines are on opposite sides of the double bond. Construct models of both geometric isomers.

9. Make a model of butene, C_4H_8. This compound has two structural isomers. Name these isomers and, in Data Table 2B, give their molecular and structural formulas. Are there also geometric (*cis* and *trans*) isomers for butene?

_____

Park D. Alkynes

10. Make a model of ethyne, C_2H_2. In the space provided in Data Table 2B, describe the shape of the molecule. Can you rotate the molecule about the triple bond?

_____

Part E. Arenes

11. Make a model of benzene, C_6H_6, using alternating single and double bonds to approximate the aromatic bonds. Do all the atoms in this molecule lie in the same plane?

_____

Can benzene exist in the boat and chair conformations?

_____

Name _____ Date _____ Class _____

OBSERVATIONS

DATA TABLE 2A: INFORMATION ON MOLECULAR MODELS

Methane molecular formula _____ Structural Formula: Sketch: H—C—H angle? _____	Ethane molecular formula _____ Structural Formula: Sketch: Rotation around C—C bond? _____
Propane molecular formula _____ Structural Formula: Sketch: Isomers? _____	Butane molecular formula _____ Structural Formula: Sketch:
Pentane molecular formula _____ Structural Formula: Sketch: 	Cyclohexane molecular formula _____ Structural Formula: Sketch: Conformations Chair: Boat: Rotation around C—C bond? _____

Name _____ Date _____ Class _____

DATA TABLE 2B: INFORMATION ON MOLECULAR MODELS

Ethene   molecular formula _____
Structural Formula: Sketch:

Rotation around C=C bond? _____

Butene   molecular formula _____

Structural Isomers
Structural Formulas: Sketch:

Geometric Isomers   Sketch:

1,2-dichloroethene   molecular formula _____
Structural Formula: Sketch:

cis-

trans-

Ethyne   molecular formula _____
Structural Formula: Sketch

Shape? _____

Rotation around C≡C bond? _____

Benzene   molecular formula _____
Structural Formula: Sketch:

Is the molecule planar? _____

Chair and boat conformations? _____

GOING FURTHER

Do Research

The pigment in your eyes that responds to visible light is a compound known as 11-*cis*-retinal. This compound is a *polyene*, a hydrocarbon derivative that consists of a network of alternating single and double bonds. 11-*cis*-retinal interacts with visible light in a process known as *photoisomerization*. The energy of light is converted into atomic motion—a necessary part of vision. Do research on the structure of 11-*cis*-retinal and its role in vision. Construct a model to show how the *cis-trans* isomerization leads to a dramatic change in the shape of the molecule, and explain the role that this conformational change plays in vision.

_____

_____

_____

_____

_____

_____

_____

_____

_____

50 ESTERS OF CARBOXYLIC ACIDS

Text Reference
Section 23.3

PURPOSE

To synthesize various esters from carboxylic acids and alcohols.

BACKGROUND

Did you know the aromas of bananas, strawberries, and other fruits are the result of organic chemistry? Esters account for the distinctive odors of many fruits. Many of these ester compounds have pleasant odors. You can synthesize an ester in the lab by heating a carboxylic acid in an alcohol solution containing a small amount of strong acid as a catalyst.

$$R\text{—}CO_2H + R'\text{—}OH \overset{H^+}{\rightleftharpoons} R\text{—}CO_2R' + H_2O$$
carboxylic acid   alcohol   ester   water

In this experiment, you will react carboxylic acids and alcohols, in the presence of a strong acid catalyst, to form esters.

MATERIALS (PER PAIR)

safety goggles
glass-marking pencil
5 medium test tubes
test-tube rack
10-mL graduated cylinder
dropper pipet
ring stand
ring support
2 250-mL beakers
wire gauze
gas burner
thermometer
90% methanoic acid,
   HCOOH [T] [F] [C]

glacial ethanoic acid,
   CH_3COOH [T] [F] [C]
salicylic acid, $C_6H_4OHCOOH$ [T]
methanol, CH_3OH [T] [F]
ethanol, $C2H5OH$ [T] [F]
2-methyl-1-propanol,
   C_4H_9OH [T] [F]
1-pentanol, $C_5H_{11}OH$ [T] [F]
1-octanol, $C_8H_{17}OH$ [T] [F]
18M sulfuric acid, H_2SO_4 [T] [C]
ice
distilled water

SAFETY FIRST!

In this lab, concentrated H_2SO_4 is used to catalyze a chemical reaction. It is strongly recommended that your teacher assist during this procedure. Observe all precautions, especially the ones listed below. If you see a safety icon beside a step in the Procedure, refer to the list below for its meaning.

 Caution: Wear your safety goggles. (All steps.)

Caution: All acids are corrosive, and several of the carboxylic acids used in this experiment are concentrated and particularly hazardous. (All steps.)

 Caution: The chemicals used in this experiment are toxic. Avoid contact with these chemicals. (All steps .)

 Caution: Alcohols are flammable liquids. Do not dispense these compounds near an open flame. (Step 2.)

Caution: Mix chemicals only according to directions. Never add water to 18*M* sulfuric acid. Never add 18*M* sulfuric acid to any other concentrated acid or to an alcohol.

 Note: Return or dispose of all materials according to the instructions of your teacher. (Step 4.)

PROCEDURE

As you perform the experiment, record your observations in Data Table 1.

 1. **CAUTION:** *The acids used in this experiment are extremely corrosive.* Label five medium test tubes with the numbers 1–5. Put the tubes in a test-tube rack. To each of the tubes, add 1 mL of a carboxylic acid and 1 mL of an alcohol, as listed in Data Table 1. In the case of the solid carboxylic acid, salicylic acid, add 1 g of acid and 1 mL of alcohol to the tube.

2. **CAUTION:** *Keep containers of alcohols and carboxylic acids away from flames.* Add 3–5 drops of concentrated sulfuric acid to each tube and heat the tubes in a water bath at 60°C for 10–15 minutes.

3. Turn off the burner and remove the test tubes from the hot water bath. Cool the tubes in an ice bath. Add 5 mL of distilled water to each tube. Any ester produced in the reaction will float on the water in the tube. Note the odor of the ester by wafting the fumes toward your nose with your hand. Try to relate each odor to a familiar fruit, flower, or vegetable. Record your observations in Data Table 1.

 4. Follow your teacher's instructions for proper disposal of the materials.

OBSERVATIONS

DATA TABLE 1: RESULTS AND CONCLUSIONS				
Test Tube	Carboxylic Acid	Alcohol	Ester Synthesized	Odor of Ester
1	methanoic acid	2-methyl-1-propanol		
2	glacial ethanoic acid	ethanol		
3	glacial ethanoic acid	1-pentanol		
4	glacial ethanoic acid	1-octanol		
5	salicylic acid	methanol		

ANALYSES AND CONCLUSIONS

1. Complete Data Table 1 by naming the esters that were synthesized in the experiment.

2. Write a general equation for the acid-catalyzed formation of an ester from an alcohol and a carboxylic acid.

   _____

3. Why was water added to the tube before you were asked to smell it? (**Hint:** What was in the water layer in the test tube?) To answer this question, discuss the relative solubility of acids, alcohols, and esters in water.

   _____

   _____

   _____

   _____

4. Why were the reactions kept free of water during heating?

   _____

   _____

   _____

   _____

   _____

   _____

5. Write equations for each of the esterfication reactions in this experiment. Use structural formulas in the equations and write the name of each compound below its structural formula.

6. In esterfication reactions, the products are in chemical equilibrium with the reactants. Suggest several ways of causing the equilibrium to shift in favor of the production of additional ester.

_____

_____

_____

_____

_____

_____

Name _____ Date _____ Class _____

GOING FURTHER

Develop a Hypothesis

Based on the results of this lab, predict the product formed when 5-hydroxypentanoic acid is treated with acid catalyst.

Propose a mechanism for this reaction. How does the acid catalyze the reaction?

_____

_____

_____

_____

Design an Experiment

Propose an experiment to test your idea(s). If resources are available and you have your teacher's permission, perform the experiment.

_____

_____

_____

_____

51 PREPARATION OF SOAP

Text Reference
Section 24.4

PURPOSE

To prepare and isolate a soap by saponification of a triglyceride.

BACKGROUND

Have you ever considered that soap is one of society's major defenses against disease? The cleansing power of soap helps rinse away many disease-causing organisms, making your home and school healthier places than they otherwise would be. Soaps are alkali metal salts of carboxylic acids. They are generally produced by the reaction of metallic hydroxides with animal fats and vegetable oils. The major components of these fats and oils are triglycerides, esters of glycerol, and various fatty acids. Typically, soaps are made by hydrolyzing the ester bonds of triglycerides with solutions of sodium hydroxide. This soap-making reaction is called saponification (in Greek, *sapon* means "soap"). The products of the hydrolysis reaction are soap and glycerol.

In this experiment, you will saponify a vegetable oil and examine some properties of your product. You will compare the properties of the soap you make with the properties of a commercial detergent and a commercial hand soap.

MATERIALS (PER PAIR)

safety goggles and apron
2 250-mL beakers
2 50-mL beakers
10-mL graduated cylinder
gas burner
ring stand
ring support
wire gauze
glass stirring rod
50-mL graduated cylinder
spatula
3 medium test tubes
centigram balance
glass-marking pencil
test-tube rack
dropper pipet
3 cork stoppers

plastic wash bottle
scoopula
vegetable oil
50% (v/v) ethanol-water mixture
sodium hydroxide, NaOH [C] [T]
saturated sodium chloride
    solution, NaCl
paper towels
laundry detergent [I]
hand soap
wide-range indicator solution or
    wide-range test paper
0.1M calcium chloride, $CaCl_2$ [T]
0.1M iron(III) chloride,
    $FeCl_3$ [T] [I]
0.1M magnesium chloride,
    $MgCl_2$ [T]

Name _____ Date _____ Class _____

SAFETY FIRST!

In this lab, observe all precautions, especially the ones listed below. If you see a safety icon beside a step in the Procedure, refer to the list below for its meaning.

 Caution: Wear your safety goggles. (All steps.)

 Caution: Wear your lab apron. (All steps.)

 Caution: Sodium hydroxide is corrosive and can cause severe burns. Never handle sodium hydroxide pellets with your fingers; use a small beaker and a scoopula. Solid sodium hydroxide will absorb water from the atmosphere; do not leave the container of sodium hydroxide open. (Steps 2, 3.)

Caution: Aqueous iron(III) chloride will stain clothes permanently and is irritating to the skin. Avoid contact with this material. (Step 9.)

 Caution: Keep ethanol and ethanol-water mixtures away from open flames. (Step 3.)

 Note: Return or dispose of all materials according to the instructions of your teacher. (Step 12.)

PROCEDURE

Part A. Preparation of Soap

 1. Pour 5 mL (5.0 g) of vegetable oil into a 250-mL beaker.

 2. Measure 15 mL of 50% ethanol-water mixture into a 50-mL beaker. Slowly dissolve 2.5 g of NaOH pellets in the ethanol-water mixture.

 3. Add 2–3 mL of the NaOH solution to the beaker containing the oil. **CAUTION:** *Keep your face away from the beaker.* Heat the mixture over a *low flame* while stirring. Every few minutes, for about 20 minutes, add a portion of the ethanol-water mixture while continuing to stir. Heat and stir for about 10 more minutes. The oil should be dissolved and a homogeneous solution should be obtained.

4. Add 25 mL of cold water to the hot solution. Using a towel "handle," as shown in Figure 30.1, pour this solution into a 250-mL beaker containing 150 mL of saturated NaCl. Stir this mixture gently and allow it to cool for several minutes.

5. Using a spatula, skim off the top layer of soap and place it in a 50-mL beaker.

Name _____ Date _____ Class _____

Part B. Properties of Soaps and Detergents

6. Place a pea-sized lump of your soap into a test tube. Use a scoopula to put a similar amount of laundry detergent in a second tube and a similar amount of hand soap in a third tube. Add 10 mL of water to each tube, stopper them, and shake the tubes thoroughly. In this step and throughout this experiment, use a test-tube rack as needed.

7. Estimate the pH of the solutions, using wide-range indicator solution or wide-range test paper. Record the results. Pour the contents of the test tubes down the drain. Rinse the test tubes and stoppers with water.

8. Mark three test tubes with the labels "$CaCl_2$," "$FeCl_3$," and "$MgCl_2$," respectively.

9. Prepare a detergent solution by dissolving 0.3 g of detergent in 30 mL of water. Divide this solution equally among the three test tubes. Add solutions to the test tubes as follows.

   $CaCl_2$ test tube: 1.0 mL (or 20 drops) of $0.1M$ $CaCl_2$

   $FeCl_3$ test tube: 1.0 mL of $0.1M$ $FeCl_3$

   $MgCl_2$ test tube: 1.0 mL of $0.1M$ $MgCl_2$

   Stopper each test tube and shake it to mix. Record your observations. Pour the contents of the test tubes down the drain. Rinse the test tubes and stoppers with water.

10. Repeat Step 9, but replace the detergent solution with a hand-soap solution of the same strength. Record your observations.

11. Repeat Step 9, but replace the detergent solution with a solution of your soap of the same strength. Record your observations.

12. Follow your teacher's instructions for proper disposal of the materials.

OBSERVATIONS

DATA TABLE 1: PROPERTIES OF SOAPS AND DETERGENTS				
Substance	pH of Solution	Effect of Adding Salts		
		$CaCl_2$	$FeCl_3$	$MgCl_2$
your soap				
detergent				
hand soap				

ANALYSES AND CONCLUSIONS

1. Write the reaction for saponification of a typical fat (or oil) with sodium hydroxide. Include structural formulas.

2. How does the pH of the soap solution that you prepared compare with those of the solution of commercial laundry detergent and the solution of hand soap? Which of these products would have the harshest effect on the skin?

   _____

   _____

   _____

   _____

3. The metal ions Ca^{2+}, Fe^{3+}, and Mg^{2+} all contribute to the formation of *hard water*. What differences did you observe when the metal ions Ca^{2+}, Fe^{3+}, and Mg^{2+} were added to a soap or detergent? Do you think that a soap or detergent would make a better cleansing agent in hard water? Explain.

   _____

   _____

   _____

   _____

GOING FURTHER

Develop a Hypothesis

Based on the results of this lab, develop a hypothesis to explain why commercial laundry detergents do not form insoluble salts when mixed with calcium, iron, or magnesium salts.

_____

_____

_____

_____

Design an Experiment

Propose an experiment to test your hypothesis. If resources are available and you have your teacher's permission, perform the experiment. Alternatively, do research to learn more about what properties of laundry detergent enhance their solubility in hard water.

_____

_____

_____

_____

52 RADIOACTIVITY AND RADIATION

Text Reference
Section 25.4

PURPOSE

To investigate the effects of distance, shielding, and time on radiation exposure.

BACKGROUND

Although radiation is generally considered dangerous to living things, radiation and radioisotopes are very important in the diagnosis and treatment of some diseases. Nevertheless, the penetrating power of some types of radiation and the ionizations they produce in the body are potentially hazardous. When radioactive elements decay, they can emit three types of radiation: alpha (α), beta (β), and gamma (γ). Radiation cannot be seen, but its presence can be detected through the ionizations produced when it interacts with matter.

How can X-ray technicians and other people who work with radioactive materials minimize their exposure to the potentially hazardous effects of radiation? In this experiment, you will investigate how to minimize your exposure to radiation from low-level radioactive sources.

MATERIALS (PER GROUP)

safety goggles   ring stand
Geiger-Müller counter   ring support
forceps   utility clamp
meter stick
radioactive sources, sealed and kept in shielded container when not in use:
    carbon-14, ^{14}C   cesium-137, ^{137}Cs
    thallium-204, ^{204}Tl
shielding materials, 10-cm × 10-cm squares, 1 of each of the following:
    paper   lead foil
    wood, 3 mm thick   cotton fabric
    aluminum foil   plastic (film)
    glass, picture

SAFETY FIRST!

In this lab, observe all precautions, especially the ones listed below. If you see a safety icon beside a step in the procedure, refer to the list below for its meaning.

 Caution: Wear your safety goggles. (All steps.)

 Caution: The amount of radiation from the sources used in this experiment presents a negligible health hazard. Nevertheless, proper handling of radioactive materials should always be practiced.

PROCEDURE

Your teacher will describe the Geiger-Müller tube and counter, and will demonstrate proper procedures for handling the sealed radioactive sources. Follow your teacher's directions! As the experiment is performed, record observations in Data Tables 1, 2, and 3.

Part A. Background Radiation

 1. Remove all radioactive material from the region near the Geiger-Müller tube. Measure the detected background radiation in counts per minute and record the measurements in Data Table 1.

Part B. Effect of Distance

2. Place the Geiger-Müller tube at one end of the meter stick with a sealed source (preferably a gamma emitter) at the other end, as shown in Figure 52.1.

3. Measure the detected radiation at distances between the source and the detector of 4 cm, 2 cm, and 1 cm. Record your measurements in Data Table 1.

Figure 52.1

Counter

Meter stick

Sealed radioactive source

Geiger-Müller tube

Part C. Effect of Shielding

4. Place a sealed source 5–10 cm below a Geiger-Müller tube, as shown in Figure 52.2. Measure the detected radiation and record your measurement in Data Table 2.

5. Place thin pieces of the various materials (paper, wood, aluminum, glass, lead, cotton fabric, and plastic) between the sealed source and the Geiger-Müller tube. Measure and record the detected radiation for each of the various materials.

Part D. Effect of Time

6. Measure and record the counts per minute from a radiation source. Calculate the total counts for 5 minutes, 30 minutes, and 60 minutes. Record your results in Data Table 3.

Figure 52.2

Name _____ Date _____ Class _____

OBSERVATIONS

DATA TABLE 1: EFFECT OF DISTANCE ON RADIATION INTENSITY

Distance from Source (cm)	Radiation Intensity (cpm)

(Source: _____)   Background radiation: _____ cpm

DATA TABLE 2: EFFECT OF SHIELDING ON RADIATION INTENSITY

Shielding Material	Radiation Intensity (cpm) Sealed Source _____ Radiation Type _____	Radiation Intensity (cpm) Sealed Source _____ Radiation Type _____
none		
paper		
wood		
aluminum		
glass		
lead		
cotton fabric		
plastic		

DATA TABLE 3: EFFECT OF TIME ON RADIATION EXPOSURE (SOURCE: _____)

Time (min)	Total Counts

ANALYSES AND CONCLUSIONS

1. What types of radiation—alpha, beta, or gamma—can be detected with a Geiger-Müller counter?

   _____

2. Graph the radiation intensity (in counts per minute) versus distance (in centimeters) from the source. Be certain to identify the type of sealed source the data represents.

3. What did you find to be the best shielding material?

   _____

   _____

   _____

4. When you double the distance from the radiation source, how do the counts per minute change?

   _____

   _____

   _____

   _____

   _____

5. Is there an advantage in limiting your exposure to a radiation source to the shortest time possible? Explain.

   _____

   _____

   _____

   _____

GOING FURTHER

Develop a Hypothesis

Based on the results of this lab, develop a hypothesis to explain why the radiation from the ^{14}C source could be shielded more effectively than the radiation from the ^{137}Cs source. What do your results suggest about the decay mode of each radioactive isotope?

_____

_____

_____

Do Research

Do research to find scientific evidence that supports or refutes your hypothesis.

_____

_____

_____

Sample Laboratory Report

Name: Janet Blair   **Class:** 2   **Date:** October 5, 2004

Experiment Number and Title: Experiment 5: Mass, Volume, and Density

Purpose: (Give a clear, concise description of exactly what the experiment was intended to demonstrate.)

The purpose of this experiment was to investigate the relationship between mass and volume for a metal and to determine if that relationship can be used as an identifying property of the metal.

Equipment/Materials: (List the equipment and materials that you actually used in the experiment.)

graduated cylinder (25-mL)   centigram balance
metal A   ruler (cm)
metal B

Methods: (Describe all laboratory techniques and types of calculations that you used in the experiment.)

Mass measurements were made by measuring clean, dry samples of metals on a centigram balance. The mass measurements were made to the nearest 0.01 g.

Volume measurements were made by the method of water displacement. A 25-mL graduated cylinder was half-filled with water and the volume recorded. The volume was read at the bottom of the meniscus. Then the metal sample was immersed in the water in the graduated cylinder. The new volume of the water and the metal sample together was read and recorded. The volume of the metal sample was determined by subtracting the initial volume of the water from the final volume. The density of each sample was calculated by dividing the mass of the sample by its volume.

Other groups in the class had different-sized samples of the same metals, A and B. Class data was pooled to obtain data points for graphing mass (the manipulated or independent variable) versus volume (the responding or dependent variable) for each metal. The slope of the line obtained for each metal is equal to mass/volume and represents the density of the metal. The slope was determined according to the formula $y = mx + b$, where x = mass value, y = the volume associated with that mass, m = slope of the line, and b = y-intercept of the line.

Procedure: (Describe the major steps of the procedure, exactly as you carried them out. Include here any qualitative observations you made during the experiment.)

We received one sample of metal A and one sample of metal B from the teacher. Metal A was shiny, smooth, and black. Metal B was dull, rough, and tan. We cleaned and dried the samples, using tap water and paper towels. Metal B was more difficult to dry than metal A. We then measured each sample on the centigram balance as described above and recorded the masses. We determined the mass of metal A first and metal B second. I did the measurements, and Paul recorded the data.

We then made the volume measurements, using the water displacement method described in the Methods section. Paul added the samples to the water, and I made the initial and final volume readings. We did this first for metal A and then for metal B. After making these measurements, we dried the samples and returned them to the teacher.

Observations: (Record here any measurements and calculations that you make during the experiment. Make sure to clearly distinguish between the two. Include units for all measurements and all calculations. Pay close attention to significant figures. If possible, present your data in the form of a table and/or graph so that patterns in the data may be more easily recognized.)

Group 1 Data and Calculations		
Quantity	Metal A	Metal B
mass	10.10 g	33.41 g
volume of water alone	12.0 mL	19.7 mL
volume of water and metal	15.8 mL	23.5 mL
volume of metal	3.8 mL (15.8 mL − 12.0 mL)	3.8 mL (23.5 mL − 19.7 mL)
density of metal	2.7 g/mL (10.10 g/3.8 mL)	88 g/mL (33.41 g/3.8 mL)

Class Data and Calculations						
Lab Group*	Metal A			Metal B		
	Mass	Volume	Density	Mass	Volume	Density
1	10.10 g	3.8 mL	2.7 g/mL	33.41 g	3.8 mL	8.8 g/mL
2	4.31 g	1.7 mL	2.6 g/mL	34.62 g	3.9 mL	8.9 g/mL
3	8.05 g	3.0 mL	2.7 g/mL	27.63 g	3.1 mL	8.9 g/mL
4	9.00 g	3.4 mL	2.6 g/mL	21.00 g	2.4 mL	8.4 g/mL
5	6.25 g	2.5 mL	2.5 g/mL	20.92 g	2.5 mL	8.4 g/mL

*1 = Janet & Paul   2 = Lin & Pat   3 = Ellen & Emilio   4 = Dave & Alice   5 = Fariq & Bill

Graph of Class Data for Metal A (Remember to plot the manipulated variable on the *x*-axis, the horizontal axis, and the responding variable on the *y*-axis, the vertical axis.)

mass (x)	volume (y)
10.10 g	3.8 mL
4.31 g	1.7 mL
8.05 g	3.0 mL
9.00 g	3.4 mL
6.25 g	2.5 mL

Class Data for Metal A
(mass versus volume)

Analyses and Conclusions: (Record here the answers to all the questions in the Analyses and Conclusions section of the experiment. Also answer any additional questions that your teacher may ask.)

6. The results of this experiment indicate that the density of a specific substance is a constant. They indicate also that the densities of different substances can be quite different. For these reasons, density should be useful in the identification of substances.

(Use this model for the questions posed in the lab manual.)

Table A.1 Symbols of Common Elements

Ag	silver	Cu	copper	O	oxygen
Al	aluminum	F	fluorine	P	phosphorus
As	arsenic	Fe	iron	Pb	lead
Au	gold	H	hydrogen	Pt	platinum
Ba	barium	Hg	mercury	S	sulfur
Bi	bismuth	I	iodine	Sb	antimony
Br	bromine	K	potassium	Sn	tin
C	carbon	Mg	magnesium	Sr	strontium
Ca	calcium	Mn	manganese	Ti	titanium
Cl	chlorine	N	nitrogen	U	uranium
Co	cobalt	Na	sodium	W	tungsten
Cr	chromium	Ni	nickel	Zn	zinc

Table A.2 Symbols of Common Polyatomic Ions

$C_2H_3O_2^-$	ethanoate	$Cr_2O_7^{2-}$	dichromate	NO_3^-	nitrate
ClO^-	hypochlorite	HCO_3^-	hydrogen carbonate	NO_2^-	nitrite
ClO_2^-	chlorite	H_3O^+	hydronium	O_2^{2-}	peroxide
ClO_3^-	chlorate	HPO_4^{2-}	hydrogen phosphate	OH^-	hydroxide
ClO_4^-	perchlorate	HSO_3^-	hydrogen sulfite	PO_4^{3-}	phosphate
CN^-	cyanide	HSO_4^-	hydrogen sulfate	SiO_3^{2-}	silicate
CO_3^{2-}	carbonate	MnO_4^-	permanganate	SO_3^{2-}	sulfite
CrO_4^{2-}	chromate	NH_4^+	ammonium	SO_4^{2-}	sulfate

Table A.3 Solubilities of Compounds at 25°C and 101 kPa

	bromide	carbonate	chlorate	chloride	ethanoate	hydroxide	iodide	nitrate	oxide	perchlorate	phosphate	sulfate	sulfide
aluminium	S	—	S	S	S	I	S	S	I	S	I	S	d
ammonium	S	S	S	S	S	S	S	S	—	S	S	S	S
barium	S	I	S	S	S	S	S	S	sS	S	I	I	d
calcium	S	I	S	S	S	S	S	S	sS	S	I	sS	I
copper(II)	S	—	S	S	S	I	S	S	I	S	I	S	I
iron(II)	S	I	S	S	S	I	S	S	I	S	I	S	I
iron(III)	S	—	S	S	S	I	S	S	I	S	I	sS	d
lithium	S	sS	S	S	S	S	S	S	S	S	sS	S	S
magnesium	S	I	S	S	S	I	S	S	I	S	I	S	d
potassium	S	S	S	S	S	S	S	S	S	S	S	S	S
silver	I	I	S	I	sS	—	I	S	I	S	I	sS	I
sodium	S	S	S	S	S	S	S	S	S	S	S	S	S
strontium	S	I	S	S	S	S	S	S	S	S	I	I	I
zinc	S	I	S	S	S	I	S	S	I	S	I	S	I

Key:
S = soluble
sS = slightly soluble
I = insoluble

d = decomposes in water
— = no such compound

Table A.4 Some Properties of the Elements

Element	Symbol	Atomic Number	Atomic Mass	Melting Point (°C)	Boiling Point (°C)	Density (g/cm³) (gases at STP)	Major Oxidation States
actinium	Ac	89	(227)	1050	3200	10.07	+3
aluminium	Al	13	26.98154	660.37	2467	2.6989	+3
americium	Am	95	(243)	944	2607	13.67	+3, +4, +5, +6
antimony	Sb	51	121.75	630.74	1950	6.691	−3, +3, +5
argon	Ar	18	39.948	−189.2	−185.7	0.0017837	
arsenic	As	33	74.9216	817	613	5.73	−3, +3, +5
astatine	At	85	(210)	302	337	—	
barium	Ba	56	137.33	725	1640	3.5	+2
berkelium	Bk	97	(247)	986	—	14.78	
beryllium	Be	4	9.01218	1278	2970	1.848	+2
bismuth	Bi	83	208.9804	271.3	1560	9.747	+3, +5
bohrium	Bh	107	(264)	—	—	—	
boron	B	5	10.81	2079	3675	2.34	+3
bromine	Br	35	79.904	−7.2	58.78	3.12	−1, +1, +5
cadmium	Cd	48	112.41	320.9	765	8.65	+2
calcium	Ca	20	40.08	839	1484	1.55	+2
californium	Cf	98	(251)	900	—	14	
carbon	C	6	12.011	3550	4827	2.267	−4, +2, +4
cerium	Ce	58	140.12	799	3426	6.657	+3, +4
cesium	Cs	55	132.9054	28.40	669.3	1.873	+1
chlorine	Cl	17	35.453	−100.98	−34.6	0.003214	−1, +1, +5, +7
chromium	Cr	24	51.996	1857	2672	7.18	+2, +3, +6
cobalt	Co	27	58.9332	1495	2870	8.9	+2, +3
copper	Cu	29	63.546	1083.4	2567	8.96	+1, +2
curium	Cm	96	(247)	1340	—	13.51	+3
darmstadtium	Ds	110	(269)	—	—	—	
dubnium	Db	105	(262)	—	—	—	
dysprosium	Dy	66	162.50	1412	2562	8.550	+3
einsteinium	Es	99	(252)	—	—	—	
erbium	Er	68	167.26	159	2863	9.006	+3
europium	Eu	63	151.96	822	1597	5.243	+2, +3
fermium	Fm	100	(257)	—	—	—	
fluorine	F	9	18.998403	−219.62	−188.54	0.001696	−1
francium	Fr	87	(223)	27	667	—	+1
gadolinium	Gd	64	157.25	1313	3266	7.9004	+3
gallium	Ga	31	69.72	29.78	2204	5.904	+3
germanium	Ge	32	72.59	937.4	2830	5.323	+2, +4
gold	Au	79	196.9665	1064.43	3080	19.3	+1, +3
hafnium	Hf	72	178.49	2227	4602	13.31	+4
hassium	Hs	108	(265)	—	—	—	
helium	He	2	4.00260	−272.2	−268.934	0.001785	
holmium	Ho	67	164.9304	1474	2695	8.795	+3
hydrogen	H	1	1.00794	−259.14	−252.87	0.00008988	+1
indium	In	49	114.82	156.61	2080	7.31	+1, +3
iodine	I	53	126.9045	113.5	184.35	4.93	−1, +1, +5, +7
iridium	Ir	77	192.22	2410	4130	22.42	+3, +4
iron	Fe	26	55.847	1535	2750	7.874	+2, +3
krypton	Kr	36	83.80	−156.6	−152.30	0.003733	
lanthanum	La	57	138.9055	921	3457	6.145	+3
lawrencium	Lr	103	(262)	—	—	—	+3
lead	Pb	82	207.2	327.502	1740	11.35	+2, +4
lithium	Li	3	6.941	180.54	1342	0.534	+1
lutetium	Lu	71	174.967	1663	3395	9.840	+3
magnesium	Mg	12	24.305	648.8	1090	1.738	+2
manganese	Mn	25	54.9380	1244	1962	7.32	+2, +3, +4, +7
meitnerium	Mt	109	(268)	—	—	—	
mendelevium	Md	101	(257)	—	—	—	+2, +3
mercury	Hg	80	200.59	−38.842	356.58	13.55	+1, +2

Table A.4 Some Properties of the Elements

Element	Symbol	Atomic Number	Atomic Mass	Melting Point (°C)	Boiling Point (°C)	Density (g/cm³) (gases at STP)	Major Oxidation States
molybdenum	Mo	42	95.94	2617	4612	10.22	+6
neodymium	Nd	60	144.24	1021	3068	6.90	+3
neon	Ne	10	20.179	−248.67	−246.048	0.0008999	
neptunium	Np	93	(237)	640	3902	20.25	+3, +4, +5, +6
nickel	Ni	28	58.69	1453	2732	8.902	+2, +3
niobium	Nb	41	92.9064	2468	4742	8.57	+3, +5
nitrogen	N	7	14.0067	−209.86	−195.8	0.0012506	−3, +3, +5
nobelium	No	102	(259)	—	—	—	+2, +3
osmium	Os	76	190.2	3045	5027	22.57	+3, +4
oxygen	O	8	15.9994	−218.4	−182.962	0.001429	−2
palladium	Pd	46	106.42	1554	2970	12.02	+2, +4
phosphorus	P	15	30.97376	44.1	280	1.82	−3, +3, +5
platinum	Pt	78	195.08	1772	3827	21.45	+2, +4
plutonium	Pu	94	(244)	641	3232	19.84	+3, +4, +5, +6
potassium	K	19	39.0982	63.25	760	0.862	+1
praseodymium	Pr	59	140.9077	931	3512	6.64	+3
promethium	Pm	61	(145)	1168	2460	7.22	+3
protactinium	Pa	91	231.0359	1560	4027	15.37	+4, +5
radium	Ra	88	(226)	700	1140	5.5	+2
radon	Rn	86	(222)	−71	−61.8	0.00973	
rhenium	Re	75	186.207	3180	5627	21.02	+4, +6, +7
rhodiuim	Rh	45	102.9055	1966	3727	12.41	+3
rubidium	Rb	37	85.4678	38.89	686	1.532	+1
ruthenium	Ru	44	101.07	2310	3900	12.41	+3
rutherfordium	Rf	104	(261)	—	—	—	
samarium	Sm	62	150.36	1077	1791	7.520	+2, +3
scandium	Sc	21	44.9559	1541	2831	2.989	+3
seaborgium	Sg	106	(263)	—	—	—	
selenium	Se	34	78.96	217	684.9	4.79	−2, +4, +6
silicon	Si	14	28.0855	1410	2355	2.33	−4, +2, +4
silver	Ag	47	107.8682	961.93	2212	10.50	+1
sodium	Na	11	22.98977	97.81	882.9	0.971	+1
strontium	Sr	38	87.62	796	1384	2.54	+2
sulfur	S	16	32.06	112.8	444.7	2.07	−2, +4, +6
tantalum	Ta	73	180.9479	2996	5425	16.654	+5
technetium	Tc	43	(98)	2172	4877	11.50	+4, +6, +7
tellurium	Te	52	127.60	449.5	989.8	6.24	−2, +4, +6
terbium	Tb	65	158.9254	1356	3123	8.229	+3
thallium	Tl	81	204.383	303.5	1457	11.85	+1, +3
thorium	Th	90	232.0381	1750	4790	11.72	+4
thulium	Tm	69	168.9342	1545	1947	9.321	+3
tin	Sn	50	118.69	231.968	2270	7.31	+2, +4
titanium	Ti	22	47.88	1660	3287	4.54	+2, +3, +4
tungsten	W	74	183.85	3410	5660	19.3	+6
ununbium	Uub	112	(277)	—	—	—	
ununquadium	Uuq	114					
unununium	Uuu	111	(272)	—	—	—	
uranium	U	92	238.0289	1132.3	3818	18.95	+3, +4, +5, +6
vanadium	V	23	50.9415	1890	3380	6.11	+2, +3, +4, +5
xenon	Xe	54	131.29	−111.9	−107.1	0.005887	
ytterbium	Yb	70	173.04	819	1194	6.965	+2, +3
yttrium	Y	39	88.9059	1522	3338	4.469	+3
zinc	Zn	30	65.38	419.58	907	7.133	+2
zirconium	Zr	40	91.22	1852	4377	6.506	+4

Periodic Table of the Elements

This numbering system is used by the International Union of Pure and Applied Chemistry (IUPAC)

Key

State
2
8
1
$\overline{S}$ **11** Atomic number
Na — Element symbol
Sodium
22.990 — Average atomic mass

- Electrons in each energy level

State
- S Solid
- L Liquid
- G Gas
- N Not found in nature

Group 1 / 1A

| G 1 **H** Hydrogen 1.0079 |
| S 3 **Li** Lithium 6.941 |
| S 11 **Na** Sodium 22.990 |
| S 19 **K** Potassium 39.098 |
| S 37 **Rb** Rubidium 85.468 |
| S 55 **Cs** Cesium 132.91 |
| S 87 **Fr** Francium (223) |

Group 2 / 2A

| S 4 **Be** Beryllium 9.0122 |
| S 12 **Mg** Magnesium 24.305 |
| S 20 **Ca** Calcium 40.08 |
| S 38 **Sr** Strontium 87.62 |
| S 56 **Ba** Barium 137.33 |
| S 88 **Ra** Radium (226) |

3 / 3B

| S 21 **Sc** Scandium 44.956 |
| S 39 **Y** Yttrium 88.906 |
| S 71 **Lu** Lutetium 174.97 |
| N 103 **Lr** Lawrencium (262) |

4 / 4B

| S 22 **Ti** Titanium 47.90 |
| S 40 **Zr** Zirconium 91.22 |
| S 72 **Hf** Hafnium 178.49 |
| N 104 **Rf** Rutherfordium (261) |

5 / 5B

| S 23 **V** Vanadium 50.941 |
| S 41 **Nb** Niobium 92.906 |
| S 73 **Ta** Tantalum 180.95 |
| N 105 **Db** Dubnium (262) |

6 / 6B

| S 24 **Cr** Chromium 51.996 |
| S 42 **Mo** Molybdenum 95.94 |
| S 74 **W** Tungsten 183.85 |
| N 106 **Sg** Seaborgium (263) |

7 / 7B

| S 25 **Mn** Manganese 54.938 |
| N 43 **Tc** Technetium (98) |
| S 75 **Re** Rhenium 186.21 |
| N 107 **Bh** Bohrium (264) |

8 / 8B

| S 26 **Fe** Iron 55.847 |
| S 44 **Ru** Ruthenium 101.07 |
| S 76 **Os** Osmium 190.2 |
| N 108 **Hs** Hassium (265) |

9 / 8B

| S 27 **Co** Cobalt 58.933 |
| S 45 **Rh** Rhodium 102.91 |
| S 77 **Ir** Iridium 192.22 |
| N 109 **Mt** Meitnerium (268) |

10 / 8B

| S 28 **Ni** Nickel 58.71 |
| S 46 **Pd** Palladium 106.4 |
| S 78 **Pt** Platinum 195.09 |
| N 110 **Ds** Darmstadtium (269) |

11 / 1B

| S 29 **Cu** Copper 63.546 |
| S 47 **Ag** Silver 107.87 |
| S 79 **Au** Gold 196.97 |
| N 111 *Uuu Unununium (272) |

12 / 2B

| S 30 **Zn** Zinc 65.38 |
| S 48 **Cd** Cadmium 112.41 |
| L 80 **Hg** Mercury 200.59 |
| N 112 *Uub Ununbium (277) |

13 / 3A

| S 5 **B** Boron 10.81 |
| S 13 **Al** Aluminum 26.982 |
| S 31 **Ga** Gallium 69.72 |
| S 49 **In** Indium 114.82 |
| S 81 **Tl** Thallium 204.37 |

14 / 4A

| S 6 **C** Carbon 12.011 |
| S 14 **Si** Silicon 28.086 |
| S 32 **Ge** Germanium 72.59 |
| S 50 **Sn** Tin 118.69 |
| S 82 **Pb** Lead 207.2 |
| N 114 *Uuq Ununquadium |

15 / 5A

| S 7 **N** Nitrogen 14.007 |
| S 15 **P** Phosphorus 30.974 |
| S 33 **As** Arsenic 74.922 |
| S 51 **Sb** Antimony 121.75 |
| S 83 **Bi** Bismuth 208.98 |

16 / 6A

| S 8 **O** Oxygen 15.999 |
| S 16 **S** Sulfur 32.06 |
| S 34 **Se** Selenium 78.96 |
| S 52 **Te** Tellurium 127.60 |
| S 84 **Po** Polonium (209) |

17 / 7A

| G 9 **F** Fluorine 18.998 |
| G 17 **Cl** Chlorine 35.453 |
| L 35 **Br** Bromine 79.904 |
| S 53 **I** Iodine 126.90 |
| S 85 **At** Astatine (210) |

18 / 0

| G 2 **He** Helium 4.0026 |
| G 10 **Ne** Neon 20.179 |
| G 18 **Ar** Argon 39.948 |
| G 36 **Kr** Krypton 83.80 |
| G 54 **Xe** Xenon 131.30 |
| G 86 **Rn** Radon (222) |

*Name not officially assigned

Lanthanide Series

| S 57 **La** Lanthanum 138.91 |
| S 58 **Ce** Cerium 140.12 |
| S 59 **Pr** Praseodymium 140.91 |
| S 60 **Nd** Neodymium 144.24 |
| S 61 **Pm** Promethium (145) |
| S 62 **Sm** Samarium 150.4 |
| S 63 **Eu** Europium 151.96 |
| S 64 **Gd** Gadolinium 157.25 |
| S 65 **Tb** Terbium 158.93 |
| S 66 **Dy** Dysprosium 162.50 |
| S 67 **Ho** Holmium 164.93 |
| S 68 **Er** Erbium 167.26 |
| S 69 **Tm** Thulium 168.93 |
| S 70 **Yb** Ytterbium 173.04 |

Actinide Series

| S 89 **Ac** Actinium (227) |
| S 90 **Th** Thorium 232.04 |
| S 91 **Pa** Protactinium 231.04 |
| S 92 **U** Uranium 238.03 |
| N 93 **Np** Neptunium (237) |
| N 94 **Pu** Plutonium (244) |
| N 95 **Am** Americium (243) |
| N 96 **Cm** Curium (247) |
| N 97 **Bk** Berkelium (247) |
| N 98 **Cf** Californium (251) |
| N 99 **Es** Einsteinium (252) |
| N 100 **Fm** Fermium (257) |
| N 101 **Md** Mendelevium (258) |
| N 102 **No** Nobelium (259) |